Virtual Methods

Issues in Social Research on the Internet

Edited by Christine Hine

⊛BERG

Oxford • New York

First published in 2005 by
Berg
Editorial offices:
1st Floor, Angel Court, 81 St Clements Street, Oxford, OX4 1AW, UK
175 Fifth Avenue, New York, NY 10010, USA

Berg is the imprint of Oxford International Publishers Ltd.

Library of Congress Cataloguing-in-Publication Data
Virtual methods : issues in social research on the Internet / edited by
Christine Hine.
   p. cm.
Includes bibliographical references and index.
ISBN 1-84520-084-5 (cloth) — ISBN 1-84520-085-3 (pbk.)
1. Internet — Social aspects. 2. Internet research. 3. Computer networks.
4. Social interaction. I. Hine, Christine.
HM851.V575 2005
303.48'33'072—dc22   2005001815

British Library Cataloguing-in-Publication Data
A catalogue record for this book is available from the British Library.

ISBN-13 978 184520 084 8 (Cloth)
ISBN-10 1 84520 084 5 (Cloth)

ISBN-13 978 184520 085 5 (Paper)
ISBN-10 1 84520 085 3 (Paper)

Typeset by Avocet Typeset, Chilton, Aylesbury, Bucks
Printed in the United Kingdom by Antony Rowe, Chippenham, Wiltshire

www.bergpublishers.com

Contents

Part II Research Sites and Strategies

Figures

Notes on Contributors

Anne Beaulieu (http://www.niwi.knaw.nl/en/nerdi2/) is a senior researcher with Networked Research and Digital Information, Royal Netherlands Academy of Arts and Science, Amsterdam. Her work focuses on the interaction between new technologies and scientific research practices. She has pursued analyses of the development and consequences of digital imaging and databasing technologies for biomedical knowledge, including an ethnographic study of brain imaging in neuroscience. She has written about methodological issues regarding laboratory studies and online research, and about the intellectual agenda of current ethnographic research on the Internet. She is currently investigating issues of trust and space in the development of online infrastructure (collaboratories and data-sharing tools) for knowledge production.

Martin Dodge works at University College London, UK, as a researcher in the Centre for Advanced Spatial Analysis and lecturer in the Department of Geography. He has a degree in geography and computing, an MSc in geographical information systems and is currently completing his PhD. His work has been primarily concerned with developing a new research area of the geography of cyberspace, focusing in large part on the ways to map and visualize the Internet and the Web. He is the curator of a web-based *Atlas of Cyberspace* (http://www.cybergeography.org/atlas) and has co-authored two books with Rob Kitchin, *Mapping Cyberspace* (Routledge 2000) and *Atlas of Cyberspace* (Addison-Wesley 2001).

Kirsten A. Foot is an Assistant Professor in the Department of Communication at the University of Washington, USA. As co-director of the WebArchivist.org research group, she is developing new techniques for studying social and political action on the Web. Her research interests include co-production and mobilization on the Web, and online campaigning practices. She co-edits the *Acting with Technology* series at MIT Press, and her work has been published in journals such as *Communication Theory*, the *Journal of Broadcasting and Electronic Media* and the *Journal of Computer-Mediated Communication*.

Maximilian C. Forte is an Assistant Professor in Anthropology at the University College of Cape Breton, Canada. His doctoral research concerned practices of representation and the cultural politics of indigeneity in the contemporary Caribbean, with specific reference to Trinidad. He is the founding editor of the *Caribbean Amerindian Centrelink* (http://www.centrelink.org) and *Kacike: The Journal of Caribbean Amerindian History and Anthropology* (http://www.kacike.org). He has published articles on indigenous peoples and the Internet in the Caribbean in *Indigenous Affairs*, on action research and virtual ethnography in *Virtual Research Ethics: Issues and Controversies*, edited by Elizabeth Buchanan (Idea Publishing Group 2003) and on the transformative potential of the Internet for anthropological research and communication practice in various issues of *Anthropology News*.

Mário J. L. Guimarães Jr is an anthropologist interested in the relationship between technology and social life, especially the study of social spaces created by and through ICTs: cyberspace. His latest project, developed in the Social Anthropology department of the Federal University of Santa Catarina, Brazil, investigated the ways in which avatars' physical performance is related to the sociability practices of a virtual community. The outcomes of that project led to his PhD research, currently being done at the Centre for Research into Culture and Technology (CRICT), Brunel University, UK, where he is exploring how conceptions of body and personhood contribute to the design, use and transformation of avatar-related technologies.

Christine Hine is a Lecturer in the Department of Sociology at the University of Surrey, UK. Her research centres on the sociology of science and technology, including ethnographic studies of scientific culture, information technology and the Internet. She is author of *Virtual Ethnography* (Sage 2000) and has taken a prominent interest in the development of methodological approaches to the understanding of virtual technologies. She is currently engaged in an ethnographic exploration of patterns of communication and information flow in contemporary scientific research.

Nicholas W. Jankowski is Associate Professor in the Department of Communication, University of Nijmegen. He has studied community media and other small-scale forms of communication since the mid-1970s. His publications include *The Contours of Multimedia* (with L. Hanssen, Luton 1996), *Community Media in the Information Age* (Hampton 2002); and *A Handbook of Qualitative Methodologies for Mass Communication Research* (with K. B. Jensen, Routledge 1991). He is preparing a textbook on new media research with Martine van Selm. Nicholas is initiator and co-editor of the journal *New Media and Society*, a founding board member of the European Institute of Communication and Culture (Euricom) and editor of the Hampton Press book series *Euricom Monographs: Communicative Innovations and Democracy*.

Adam N. Joinson is a Lecturer in the use of Information Communication Technology (ICT) in the Social Sciences at The Open University, UK. His current research interests include self-disclosure in computer-mediated communication, personalization technologies, audience effects and socially desirable behaviour in online research. He is the author of *Understanding the Psychology of Internet Behaviour* (Palgrave Macmillan 2003) and numerous research articles and book chapters on computer-mediated communication, Internet behaviour and online research methods. Pre-print versions of much of his work are available at http://www.joinson.com.

Joëlle Kivits is currently a research student at the London School of Economics and Political Science (LSE), UK. Her doctoral research project focuses on the significance of information practices for individuals' everyday health. She is particularly interested in the role of mediated information, especially online health information, in individuals' management of personal health and its implications for the contemporary definition and experience of health. Her other research interests concern the use of Internet research methods, both quantitative and qualitative, in social and health sciences.

Hugh Mackay is Senior Lecturer at The Open University, based in Wales. He is a sociologist of technology, with an interest in technology and culture. Research has focused on how users shape, and are configured by, technology. He has explored ethnographically the development of computer systems and new media technologies. Authored work includes Reconfiguring the User (*Social Studies of Science* 2000), *Doing Cultural Studies: The Story of the Sony Walkman* (with Stuart Hall et al., Sage 1997); *Investigating the Information Society* (with W. Maples et al., Routledge 2002) and *Modern Media in the Home: An Ethnographic Study* (with Darren Ivey, University of Luton Press 2004).

Shani Orgad is a Lecturer in the Department of Media and Communications at the London School of Economics and Political Science, UK. She lectures on Internet, communications and globalization, media, culture and society; and methods of research in media and communications. Her research interests include media and everyday life, media and globalization, narrative and media, health and new media and methodological aspects of doing Internet research. Her PhD research focused on narrativization and storytelling in the online communication of breast cancer patients. Her first degree was in Media and Communications with Sociology and Anthropology from The Hebrew University, and she has a master's degree in Media and Communications from the LSE.

Han Woo Park (http://www.hanpark.net) currently works for the Department of Communication and Information at YeungNam University in South Korea. He obtained his PhD in the School of Informatics at the State University of New York (SUNY) at Buffalo, USA. He was a research fellow at the Korean Agency for Digital Opportunity (1997–8) and Royal Netherlands Academy of Arts and Sciences (2002–3). His research focuses on examining cyber-communication using hyperlink network analysis. He guest edited the *Journal of Computer-Mediated Communication*'s special issue on Internet Networks. His research has appeared in international journals such as *First Monday, Journal of American Society of Information Science and Technology, Journal of Computer-Mediated Communication, Electronic Journal of Communication* and *NETCOM: Networks and Communication Studies.*

Jason Rutter is a Research Fellow at the ESRC Centre for Research on Innovation & Competition (CRIC) at the University of Manchester, UK. His current research and publication interests centre on social and routine aspects of ICT use and consumption particularly in the context of digital gaming, entertainment and mobile devices. He is currently co-editing *Understanding Digital Games* for publication with Sage.

Teela Sanders is a Lecturer in the School of Sociology and Social Policy at the University of Leeds, UK, and specializes in crime and deviance. Her main research interests are in the female sex industry examining the social organization of sex work and the management of occupational hazards. She is also interested in qualitative research methods and in particular ethnography. She has recently published in journals such as *Sociology, Urban Studies, International Journal for Urban and Regional Research* and *Sociology of Health and Illness.* Her first book is *Sex Work: A Risky Business* (Willan 2004).

Steven M. Schneider is an Associate Professor of Political Science at the SUNY Institute of Technology, New York, USA. He is a co-founder and co-director of the WebArchivist.org research group (http://webarchivist.org), within which he has developed tools and systems to support collection and analysis of large-scale collections of digital objects, and, in partnership with the US Library of Congress, produced the 2002 Election Web Archive and the September 11 Web Archive. Recent publications have appeared in *New Media & Society, Journal of Computer Mediated Communication* and *Journal of Broadcasting and Electronic Media.* He obtained his PhD from the Massachusetts Institute of Technology (MIT), USA.

Gregory W. H. Smith has been an undergraduate, postgraduate, Lecturer and Senior Lecturer at the University of Salford, UK, where he is now Reader in Sociology. His main research and teaching interests are in theory, ethnography, interaction, embodiment and visual sociology. His books include *Analyzing Visual*

Data (with M. S. Ball, Sage 1992), *Introducing Cultural Studies* (with E. Baldwin, B. Longhurst, S. McCracken and M. Ogborn, Prentice-Hall 1999/2004), *Goffman and Social Organization* (Routledge 1999) and *Erving Goffman*, 4 vols (co-edited with G. A. Finem Sage 2000).

Mike Thelwall is head of the Statistical Cybermetrics Research Group (http://cybermetrics.wlv.ac.uk) at the University of Wolverhampton, UK. He obtained his PhD in Pure Maths at the University of Lancaster, UK. He researches into the application of hyperlink analysis in a variety of contexts, from computer science to sociology. His research contributions include the development of network graphing methods and techniques for improving the reliability of hyperlink counts between web sites, as well as the development of a theoretical model for academic web linking. He is on the editorial board of two journals and two book series, and has published sixty-five refereed journal articles.

Martine van Selm is Associate Professor in the Department of Social Science Research Methodology, Faculty of Social Sciences at the University of Nijmegen in the Netherlands. Her research interests are elderly people and the media (media-use and portrayal), Internet research, use of ICT in various contexts (such as Internet and citizen participation, ICT use in organizations) and traditional media that meet the Internet (Web radio, on line news media and interactive television).

Virtual Methods and the Sociology of Cyber-Social-Scientific Knowledge

Christine Hine

Introduction

The coming of the Internet has posed a significant challenge for our understanding of research methods. Across the social sciences and humanities people have found themselves wanting to explore the new social formations that arise when people communicate and organize themselves via email, web sites, mobile phones and the rest of the increasingly commonplace mediated forms of communication. Mediated interactions have come to the fore as key ways in which social practices are defined and experienced. Indeed, there are few researchers in the social sciences or humanities who could not find some aspect of their research interest manifested on the Internet. There is, then, a considerable will to research and understand technologically mediated interactions, both as a topic in their own right and as an important conduit for contemporary social life. At the same time, however, there is considerable anxiety about just how far existing tried and tested research methods are appropriate for technologically mediated interactions. New media seem to offer the hope of reaching different populations of research subjects in new ways, but their promise is tinged with anxiety. Methodological solutions gain much of their authority through precedent, and it is not clear as yet just how far the heritage of research methodology applies to new media and what gaps in our understanding are still to be exposed.

This volume contains a series of case studies and reviews which explore methodological solutions to understanding the social interactions mediated by information and communications technologies. Each of the case studies here involved its author(s) in working out a situated response to the research question they wished to address, appropriate to the conditions which they found in context. In each of the chapters general methodological lessons are drawn from these situated responses. By looking at research methods in this way, the aim is to provide guidance for researchers starting out on projects involving mediated interactions.

Our aim in this volume is to offer precedents as a confidence boost for researchers developing solutions to their own research needs, and to provide fuel for the methodological imagination. This is not to say that previous methodological thinking is deemed irrelevant. A major part of the contribution made by the authors of chapters in this volume is in working out just where the existing heritage of methodological thinking applies, and where they felt the need to question or move forward from established thinking.

Like all practical skills, the only real way to learn to be a researcher is by experience. You can read about the theory of research methods but, most noticeably in qualitative research, these theories become meaningful only when you start to try them out for yourself. Part of the reason for this is the very unpredictability of the situations which will form the setting for the research. When we set out to research social interactions we cannot specify in advance just what form those interactions will take, nor how we will be able to participate in or observe them. The whole reason for doing the research is to find out something about the setting, and it is quite possible that some of the things we do not know about the setting impact upon the design and conduct of the research we carry out. To a certain extent, then, social research methods have always had to be adaptive. However, there are some regularities to the problems which researchers face, and thus much to be gained by sharing solutions to these problems. New ways of doing research deserve to be shared, in order to boost the collective stock of models for the research process. This volume provides a way of sharing research solutions in order to support researchers in developing their own adaptive approaches.

The chapters collected here are versions of papers first presented at a series of seminars on Virtual Methods, held at universities in southern England between 2001 and 2003.[1] This seminar series aimed to provide a forum for the sharing of expertise on the use of information and communication technologies in social research. While we cannot in this printed volume hope to reproduce the informal interactions that are such a valuable part of a seminar series, we can use this outlet to give a more formalized presentation of some of the papers and hence widen the network of expertise sharing. We can also draw out more clearly the general lessons from specific cases, and explore resonances between the solutions which different authors adopt. Subsequent chapters are grouped into two parts, reflecting important aspects of the research process: Part I focuses on research relationships and online relationships, and Part II on research sites and strategies. Each part begins with a short introduction which explores the theme and presents the individual chapters. The two themes have been chosen to bring out the broadly applicable methodological insights from the chapters. Alternative ways of organizing the chapters, either by methodological approach (interview, ethnography, survey) or by mode of communication (electronic mail, World Wide Web (WWW), text-based online community, chat room, graphical environment) were rejected as obscuring the more general methodological issues: these methodological and substantive connections between chapters are brought out in a final section of this introduction, for the benefit of readers with particular specialist interests. First, however, I will further explore the question of virtual research methods, discussing some themes from sociology of scientific knowledge which help to understand why this area has been a source of such hope and anxiety.

The Literature on New Research Methods: Innovation and Anxiety

Social science research intrinsically involves communication, whether that communication is a researcher's observations of social behaviour, an interview encounter or the administration of a survey. In most fields of social research the methods and their preferred modes of communication are well established. The problems associated with each medium are well rehearsed and the means of minimizing the impact of these problems widely known. The introduction of a new communications medium provides the occasion for examination of the new problems which might be occasioned by use of this new technology. Logically speaking, if social research always involves communication, then it is reasonable to ask if changing the mode of communication affects any methodological assumptions or practices. Recent years have indeed seen high levels of interest in the administration of social science research methods via the Internet. One demonstration of the scale of the phenomenon comes from an online bibliography of papers and articles on web survey methodology published by Research on Internet in Slovenia. This site, http://websm.org, provides its bibliography organized alphabetically by author and thematically by subject, but also in a form useful for exploring the development of the field, chronologically by date of publication (Figure 1.1).

The bibliography contains some 1,032 references to the end of 2002, including conference presentations and published articles (while apparently complete figures for 2003 are available, there is bound to be some lag in identifying references, and it seems likely at the time of writing that more will come to light). The graph shows that publishing activity appears to have peaked in 2000, but continues at significant levels. There is obviously a lot to say about web survey methodology!

While many of the earlier items in the web survey bibliography report on the demographics of the web population, later articles focus on the technical details of web survey methodology (broadly construed): efficiency, costs, response rates, data quality, ethics, incentives. The potential of web surveys is frequently assessed by comparing results with familiar paper- or telephone-based methods, and small-scale adjustments carried out to enable the continued application of the method via the new medium. There is emphasis on a desire to capitalize on potential gains (largely in efficiency, costs and breadth of geographic reach) offered by the new

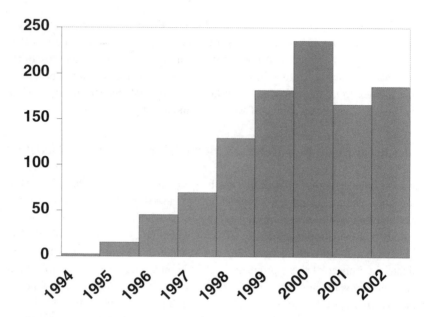

Figure 1.1 References in http://websm.org bibliography by year of publication.

technologies while minimizing losses (in response rates, representativeness of population and quality of data). New technologies are presented therefore both as an opportunity to be grasped and a threat to be countered. A similar phenomenon is encountered for other social research methods. The challenge of using electronic communications to conduct interviews has received similar attention to survey methods (see for examples Selwyn and Robson 1998; Chen and Hinton 1999; Illingworth 2001; O'Connor and Madge 2001; Bampton and Cowton 2002; Madge and O'Connor 2002). Again the concern is to exploit the benefits of the medium while avoiding its possible pitfalls. A key problem to be averted is a loss in quality of data. Face-to-face interaction here becomes the gold standard against which the performance of the computer-mediated interaction is judged.

Methods of analysis as well as methods of data collection have come under examination. For example, a growing literature examines computer-mediated discourse analysis, and considers how far the methods developed for spoken discourse or texts are applicable to computer-mediated communication or CMC (Herring 1997, 2003). Content analysis has experienced a similar revival in the face of challenges posed by web sites (for a review see Halavais 2003; see also Schneider and Foot, Chapter 11 in this volume). Social network analysis has also been thoroughly enlivened both by the new phenomena and the new visibility of networking that computer mediation provide (see for example Garton, Haythornthwaite and Wellman 1997). Ethnography also has made a considerable bid for applicability to online contexts, which I address more specifically later.

The growth of literature discussing CMC as a tool for social science research marks the question of research methods and new technologies as one of considerable interest and concern. Research 'on the Internet' is marked as a distinct topic worthy of specific note by the introduction of new epithets to familiar methods. We seem to feel the need to speak of virtual focus groups, online ethnography, cyber-research and web experiments to distinguish old familiar methods from their new offspring. This usage marks the air of innovation around the field and also provides for a sense of anxiety. The formulation of the online world as new territory for social research also creates a perception that nothing can be taken for granted.

One of the specific anxieties which has arisen in relation to use of the Internet for social research is indicated by the prominent debate over the ethics of online research. Online research is marked as a special category in which the institutionalized understandings of the ethics of research must be re-examined. Characterizations of the problem depend on the fears awakened by particular capacities of the new technology, as the report of a workshop on Ethical and Legal Aspects of Human Subjects Research in Cyberspace demonstrates:

> As cyberspace rapidly becomes a rich medium for communication and the number of users increases, it is becoming an attractive target for social and behavioural research. The ease with which the cyberspace medium allows for these types of studies also raises issues about the ethical and legal dimensions of such research. The ability of a researcher to anonymously or pseudonymously record interactions on a site without the knowledge of participants, the complexities of obtaining informed consent, the overrated expectation, if not the illusion of privacy in cyberspace, and the blurred distinction between public and private domains fuel questions about the interpretation and applicability of current policies for governing the conduct of social and behavioural research involving human subjects. (Frankel and Siang 1999)

This extract portrays a situation in which uncertainties about what participants in online settings expect, coupled with an apparent expansion in the data that researchers can collect, creates the potential for researchers to overstep accepted ethical boundaries. In response to this kind of fear one of the early actions of the newly formed Association of Internet Researchers was to set up a working committee to consider recommendations on the ethics of Internet research. The resulting statement (Ess and the Association of Internet Researchers Ethics Committee 2002) formulates a set of questions which researchers can ask themselves to explore just how the setting they are about to study might differ from more familiar contexts in terms of the expectations of users and the ethical responsibilities of researchers. The decision to frame advice in terms of questions to ask marks at once the extent to which applications of ethical principles are always situated and the diverse and contingent situations that CMC provides. The statement also aims to help users come to decisions on the ethics of their own practice by providing case studies. There is, in this understanding, no prospect of formulating a single position on the ethics of Internet research.

The Sociology of Cyber-Social-Scientific Knowledge

The air of anxiety and innovation around online methods, and the sheer burgeoning of literature on the topic might be taken, in the terms of the sociology of scientific knowledge, as pointing to the birth of a new research network around a freshly identified focus, in this case CMC. As a new research area gathers momentum, one would expect a proliferation of publications proposing methodological approaches to the new problem. We might therefore simply be witnessing, if not a period of Kuhnian revolution (Kuhn 1970 [1962]), then at least the emergence of a new problem area around which researchers can orient their interests (Mulkay, Gilbert and Woolgar 1975). The 'pioneering' ethos may render online research in general, and online methods in particular, a fruitful field to enter: rewards can be high for being among the first to enter uncharted territory. There is no doubt that the perceived newness of the new technologies is a powerful resource in stimulating the development of the field. However sceptical we might be of the hype surrounding the new technologies, their self-evident newness and the radical potential which is proposed for them provides a powerful resource to which researchers can hitch their own research agendas. A common rhetorical strategy in research proposals is to link one's agenda to a substantive phenomenon of importance, and to hope that some of the import transfers (Callon, Law and Rip 1986). The same is undoubtedly true of research into new technologies, and the editor of this book has hardly been exempt from this! At the same time, while there may be opportunities stemming from the novelty of new research areas, it is probably a mistake to expect these to be available all researchers to the same extent: we already know that the reactions to new technologies tend to be unevenly socially distributed (Woolgar 2002). What to a more established researcher might be an opportunity to experiment with new approaches might to a PhD student without a track record be a source of anxiety and self-doubt. The converse of course might also apply, with a PhD student feeling able to take risks in a way that an established researcher might not. Suffice to say that while responses to the apparent newness of new technologies in social research may be unevenly distributed, that newness can for many be a useful resource.

Perspectives from the sociology of scientific knowledge are an important reminder not to take for granted the discontinuities between what we are doing now and what has gone before. These distinctions are achieved in the ways we research and write about the new technologies, and the ways in which we organize our disciplinary boundaries. One way to pursue this insight in more detail is to consider what methods have been employed to understand CMC as a topic, and in what ways these methods have shaped our understanding of the field. Methods, after all, are not neutral devices. In laboratory studies, we know that the methods employed by researchers play a large part in shaping the phenomena which are observed, and that a large amount of work goes into sustaining a scientific instrument as a transparent spokesmachine for natural phenomena (see, for example, Latour and Woolgar 1986; Woolgar 1988). We might similarly expect, therefore, that our knowledge of the new technologies would be shaped in significant ways by the methods through which we choose to know them and the underlying epistemological commitments on which those methods rely. In illustration of this point it is worth discussing one particular methodological move, the establishment of the Internet as a cultural context.

Previously I have argued (Hine 2000) that social research into CMC to date can crudely be characterized as consisting of two phases. The first phase corresponds to the use of psychological approaches depending on experimental methods to understand the potential of computer-mediated conferencing. This approach helped to establish knowledge of CMC as an impoverished medium, stripped of social context cues and therefore prone on the one hand to promote social equality, and on the other to permit disinhibition and the display of aggression which would be deemed inappropriate in other media (Kiesler, Siegel and Mcguire 1984; Sproull and Kiesler 1986, 1991). It is possible to point to particular features of the experimental set-up which provided for this set of findings (Spears, Lea and Lee 1990; Lea and Spears 1991), and in this sense to highlight features of the method which shaped the phenomenon. It is also possible, however, to question whether experimental methods can ever give a characterization of inherent effects of the new technologies (Mantovani 1994). Naturalistic approaches based on observations in actual contexts of use might therefore seem to be the answer. Not coincidentally, a wealth of observational studies accompanied the growth in use of CMC outside experimental contexts.

The second phase of research into CMC corresponds to the growing application of naturalistic approaches to online phenomena and the subsequent claiming of the Internet as a cultural context. Participant observation and explicitly ethnographic approaches have increasingly claimed online contexts as field sites in their own right. Rheingold's (1993a) accounts of his participation in an online network were crucial in establishing the possibility of virtual community. Curtis (1992) and Bruckman (1992) wrote about the social structures which emerged in the MUDs (multi-user dimensions) they helped to design. A generation of researchers, most notably Baym (1995a, 2000), have come to apply ethnographic approaches to understanding how groups form and are sustained online. Perceptions that the medium is too restricted to promote true sociality, stemming from the earlier experimental studies, have increasingly come into question, thanks to the compelling descriptions of sustained online interaction and the formation of social structures.

We might suggest, then, that a methodological shift, the claiming of the online context as an ethnographic field site, was crucial in establishing the status of Internet communications as culture. While psychological experiments demonstrated its paucity, ethnographic methods were able to demonstrate its cultural richness. It is possible to go further and to suggest that our knowledge of the Internet as a cultural context is intrinsically tied up with the application of ethnography. The method and the phenomenon define one another in a relationship of mutual dependence. The online context is defined as a cultural context by the demonstration that ethnography can be applied to it. If we can be confident that ethnography can successfully be applied to online contexts then we can rest assured that these are indeed cultural contexts, since ethnography is a method for understanding culture.

It is not clear that what counts as ethnographic is as settled as the above suggests. I have found that an experiment in ethnographic form (Hine 2000) provokes diametrically opposed reactions from audiences. Some audiences consider the experiment in form simply ethnography as it is already practised by anthropologists in face-to-face settings, while others consider the new version to be so altered as not to constitute an ethnography at all. The problem is that there is no incontrovertible basis on which to decide whether an approach is or is not ethnographic. This point has much in parallel with Collins' (1975) discussions of the problems surrounding the replication of an experiment in science. Collins points out that the only resource we have for determining whether an experiment has been successfully replicated is whether a scientist produces something which is seen by other scientists to count as a working replication of the experiment. There is no external criterion by which we may judge successful replication. In the same way, we have no essential criteria to judge whether an ethnography in an online context is indeed an ethnography.

In claiming the method as ethnographic an author is making a performance of community (Cooper and Woolgar 1996), which is either accepted or rejected by audiences to the performance. In these interactions we can see negotiations about the meaning of a competent ethnography. When we talk about methodology we are implicitly talking about our identity and the standards by which we wish our work to be judged. It is no wonder, then, that the breaks with past methods which we declare by calling our new approaches 'virtual', 'cyber' and 'online' methods can provoke anxiety. We threaten the security of membership of a community of research practice. In this sense, then, claims about the applicability of methods to online settings and the success of particular methodological claims have the potential to shape our understanding of what the technology is and who we as researchers are at the same time. This suggests that it may be less than profitable to rest on methodological security as a means of understanding the new technologies. The question is much more interesting, potentially, than whether old methods can be adapted to fit new technologies. New technologies might, rather, provide an opportunity for interrogating and understanding our methodological commitments. In the moments of innovation and anxiety which surround the research methods there are opportunities for reflexivity. Seizing these moments of reflexivity depends, however, on not taking the radical capacities of the new technologies for granted, nor treating them as poor substitutes for a face-to-face gold standard.

This volume aims to go some way towards addressing the air of innovation and anxiety around virtual methods head on, by providing examples of innovation, and by setting precedents to quell anxiety. It also, however, provides fuel for reflexive consideration of just what methods we aim to use to explore the social formations which arise through use of information and communication technologies and how those methods will shape our understanding. It is this potential for reflexive engagement with our own practices that I aim to capture with the term the Sociology of Cyber-Social-Scientific Knowledge (SCSSK). Not a catchy term, but worth practising. Focusing on SCSSK is a reminder to capitalize on the potential that new technologies provide for social science itself, in examining epistemological and methodological commitments afresh, opening up possibilities for new research designs and new approaches, and seizing on the opportunity for reflexive engagement.

In thinking about the implications of the Internet for research methods from an SCSSK perspective, it is important to remember that the Internet is both cultural context and cultural artefact (Hine 2000). The Internet as cultural context is established, as we saw earlier, through application of ethnographic methods to online settings. That the Internet is also a cultural artefact is apparent from the extent to which it is manifested as a varying and variably used set of technologies that have different meanings for different groups of people. In this sense, using the Internet is a culturally located experience (Miller and Slater 2000). Using a term from the sociology of technology, the Internet is an interpretively flexible object (for extended discussion of this concept see Bijker 1995). It means different things to different people, and they will see its functions, risks and opportunities in ways that reflect their own concerns. Any given cultural event we might want to study incorporates both of these dimensions of the Internet to differing degrees. This complicates the use of the Internet as a research tool considerably, since we cannot be sure that using the Internet means the same thing to our informants as to us, nor that it is the same thing to all of our informants (or indeed all of our colleagues). This observation brings the mediation of research methods to the fore. Far more contingencies in the research process become apparent, since we cannot assume that our choices of medium reflect the experience of our informants nor that our choices will have predictable effects. Whatever the ostensive topic of the research, a sensitivity to its mediation becomes important.

The interrogation of methodological assumptions from different perspectives is not new, of course. The mechanics of methods have been made visible by turning a feminist epistemological commitment not just on to the substance of the research project, but onto the processes by which it generates its knowledge as well, as in Ann Oakley's discussion of reactions to experimental and qualitative methodologies (Oakley 1999). Virtual methods could act as interrogators of traditional method in a similar fashion: in pondering on whether a virtual interview qualifies as a real interview, we also can think more deeply about what it is that we valued about interviews as a methodological stance. To return to the point at which this section began, if even some of the burgeoning literature on web survey methodology contains reflection on the aims and upshots of the survey process in general, then this represents a healthy process for disciplines as a whole and not just the interdiscipline of Internet studies.

In summary then, SCSSK offers the opportunity to seize upon the power of reflexivity to examine methods afresh and to open up possibilities for new designs and approaches, sensitive to the varying interpretations of technologies of mediation. It also prompts us to be wary of the risks of over-asserting differences between virtual methods and their traditional counterparts. These risks include: distancing ourselves from useful resources and valuable allies in established disciplines; neglecting existing ethical frameworks; and assuming what we instead need to explore. The chapters which make up this volume do not explicitly take up the SCSSK framework, but through their discussion of situated methodological solutions they provide ample evidence of the power of reflexive thinking in methodology.

Subsequent to this chapter the volume divides into two parts, which reflect dominant ways of thinking about research in social science. Each part has an introduction which explores the issues covered chapter by chapter, so here I shall give only a brief overview. The first aspect of research which has come to the fore through use of CMC is the research encounter, and research as a form of interaction. Given the focus on new forms of interaction that the Internet has prompted, it seems only right that the first part of this book focus on research relationships and online relationships. In Part I, chapters examine the extent to which the relationships formed in online encounters can act as satisfying research occasions, both alone and when combined with offline interactions. The second aspect of research explored in this volume is the shaping of research objects. Online social formations seem to challenge existing ways of conceptualizing research sites and ask for new strategies of exploration. Part II of the book on research sites and strategies explores some of the ways, both innovative and more traditional, that CMC can be conceptualized as research object and made amenable to research explorations.

Given the emphasis on reflexivity that I have argued for in this introduction, it is appropriate for the collection to end on a thoughtful note. In their epilogue Jankowski & van Selm look back on the nature of the methodological innovations that the chapters have proposed, and consider the future agenda for virtual methods. They urge us to make connections across the grand methodological divides, to continue to innovate in order to facilitate cross-national, longitudinal and multi-method studies, and to continue to develop approaches to the ethics of online research. Above all, they encourage dialogue, to provide an ongoing basis for innovation as our understandings develop and as the scope of the projects we want to tackle expands.

Methodological Approaches, Modes of Communication

As described previously, the volume is divided into two parts which represent broad themes of methodological interest. It is likely, however, that some readers will approach the volume with questions that focus on particular methodological approaches or modes of communication, asking, for example, what the volume has to say about online interviews, or how it can help to research the World Wide Web. For those readers, I provide here a summary of the chapters focusing on their treatment of some key approaches and technologies.

Joinson begins the volume with a discussion of Internet behaviour that is applicable to a wide range of methodological approaches. While he explicitly discusses factors that might promote compliance with and disclosure in online surveys, his observations are also provocative for thinking about interviews and ethnographic encounters. A number of the authors discuss interviews, including Kivits, Orgad, Sanders, and Rutter & Smith. Each conceptualizes the prospects for online interviews in a different way, with only Kivits conducting a study without use of face-to-face encounters to complement online research. The others find rationales for face-to-face interviews either as a means to explore different facets of informants' lives, or as a factor in developing trusting and rich research relationships. Ethnography is the specific focus of Sanders, Rutter & Smith, Forte, Mackay, Guimarães and Beaulieu. Again, there are some startling contrasts in the definition of field sites and the choices of communication media which are made. Different research sites also provide opportunities for collection and analysis of quite different forms of data: Mackay focuses on extended visits and interviews in domestic settings; Forte uses web site production as a means to complement and expand his geographically located ethnography; Rutter & Smith begin online but find themselves drawn offline; Guimarães focuses on social environments enacted wholly online; and Beaulieu traces emergent structures through connections online and offline with a particular focus on hyperlinks.

In terms of the modes of communication which they deploy and discuss, the chapters are also diverse. Joinson provides an overview which focuses largely on text-based and visually anonymous communication, but demonstrates along the way how dangerous it is to overgeneralize about the effects of any given communication technology on interaction. Dodge reviews ways of mapping and visualizing CMC that span across a wide range of technological platforms and social applications, stimulating recognition of the complexity and diversity of social formations to which these technologies can give rise. A focus on the web in particular is provided by Forte and Beaulieu, from an experiential ethnographic perspective, and by Schneider & Foot, and Park & Thelwall from more structured points of view. Schneider & Foot explore the use of a new object of analysis, the web sphere, while Park & Thelwall explore the extent to which analysis of hyperlinking structures can tell us about socially meaningful phenomena. Beaulieu explores web structures as part of her ethnographic strategy, finding that hyperlinks have situated and diverse meanings. Rutter & Smith focus their ethnography on a newsgroup, while Guimarães explores a social network focused around use of a graphical environment peopled by avatars. Finally, use of email to communicate with informants is discussed explicitly by Kivits, Orgad and Sanders: each of them also makes use of web sites as places for observing and recruiting people to their research.

Acknowledgements

This chapter builds on an argument in a conference paper 'New Technology/New Methodology?' written with Steve Woolgar and presented at the 4S/EASST conference (Worlds in Transition: Technoscience, Citizenship and Culture in the Twenty-first Century) 20–30 September 2000, University of Vienna, Austria. I am very grateful for the discussions with my co-author which helped to develop the ideas presented here.

Note

1. The seminars were funded by the UK Economic and Social Research Council (ESRC grant number R451265171) and organized by Christine Hine. The seven seminars were as follows:

   Open Theme 17–18 December 2001, at Royal Holloway, University of London
   Research Relationships and Online Relationships, 19 April 2002, at Brunel University
   Social Research Methods and New Cultural Geographies, 29 July 2002, at Brunel University
   Qualitative Data Collection through Online Interaction, 17 September 2002, at London School of Economics

Open Theme, 7 July 2003, at Brunel University
Web Site Analysis, 15 September 2003, at University of Surrey
Virtual Methods: Prospects and Retrospects, 15 December 2003, at University of Surrey.
Further details of the series are available at http://www.soc.surrey.ac.uk/virtual-methods/vmesrc.htm.

Part I

Research Relationships
and Online Relationships

Research Relationships and Online Relationships: Introduction

Christine Hine

Research Relationships and Online Relationships: The Problem

Much has been written about the constraints of computer-mediated communication, focusing on its limitations for the formation of intimate relationships and the expression of emotion. A tersely expressed textual communication, received and read in a context far detached in time, space and warmth of social connection from the circumstances in which it was written, provides the stereotype for a mode of communication which seems hopelessly inadequate for the formation of intimacy. Qualitative research, on the other hand, has come to be seen as dependent on the achievement of trusting relationships with informants. Research encounters are occasions for development of rich mutual understanding, and for acquiring a multifaceted perspective on experiences and lives. At the outset, then, there seems to be a problem with employing CMC in qualitative research.

If qualitative research entails particular sets of beliefs about the adequacy of data and the form of relationship which best produces that data, it appears that use of CMC in qualitative research is doomed to disaster. That this is by now patently not the case is demonstrated by a substantial body of research that now attests to the vibrant social and cultural formations that occur online, and the depth and intimacy of the social relations that can happen in cyberspace. Counter to the stereotype, online interactions can be socially rich interactions. However, just as the stereotype was not fair to CMC, so unfortunately for qualitative researchers it was not entirely untrue either. Online research encounters can still be unrewarding, stilted, terse and unenlightening (just as offline encounters can be). In order for their research not to suffer these disappointments, qualitative researchers must become skilled at making and sustaining relationships online. Just as in face-to-face interactions, researchers need to both draw on their existing social abilities and develop new talents. They need to become adept at creating comfortable spaces for informants and interviewees to share their experiences, and they have to attend to the ethical responsibilities which new forms of research relationship place upon them. They have to find ways of immersing themselves in life as it is lived online, and as it connects through into offline social spheres. Clearly, there is far more to conducting effective qualitative research online than the ability to send email. Quantitative researchers too engage in relationships with informants via surveys and questionnaires, and they too may need to learn new skills for presenting their research instruments to an online audience.

Part I explores the place of the Internet within contemporary social research, in order to find out how it adds to existing research repertoires, and to provide advice on techniques and strategies for the online researcher. The chapters include advice on forming sustained research relationships online, and insights into research designs and questions which may lead researchers to move relationships offline or rely on face-to-face data collection instead. Chapters in this part also consider the extent to which online research can learn from methodological insights developed in more conventional settings. The case studies discussed here deploy a range of modes of communication, including mail, newsgroups and web site discussion boards, together with the use of web site production skills as a route to formation of research relationships.

Case Studies for Thinking about Online Research Relationships

The first of the chapters in this part, by Adam Joinson, reviews some psychological perspectives which are provocative for thinking about how online relationships can be fruitful research relationships. A general tendency for people to disclose more about themselves online provides a considerable resource for the researcher, but at a price in terms of the need for careful and ethical design. The tendency to online disclosure is not a guaranteed feature of the medium, and can be quite sensitive to the ways in which researchers present themselves and their projects. Any difference between the ways that people present themselves online and offline is also a potential methodological drawback for the generalizability of research findings.

In the next chapter, Joëlle Kivits describes a study which used email to conduct long-term interview relationships with informants. These elongated interviews become a process of extended reflection for both researcher and informants, as adapted and shared interview agendas develop and dense and intimate questions are asked and answered. While Joinson shows that online disclosure is fruitful but fragile, Kivits demonstrates some ways in which it can be carefully nurtured.

A further study in which online interviews were conducted is described by Shani Orgad. Here, though, Orgad decided to move the research relationship offline, in order to develop a deeper understanding of the context within which Internet use arises. Some stark and interesting differences were experienced between online and offline encounters, demonstrating that neither can routinely be treated as the 'context' which explains the other. The online/offline boundary is therefore not one which should automatically be respected in research design.

In another demonstration of the troubling nature of the online/offline distinction for research purposes, Teela Sanders describes the role of the Internet in an ethnography of sex work. While the Internet made visible some features of the community which were not readily observable elsewhere, it also raised difficulties in establishing a presence as a bona fide researcher. The means for establishing trust are shown to be deeply entwined with the qualities of the social world being researched. Methodological solutions do not automatically transfer from offline to online settings.

The links between methodologies as expressed in conventional settings and in online sites are further explored by Jason Rutter and Gregory W. H. Smith. Their discussion, of ethnographic presence in the 'nebulous settings' of the social networks which permeate a newsgroup, shows how online ethnographers must both learn from and renegotiate prior thinking about the presence of the researcher and the formation of field relationships. Rutter and Smith found considerable purchase in face-to-face meetings with informants, even as they respected and attended to their online sociability practices.

Finally in this part, Maximilian C. Forte describes an innovative experiment in web site design as an ethnographic immersion strategy. Through developing web sites for and with informants, Forte is able to develop an understanding of the flows of interaction and communication surrounding the web, and to provide rich insights into the cultural connections of this field site created through his actions. Forte demonstrates that his strategy, whilst powerful for enrolling new audiences for the research and exploring new aspects of the research through the reactions of these audiences, also placed a considerable burden on the researcher. His experiments to deal with overload by the use of an intelligent agent to interact with site visitors show how enlisting new technologies into the research encounter provides yet more potent but troubling occasions for research relationships.

Online Research Relationships: Potent and Troubling

Taken collectively, the chapters in Part I have some clear advice for researchers hoping to incorporate use of the Internet into their methodologies. The key points are as follows:

- Online relationships can be highly potent ways of conducting research. Contrary to previous doubts, effective qualitative research relationships can be forged online. Online presence can be a means to enhanced understanding, both of CMC itself and of the broader cultural domains that exist in and through it.

- The benefits of online research do not arise automatically from the technology, but require considerable sensitivity and reflection on the part of the researcher. A learning process, focusing on the development of new sociability skills, is to be expected.
- The online/offline distinction should not necessarily be adhered to as a research strategy. While some research questions can be answered through research relationships conducted solely online, others will be best served by moving research relationships either from online to offline or vice versa.
- Researchers have to pay considerable attention to their self-presentation. Establishing one's presence as a bona fide researcher and trustworthy recipient of confidences is not automatic, and varies depending on the cultural context under investigation. The doubts of informants, the risks to which they feel research may expose them, and their expectations of online relationships may vary widely between settings.

–2–

Internet Behaviour
and the Design of Virtual Methods

Adam N. Joinson

The Internet, and in particular the World Wide Web, has enabled social scientists to create a virtual laboratory where data can be collected twenty-four hours a day, across the globe, without the costs (time, transcription errors and financial) associated with more traditional methods of research. Just as the video camera revolutionized observation methods, so the Internet is fundamentally changing the ways in which we can observe, measure and report on the human condition and societal structures.

However, despite the increasing popularity of the Internet as both a methodology and as the object of research, it is relatively rare for these two separate literatures to cross-reference each other. In this chapter, I argue that an understanding of the social aspects of Internet behaviour is crucial to the effective design of Internet-based methodology. While the need for an appreciation of theorizing about online interaction is clear for qualitative methodologies, online experimental methods should also be seen within the context of a social interaction for a number of reasons. First, people tend to respond to computers as social actors (Nass, Fogg and Moon 1996; Moon 2000), and as such transfer modes of interaction used with other people to their interactions with new social technologies. Second, the flexibility of Internet-based (specifically World Wide Web) research methodology has encouraged people to experiment with ways to personalize the encounter between the researcher and the participant. So, it is not uncommon to encounter quite extensive information about the researcher or line drawings/smiley faces embedded within a survey (Nass et al. 1996; Tourangeau 2004). Such techniques will tend to have unexpected effects: for instance, by encouraging participants to reciprocate disclosure (Moon 2000; Joinson 2001a), or alternatively, by increasing participants' face-saving motivation (Paulhus 1984). Finally, it is possible that all writing, from diaries to the completion of web-based survey instruments, is conducted with an audience in mind. So, minor changes in the salience or type of audience, or in the identifiability of the author, may well have noticeable effects on the nature of the information disclosed by the research participant.

Models of Internet Behaviour

Early theories of Internet behaviour (and more specifically computer-mediated communication) tended to focus on what was lost during Internet-based interaction (Sproull and Kiesler 1986). The lack of visual and feedback cues in CMC was invoked to predict that any interaction will tend to be rather formal and task-oriented, and will lack the richness of real-time face-to-face interaction (Daft and Lengel 1984). For instance, Hiltz and Turoff (1978) reported that only 14 per cent of CMC groups' communication was socio-emotional in content, compared to 33 per cent in face-to-face groups. Rice and Love (1987) studied 2,347 sentences exchanged using CMC: 28 per cent were 'positive' socio-emotional messages, 4 per cent negative socio-emotional messages and 71 per cent were task-oriented messages.

However, historical analyses strongly suggest that a loss of visual cues need not be accompanied by a concurrent reduction in the 'socialness' of interaction (see Joinson 2003). For instance, Standage (1998: 123) notes that 'despite the apparently impersonal nature of communicating by wire, [the telegraph] was in fact an extremely subtle and intimate means of communication'. Fischer (1992) also notes that telephone executives bemoaned frivolous use of the telephone in internal memoranda, and actively discouraged social uses of the telephone until the 1920s. Despite this censure, the use of the telephone for intimacy became accepted and everyday. Other instances of intimate behaviour have been recorded via letter, flashlight and radio / CB (Citizens' Band) (see Joinson 2003 for a summary). Clearly then, lack of visual or verbal cues need not lead an interaction to be task-oriented, unregulated or desocialized. Indeed, more recent work on CMC suggests that it is this lack of cues which leads CMC to be more highly social, regulated by norms and intimate than face-to-face interaction.

An accumulating body of experimental evidence, first person accounts and observation research has shown that Internet-based communication can be characterized as highly socialized – perhaps even more social than face-to-face interaction (Rheingold 1993a; Walther 1996). Moreover, issues of status and hierarchy transfer just as easily to Internet-based interactions (Spears et al. 2002), negating the contention that lack of cues leads to a reduction in concern for the audience or equalization effects.

For instance, there is evidence that Internet communication can lead people to identify highly with relevant social groups and identities (Spears and Lea 1992; Spears et al. 2002) and develop high levels of affiliation and liking (Walther 1996). Internet relationships may well be characterized by idealization of the other partner (McKenna, Green and Gleasin 2002), leading to intense feelings and 'just clicked' experiences (Joinson 2003). The prognosis for an Internet relationship is just as healthy as that for one formed face-to-face (McKenna et al. 2002). Perhaps the most widely recognized prosocial behaviour on the Internet is of particular importance to the use of the Internet as a research tool as well for building intimate relationships: self-disclosure.

Wallace (1999: 151) notes that 'The tendency to disclose more to a computer ... is an important ingredient of what seems to be happening on the Internet'. Self-disclosure via (or to) a computer has been studied in a number of different settings: for instance, in the medical field, increased levels of candid disclosure to a computer, as compared to face-to-face consultations, have been reported in psychiatric interviews and pre-interviews (Greist, Klein and Van Cura 1973; Ferriter 1993). Robinson and West report that clients at a sexually transmitted disease clinic admit to more sexual partners, more previous visits and more symptoms to a computer than to a doctor (Robinson & West 1992).

When non-medical Internet behaviour is studied, similar findings also emerge. Parks and Floyd (1996) studied the relationships formed by Internet users. They also asked their participants to report the level of self-disclosure in their Internet relationships (by responding to statements such as 'I usually tell this person exactly how I feel' and 'I would never tell this person anything intimate or personal about myself'). They found that people report disclosing significantly more in their Internet relationships compared to their real-life relationships. Bargh, McKenna and Fitzsimons (2002) found evidence that people are more able to express their 'true' selves on the Internet, which may involve disclosing information about the self that would normally be socially unacceptable. Similarly, in their study of 'coming out on the Internet', McKenna and Bargh (1998: 682) argue that participation in online newsgroups gives people the benefit of 'disclosing a long secret part of one's self'. In the series of studies reported by Joinson (2001b), levels of self-disclosure were measured using content analysis of transcripts of face-to-face and synchronous CMC discussions (Study one), and in conditions of visual anonymity and video links during CMC (Study two). In keeping with the predicted effect, self-disclosure was significantly higher when participants discussed using a CMC system as opposed to face-to-face, and when they were visually anonymous. Walther (1996: 17) termed this phenomenon 'hyperpersonal communication', that is, communication which is 'more socially desirable than we tend to experience in parallel FtF [face-to-face] interaction'.

The most common aspect of CMC invoked to explain hyperpersonal communication is visual anonymity. For instance, social identity theorists (for example, Spears and Lea 1992; Spears et al. 2002) have argued that visual anonymity increases identification with a group by increasing perceived homogeneity of the group (because you cannot see how varied the group is). McKenna et al. (2002) have argued that visual anonymity creates a 'strangers on the train' experience, where the social cost of self-disclosure is reduced through relative anonymity (and the reduction in a person's power to use the disclosed information against the discloser). Alternatively, anonymity during CMC (in particular isolation) has been argued to increase people's focus on their own attitudes and emotions (Matheson and Zanna 1988), which would increase self-disclosure (Joinson 2001b). Tidwell and Walther (2002) have argued that high levels of disclosure online are motivated by a desire to reduce uncertainty within an interaction. Joinson (2003) has noted that simply the act of having to write may increase disclosure through the need to express explicitly one's emotions and attitudes.

It is also plausible that people choose the Internet specifically because they wish to disclose information, and require a degree of anonymity. For instance, an individual may well choose to post an intimate question to a health bulletin board rather than visit a medical centre. Nicholas et al. (2003) coined the term 'search disclosure' to explain their finding that health information kiosks located in more 'private' areas tended to receive more intimate or potentially embarrassing searches: a construct easily transferred to online research methods.

In this case, the medium may not be leading to a specific behaviour (that is, high disclosure), but instead is being used strategically. To test this, Joinson (2004) asked people to rank media across a series of scenarios, some of which were more interpersonally risky than others. As the level of risk increased, so people were more likely to choose email over face-to-face as their communication medium of choice.

According to Walther (1996), hyperpersonal interaction is created by four main factors. First, because many online communicants share a social categorization, they will also tend to perceive greater similarity between themselves and their conversational partner. As we tend to like those whom we see as similar, people communicating online will be predisposed toward liking their communication partners. Second, the sender of a message can optimize their self-presentation – that is, they can present themselves in a more positive light than they might be able to face-to-face because they do not have to worry about their non-verbal behaviour. Walther also suggests that being freed from concerns about our appearance might be linked to a heightening of focus on our own inner self. This would mean that messages sent during CMC would include more content on personal feelings and thoughts, and that the senders might be more in touch with their self-ideals (again, helping with their self-presentation).

A third factor in hyperpersonal communication is the format of the CMC. Walther (1996) argues that asynchronous CMC (for example, email) is more likely to lead to hyperpersonal interaction because the communicants can devote a special time to CMC rather than being distracted by other goings on, spend more time composing or editing the message, mix social and task messages, and don't need to use up cognitive resources answering immediately, so can pay more attention to the message.

The final factor Walther invokes is a feedback loop that causes these effects to be magnified through social interaction. In line with work on self-fulfilling prophecies and behavioural confirmation, as the interaction progresses, so the inflated positive impressions will be magnified as the communicators seek to confirm their initial impressions, and in turn respond to the positive impressions conveyed by their partners (Walther 1996).

Internet Behaviour: Implications for Online Research

Clearly, if people behave differently online compared to offline, this may well have implications for social scientists who use the Internet as a research tool. Indeed, there is considerable evidence that within a research setting, people also disclose more about themselves online compared to in offline equivalents, and that much of that disclosure is more candid.

For instance, socially desirable responding is the tendency for people to present themselves in a positive light in a research setting. Compared to a pencil and paper survey, answers to an electronic survey are less socially desirable and lead to the disclosure of more information about the self (Kiesler and Sproull 1986; Weisband and Kiesler 1986; Joinson 1999; Frick Bächtiger and Reips 2001). In a meta-analysis of self-disclosure on computer forms, Weisband and Kiesler found that the effect of using a computer on self-disclosure is highest when collecting sensitive information. Compared to other research methods, when data collection is conducted via computer-aided self-interviews (where participants type their answers on to a laptop), people report more health-related problems (Epstein, Barker and Kroutil 2001), more HIV-risk behaviours (Des Jarlais et al. 1999) and more drug use (Lessler et al. 2000); men report fewer sexual partners, and women more (Tourangeau & Smith 1996). Similarly, automated or computerized telephone interviews, compared to other forms of telephone interviewing, lead to higher levels of reporting of sensitive information (see Lau, Tsui and Wang 2003; Tourangeau 2004). However, although the weight of evidence suggests high self-disclosure and low social desirability in computerized research – on the WWW, interviews and telephone – there have also been occasions when no differences are found between offline and online research methods (Fox and Schwartz 2002; Birnbaum 2004; Buchanan and Joinson 2004). It is unclear why an effect might be found in some studies and not in others, and there are often a number of confounding variables – for instance, between anonymity and being in the presence of others, timing, identifiability and sample motivation. In the following sections, five aspects of the design of virtual methods, the impact on responses, and links to general Internet behaviour, are discussed.

The Role of Privacy and Anonymity

Privacy is a prerequisite for intimacy (Fried 1970). But, such intimacy paradoxically serves to reduce people's privacy (Ben-Ze'ev 2003). The Internet, and Internet research methods, may provide people with expressive privacy, without negating their informational privacy (DeCew 1997). In this respect the Internet may well be ideally suited to preserving privacy while simultaneously allowing openness. This is because on the Internet privacy need not be expressly linked to concealment. According to Ben-Ze'ev (2003: 452), 'The relative anonymity of cyberspace decreases our vulnerability and so reduces the necessity for such secrecy in private matters'.

Most researchers are ethically bound and methodologically motivated to maintain participant confidentiality and anonymity during online research. Institutional Research Boards now tend to require that participants' confidentiality is carefully protected. In many cases, this might require a recognition that true anonymity is not strictly possible (for instance, because IP (Internet Protocol) numbers are automatically stored), but that confidentiality is assured. Detailed consent forms can be used to assuage participants' privacy concerns in most cases, although in some cases it might be necessary to take further steps (for instance, by storing identifying information and responses on separate computers).

Other aspects of the design of Internet-based research could conceivably increase the real and perceived privacy of participants. For instance, Moon (1998) found that giving responses to a geographically distant computer was seen as more private than a computer located closer to the participant. In this instance, one would assume that it is people's sense of vulnerability that is changed, rather than their sense of absolute privacy (or anonymity).

However, increasing privacy and anonymity may at times run counter to researchers' efforts to check for multiple submissions of web-based surveys. Multiple submissions of surveys can usually be guarded against through checking for multiple IP numbers, the setting of session-based cookies or the use of panels or passwords and usernames. These techniques also tend to make participants less anonymous. The student panels run at the Open University use invitations with personalized URLs (Uniform Resource Locators) to recruit panel members to studies. These URLs include an encoded personal identifier for the participant, enabling researchers to link an individual's responses with their demographic details and earlier survey answers. Clearly the participants in these cases are not anonymous, but their responses are treated confidentially.

However, such reductions in privacy may not influence responses as much as expected. Buchanan, Joinson and Ali (2002) tested the impact of increasing people's privacy concerns on self-disclosure. Participants were randomly allocated to two conditions, one of which aimed to increase their privacy concerns. Before completing a series of questions to test their willingness to disclose personal information, the privacy concern group were told:

> Warning: Remember the Internet is not a secure environment. While we undertake to keep your data confidential, you should be aware that any data you submit could be intercepted by third parties while in transit (e.g. IT staff at work or school, employees of your ISP [Internet Service Providers], hackers) and that records of your submission may be kept in WWW server log files. Your browser may also store data locally in your computer's hard drive, with the result that other people using your computer could potentially find it.

Surprisingly, this warning made little difference to people's willingness to disclose information as part of a web study, with the exception of two items – masturbation and fantasizing about an affair. It is plausible that these two items represented the most intimate, potentially embarrassing (or damaging) behaviours to disclose, hence the effect.

Accidental and Intentional Use of Social Rules and Norms

A second way to design disclosure into virtual methodologies is to exploit the theory that people tend to respond to computers as social actors (Moon 2000). As such, people's responses to web-based questionnaires should follow well-established social psychological principles derived from work on communication and persuasion. One such rule is self-disclosure reciprocity.

Reciprocity

Self-disclosure tends to be reciprocated (Archer 1980). That is, within an interaction, one person's intimacies tend to be reciprocated in terms of level and type by the communication partner. Violation of this rule can lead to discomfort and withdrawal from an interaction. To test the notion that people respond to computers as social actors, Moon (2000) tested self-disclosure reciprocity in the collection of data via stand-alone computers. She found that when the computer essentially disclosed information about itself (for example, 'Sometimes this computer is used by people who don't know how to operate it. It ends up crashing. What are some of the things that make you furious?'), the participants reciprocated in kind, leading to a greater breadth and depth of disclosure. In a pilot study testing the applicability of this effect to web-based surveys, Joinson (2001a) assigned participants to either an experimenter disclosing or experimenter non-disclosing condition. In the experimenter disclosing condition, participants were directed to a web page with information about the experimenter, while in the non-disclosing condition, participants did not receive information about the experimenter until after the experimental procedure. All participants answered six personal questions using free text. Although in the study, there was no effect of reciprocal self-disclosure on the depth of self-disclosure, there was an effect on the breadth of disclosure. That is, participants who answered the questions following self-disclosure by the experimenter went on to disclose more about themselves, but not with any greater intimacy, than those who went straight to the questions.

Diffusion of Responsibility

A second possible social rule that can be applied to online research is diffusion of responsibility. Research on bystander apathy (the tendency for groups of people not to intervene when help is needed) established the principle that the more people there are to help, the less the chance that any help will be received at all (Latane and Darley 1970). One explanation for this phenomenon is diffusion of responsibility – the obligation to help is spread across the number of potential helpers, reducing the likelihood that any one individual will provide assistance (Latane and Darley 1970).

Barron and Yechiam (2002) tested the diffusion of responsibility effect in email requests for assistance. They found that addressing an email to a single addressee (as opposed to five addresses) led to more responses, and for those responses to be both more helpful and longer in length.

Theoretically at least then, one would expect that Internet-based research should, paradoxically, gain a greater number of more committed responses by sending out individual requests for assistance in research, rather than mass mailings (but see the discussion of personalization below).

Foot in the Door

The foot-in-the-door technique is a way of improving compliance to large requests by preceding it with a small request. Freedman and Fraser (1966) found that 43 per cent of their sample would spend two hours compiling a list of their household goods if it was preceded by a small request three days earlier (an eight question survey). If there was no small request preceding it, only 22 per cent of participants acquiesced to the large request, Gueguen (2002) found that the technique also worked on the Internet: half of his participants were first asked by email to help with a small request (information on file conversion). A short time later (30 minutes) all participants were asked to complete a forty question survey requiring 15–20 minutes of their time. Gueguen found that compliance with the first small request increased people's compliance with the later large task – 76 per cent in the foot-in-the-door group completed and mailed back the second request, compared to 44 per cent in the control group.

Possible Contra-indications

However, the use of social rules to improve response rates or candour may have unintended, unexpected effects. One aspect of socially desirable responding is impression management: that is, the motivation to save face when responding to questions. Any design that increases the 'socialness' of an encounter may also lead to increases in impression management motives as well. One possible reason why touch tone telephone surveys and web-based surveys are successful in the exploration of sensitive topics may be due to the absence of an obvious audience to whom we might wish to face save.

If a social interface can be designed that also allows for participants' privacy and reduces impression management concerns, then clearly this would be a powerful methodological tool. One possible mechanism is to stress geographic distance between the server collecting data and the participant (after all, privacy is less concerning if the person completing the survey is many thousands of miles from the researcher). Indeed, any design that stresses 'strangers on the train' factors (for example, that revealing personal information does not increase vulnerability) may well improve data quality in web-based forms, while manipulations that stress the power of sanction of the researcher would be expected to increase socially desirable responding.

Triggering People's Strategic Impression Management

As noted, people may well participate in online research, even the completion of web-based surveys, with an audience in mind. Research conducted in the Open University's virtual research lab by Joinson and Reips (2004a) confirms this notion. Joinson and Reips conducted a series of experiments using Open University student panels to investigate the role of power and status differentials in volunteering to participate in web-based surveying. In the first study 10,000 students were emailed invitations from the vice-chancellor to join a panel. The salutation was varied in four ways: 'Dear Open University Student', 'Dear Student', 'Dear John Doe' and 'Dear John'. Significantly more students signed up for the panel when addressed only by their forename compared to the other three salutation conditions.

In the second study, an existing panel were mailed an invitation to end their membership of the panel (it was a twelve month commitment). In keeping with the first study, the salutation was varied, and the emails originated from the vice-chancellor of the Open University. As expected, in this study fewer students addressed as 'Dear John' or 'Dear John Doe' opted to leave the panel.

In the third study, participants were told that they were members of a small (156 members) or large (1,405) panel, and again the salutation was varied. This time the email originated from a neutral or low power source. There were no effects of either panel size or salutation, suggesting that the power and status of the person making the request interacts with a personal salutation to create higher levels of compliance.

This was tested in the fourth study: both power and salutation were manipulated. As predicted, there was an effect of salutation only when the power of the requestor was high. This suggests that the combination of high power request, and personal salutation, might lead to a strategic response (to sign up to a panel). The importance of the audience was clear throughout this series of studies – in some cases students would reply to the email from the vice-chancellor by addressing her by her forename, and the person requesting the participation would be name-checked within the surveys.

Although not tested directly in Joinson and Reips' studies, it is likely that such manipulations would serve to increase socially desirable responding in most circumstances, despite increasing response rates. It is common for research and survey advice to stress the importance of having a faculty member or other respected person to invite people to participate in a research project (Dillman 2000). The research of Joinson and Reips (2004a) suggests that the efficacy of this technique may well be due to the strategic behaviour of non-anonymous people. Since the requirement to act strategically is reduced once true anonymity is available, it is unlikely that a powerful, high status requestor to anonymous participants would elicit such a strong effect on response rates.

The Design of Specific Questions

Just as drop-out from web experiments has become an increasingly popular dependent variable (Reips 2002; Birnbaum 2004), so lack of disclosure could become the topic of similar levels of interest. In a typical web-based survey, people are rarely given the opportunity to choose not to answer a particular question. For instance, a drop-down salary question (see Figure 2.1) might have seven options, beginning with 'Please choose . . .' set as the default, through to the highest range (for example, £75,001 plus per annum). The use of the 'Please choose . . .' option is important because it enables the researcher to identify people who are leaving the default option and submitting the survey. However, participants may also be using the 'Please choose . . .' option as a proxy 'I don't want to answer that question'. To differentiate these two effects, it is worth adding the option 'I don't want to answer' to questions that people might conceivably not want to disclose (see Figure 2.1).

Joinson & Reips (2004b) tested the effect of having an 'I don't want to say' option in a salary question given to 1,076 Open University alumni. The presence and location of the option 'I don't want to say' was experimentally manipulated, as was the default selection (either 'Please choose' or 'I don't want to say'). When 'I don't want to say' was the default choice, 35 per cent of participants chose that option, compared to 9.6 per cent when 'Please choose' was the default. When there

Your annual salary	Please choose	
	Please choose	
	I don't want to say	
	£0 - £15,000 per annum	
Please subm	£15,001 - £25,000 per annum	**e button below.**
	£25,001 - £35,000 per annum	
	£35,001 - £45,000 per annum	
	£45,001 - £55,000 per annum	
	£55,001 - £75,000 per annum	
	£75,001 plus per year	

	O	I don't want to say
	O	£0 - £15,000 per annum
	O	£15,001 - £25,000 per annum
	O	£25,001 - £35,000 per annum
Your annual salary	O	£35,001 - £45,000 per annum
	O	£45,001 - £55,000 per annum
	O	£55,001 - £75,000 per annum
	O	£75,001 plus per year

Figure 2.1 Non-disclosure in drop down menus and radio button lists.

was no 'I don't want to say' option 17.8 per cent of people submitted the 'Please choose . . .' default. This reduced to 11.5 per cent when there was an 'I don't want to say' option added

Therefore, an 'I don't want to say' option, if used carefully, should improve data quality by reducing the number of default selections. Its use in a drop-down menu will reduce the amount of 'Please choose . . .' options submitted by around 50 per cent, but there will still be default submissions. This could be either because participants do not click the menu, or because even if the menu is activated, the choice of 'I don't want to say' is itself a statement that people wish to avoid making. When radio buttons were used instead of drop-down menus, the proportion of people choosing 'I don't want to say' was considerably higher (12.1 per cent) when the 'I don't want to say' option was the first button as opposed to the last button (6.1 per cent), but having 'I don't want to say' last was associated with more missing data (that is, people who click submit without choosing any option).

The data of Joinson and Reips suggest that people can be discouraged from disclosing sensitive data through the use of options within a web-based design. It also suggests that there is a subgroup of people (around 10 per cent of this sample) who do not examine the options available in either a radio button list or drop-down menu before deciding not to disclose sensitive information (in this case, salary). By placing 'I don't want to say' at the top of a list of radio buttons, some of this sub-group were enticed into selecting an option before submitting, but 6 per cent of the sample still submitted the default 'no radio button selected'.

The results of this study also tentatively suggest that the optimal design for such sensitive data collection is radio buttons (removing the need for a 'Please choose . . .' option), with an 'I don't want to say' as the first option, rather than the last. This will minimize the amount of missing data, while maximizing the number of people disclosing such information. The provision of an 'I don't want to say' option is particularly important if submissions are being checked for complete responses, since being forced to give a response might lead people to drop out of a research project if they do not want to answer all the questions, or to answer randomly (Reips 2002).

Control and Impression Management

Socially desirable responding may well contain two distinct aspects: impression formation and self-deception (Paulhus 1984). Theoretically, anonymity will reduce socially desirable responding based on the desire to impression manage (Paulhus 1984), but it will not influence participants' self-deception. Empirical results however are mixed – in some cases, anonymity has reduced only the impression formation aspect of socially desirable responding (Paulhus 1984), while in others both aspects have been reduced through anonymity (Booth-Kewley, Edwards and Rosenfeld 1992). Fox and Schwartz (2002) found that by increasing participants' control during the research process, the impression management aspect of socially desirable responding was also increased. Control was introduced into the procedure by allowing participants choice as to the type of questions they wanted to answer, allowing movement through the questions to change or check responses, and providing sample questions to inform their choice. Participants given increased control also rated the test more positively than those with no control – they had more trust in the research, were less anxious and said that they were likely to respond with more candour (even though this was not found when experimentally tested). In the condition with weakened control – where participants were given a short time to answer each question, and could not move back to previous items – impression management was reduced. Fox and Schwartz (2002) found no effect of anonymity, although this may be due to their particular sample (people undergoing selection for an elite military group).

For CMC-based interviews and focus groups, the same principle will apply. According to Walther (1996), asynchronous CMC has substantial impression management advantages over synchronous CMC – people have the time to edit and check their messages before sending. Moreover, the time afforded by asynchronous CMC should also reduce the cognitive load associated with the need to combine answering a question with impression management. While these are desirable qualities for the building of an online relationship and building affiliation, they do not sit easily with a researchers' desire to elicit candid responses. It would be expected then that synchronous CMC methods should reduce impression management, and at least in theory should provide better quality data, particularly when dealing with sensitive topics.

Conclusion

If the Internet-based research process, whether an interview or automated survey, is seen as a social encounter, then an understanding of principles underpinning behaviour on the Internet can be invaluable to a researcher. Once the research process is recognized as such, then issues of power, status, privacy and vulnerability come to the fore, and should ideally inform the design of virtual methodologies.

Although the effect of design can be subtle, the differences observed in response rates, answers to sensitive questions (or choosing not to answer) and social desirability are important enough to warrant careful consideration in any research programme.

Alas, outside of a few subdisciplines (primarily survey and experiment methodology and medical research of sensitive issues) the question of how the mode and design of a research tool can influence responses has been somewhat neglected. Similarly, it is not completely clear why computer-based research tends to lead to more candid responses than pen and paper or personal interviews. Although anonymity might seem the most obvious cause, in many cases (for example, telephone interviews or web-based surveys) it is arguable that participants are actually less anonymous than traditional methods (for example, completing a survey in class). In this case, the 'strangers on the train' explanation (Bargh & McKenna 2004) may not hold up particularly well – any reduction in anonymity is likely to be associated with an increase in the potential vulnerability following candid self-disclosure. The work of Moon (2000) on disclosure to geographically distant computers suggests that such concerns do influence people's responses to research.

We may need to look more closely at the context in which various methodologies are enacted to fully understand response differences. Many of the high disclosure methodologies are conducted in private: either via a computer terminal, typing answers on a laptop or keying numbers on a telephone. However, the lower disclosure methodologies (face-to-face interview, telephone interview) tend to reinforce not only the social presence of the researcher, but also the salience of any reaction from them to the participants' responses. A long tradition within social psychology and sociology has noted the importance of others' reactions on self-evaluation. According to this, much of our self-perception and esteem comes by evaluating others' reactions to our own behaviour (the so-called 'looking glass' of interaction). Presumably, disclosing socially undesirable information to another, and their possible reaction, would pose a threat to self-evaluation. By reducing the presence of the other – either by replacing them with a computer, or increasing the distance – we should simultaneously reduce self-protection motivation, and increase candour.

Also, the tendency to socialize computer interfaces may well have a counter-intuitive impact on the research process. While a social interface, and the use of social rules and norms, may improve some aspects of the research process, they may also introduce an awareness of the audience that would otherwise be missing. In some cases, a faceless, featureless, distant computer may well produce better quality data than a friendly, computer-generated face.

Online Interviewing
and the Research Relationship

Joëlle Kivits

Opting for the email interview as the main method for qualitative data collection requires the researcher to accept that she or he is undertaking a tentative interview project. At first sight a method free of cost, travel and transcription concerns, email interviewing is an interpersonal journey that demands from both the interviewer and interviewees a strong commitment towards the subject under study and the interviewing process, lasting long after the first email exchange. Each email interview is unique in terms of the personal contact between the researcher and the respondent and of the final quality of data. Often opted for in situations where populations are not easily accessible in an offline context (Coomber 1997), the convenient and attractive practicalities of interviewing by email generally determine its use in a research project. However, the researcher wishing to conduct interviews online needs to be aware of, and anticipate, the unusual, even sometimes troubling, research relationship.

Email interviewing is an asynchronous mode of online interviewing. The one-to-one relationship between the researcher and the respondent, as well as the repetitive email exchanges, make interviewing by email a personal and thoughtful form of communication (Mann and Stewart 2000). The technical prerequisites are for the researcher and participants to be competent and comfortable in using email. The unfamiliarity of the field (Markham 2004) comes from the necessity for the online interviewer to create a personal relationship in order to achieve the interview's purpose of collecting qualitative data. That implies a constant negotiation of the email communication where motivations waver between establishing and keeping up an interpersonal and enjoyable talk with respondents and simultaneously installing a delineated research interview situation.

Based on my novice experience as an online researcher taken by surprise by the challenging and demanding nature of email interviewing, this chapter first presents the background of the study and then discusses two interconnected aspects of the interviewer–interviewee relationship and its necessary adaptation to email communication: the interview rapport based on email exchanges and the temporal dimension of the interview interaction.

Researching Information Seekers in Healthcare: A Case for Interviewing by Email

Email interviews were conducted in the context of a research project focusing on the increasing use of the Internet in healthcare. More specifically, at the core of the study was the interest to recognize the use of the Internet as a health information source, used by a lay, non-medical public. First, it was intended to understand the significance of being informed about one's everyday health, by proposing a theoretical framework for an 'informed health' experience. Second, the research concentrated on the Internet as a mediated information environment and evaluated its role as an 'information tool' in individuals' management of personal health. The collection of qualitative data through interviewing was aimed at researching both dimensions and at interrogating the two facets of online health information seekers as they simultaneously enact the role of health-minded individuals and savvy Internet users. From the outset, interviewing was considered the most appropriate method to address the research question. The decision to undertake interviews by email rather than face-to-face arose from the difficulty in accessing the targeted individuals outside their online activity settings.

The existence of an Internet population active in searching for health information on the World Wide Web is now widely recognized (Eaton 2002; Fox and Fallows 2003). Alongside quantitative insights on the continually increasing number of health seekers, e-patients or cyberchondriacs (Harris Interactive 2003), qualitative approaches also examine the phenomenon, outlining the information and support platform in healthcare that the Internet has become in the Western world (Hardey 1999, 2002; Burrows et al. 2000; Akrich and Méadel 2002; Orgad 2004). The online health information seeker, however, has an ambiguous status. The Internet attracts information seekers of varying profiles that go beyond the definition of a patient (Ferguson 2002). An intriguing aspect is the fact that seekers of information about health and illness are generally revealed to be in good health. First, carers searching for health information for family members or friends form an important part of the healthy information seeker population (Ferguson 2002; Fox and Rainie 2002). Along with carers, a significant proportion of information seekers is also concerned with a general interest in, or an orientation towards, the aim of keeping fit and healthy (Nicholas et al. 2001). The interest of the study was precisely to reach this group of Internet users to be defined primarily as health information seekers independently of their health/illness status.

Access to this population was challenging in two ways: first, its diverse and mobile profile makes it awkward to draw a single picture of who is a health information seeker, and what she or he does. Accessing the population therefore meant exploring it in the first place. Second, beginning with the observation that non-patients constitute a significant part of this population, access in physical health care settings was not possible. The only plausible access to online health information seekers was through their sites of activity, that is, on web sites that provide health information which the users accessed. Accessing this population was therefore based on the definition and selection of UK-based web sites whose topics were related to healthy eating, fitness and general health. Twenty web sites agreed to advertise the research either as a web link on one page of the web site or as a message in discussion groups, posted by the researcher with the permission of the web site administrator.

The advertisement led people interested in the study to the project's web site where the research objectives and methods were explained. The visitor wishing to participate in an interview was free to contact me – by phone, email or mail. All participants, except one, contacted me by email. Left in abeyance until then, the form of interviewing became an issue at that point. As respondents were geographically dispersed throughout the UK, email emerged as an appropriate communication tool. Email was moreover assumed to be used by the majority of online health information seekers (Fox and Fallows 2003), therefore avoiding the exclusion of any potential interviewee. After three pilots that turned out to be exciting in terms of the three different individuals I interviewed, and of the quality of the exchange, I decided to pursue email interviews with more participants, although telephone contacts or face-to-face interviews were not excluded. The online recruitment and the voluntary contact by interviewees through email thus set the basis for a year of email interviews with thirty-one individuals.

Importance of the Research Relationship in Online Interviewing

The interview situation is primarily an interpersonal one where the interviewer works at establishing 'an atmosphere in which the subject feels safe enough to talk freely about his or her experiences and feelings' (Kvale 1996: 125). Not surprisingly, one of the main issues of email interviews discussed by online researchers (Chen and Hinton 1999; Illingworth 2001; Mann and Stewart 2000; Bampton and Cowton 2002) is precisely the question of whether text-based email communication enables such close contact between the researcher and his or her interviewees, and whether it can produce sufficient data.

Starting the Interview, Preserving the Relationship
Mann and Stewart (2000), interrogating researchers who conducted email interviews, gathered mixed perceptions on the possibility of creating a personal relationship by email. As with face-to-face interviews where the success of the

interaction is often a matter of personal affinities, online and email interview relationships will be differently experienced, and hence valued, according to the individual subjectivities involved.

In my interview project, friendly contacts were established with some participants while with others I was confined to the role of the questioner. In some cases I had to decide to what extent I could engage in the email relationship at a personal level. In other cases, I had to find ways to escape a too strict interview context and create a comfortable interview situation favouring free speech. In all interviews, however, the same conditions for establishing a personal relationship were applied throughout the project. As suggested by online researchers, a context of trust through mutual disclosure and repeated interaction (Mann and Stewart 2000; Illingworth 2001) was developed, which started with the communication of research objectives and methods as well as privacy issues. As health information seekers willing to participate in an interview were the first to email me, my reply aimed to first thank them for their interest in the study and then to communicate relevant information about the research and the conduct of interviews. For example:[1]

Dear Sophie,

I'm contacting you regarding your interest in my research project "Health information on the Internet" and your motivation to participate in an interview. First of all, I would like to thank you very much for your cooperation . . .

As briefly explained on the research website, I would like to conduct interviews with Internet users who use the Internet for health purposes. My main objective is to understand why and how you personally use the Internet in relation to your health experience, whether you do so for reasons of well-being or of illness.

I propose to conduct the interview by email. Besides being a practical facility — participants indeed come from geographically dispersed locations —, email interviewing is also convenient as it allows the exchange of questions and answers at a pace which suits you. In previous interviews, participants emailed me their answers several times a week while others answered me every 2 weeks when their work and family schedule allowed them to do so. Moreover, as my questions will be open-ended, you are free to answer in a few sentences or by longer emails. There is no right or wrong answer. It is your interview and you set the agenda! Alternatively, if you prefer to be interviewed face-to-face, let me know and I would be pleased to arrange a meeting with you . . . .

Thank you again for your help and your time. I'm looking forward to hearing from you.

Kindest regards,

Joëlle

The informed consent form was generally signed after this email. However, before asking the first interview question, one or two emails were still exchanged in which I presented myself – my age, my work, my hobbies, etc. – and asked participants to do the same. These pre-interview contacts were full of information about the person I was corresponding with: receiving a CV-style answer or a poem gave me a sense of who I was emailing. Participants also generally reacted to the information I provided, divulging elements of their personal life, often relating their individual, professional or family situation to mine: in one case, I was communicating with a mother who had a daughter the same age as myself who was a research student too; in another case, the respondent's husband had visited my former university in Belgium; or in other cases, participants were keen to have more details about my frequent travels in France and in Belgium.

Extracts 1: Linking and Getting to Know Each Other

Joëlle's second email to Rebecca (47 years old):
> Hi Rebecca!
>
> Thanks for your quick answer! We can now start the interview . . .
> Before my first question, it would be nice however to know a bit more
> about each other. Well, I'm Joëlle, I'm 26 and a PhD student . . .
>   Apart from my research, I have a passion for mountains and do
> climbing and mountaineering. I often travel to the South of France
> where my boyfriend lives and of course to Belgium where my family
> and most of my friends are. If you have any more questions about
> me, my interests, what I'm doing at the LSE . . . I'll be pleased
> to answer!
>   If you don't have any objection, it would be nice for me to hear
> a few words about you . . . Kindest regards Joëlle

Kathleen, 50 years old, emails 2 & 15:
> I have 1 daughter, . . . she is 25 this month and like you she
> is doing a PhD. She's in her final year . . . I am a very proud
> mum . . .

Charlotte, 39 years old, email 2:
> In 1999 I finally finished my MSc (this is why I'm eager to par-
> ticipate in your research — I don't know how difficult it is for
> you to recruit to the project, but I remember 3 months into my 6
> month project I only had 1 person to interview!

Ellen, 59 years old, email 2:
> Thank you very much for giving me a bit of information about your-
> self and what you're doing. My husband visited Louvain-la-
> Neuve on several occasions, giving lectures and presenting
> papers on hepatitis, many years ago! We have a house in the S. f

France . . . which we share with 2 friends, and visit 4—5 times a year.

Louisa 20 years old, email 2:
> Wow, its sounds like you have had a wonderful time!! . . . I too enjoy travelling my favourite place is Prague and love taking trips over there. I also lived in spain for six months two years ago, although I can barely remember the language at all now!! We are looking forward to visiting Canada next year as my boyfriend lived there for a while and he would like to go back.

The stage of mutual self-disclosure is essential in setting up the basis of the interview relationship as it enables participants not only to be more familiar with the project, but also to ask the researcher personal questions and to add, to the interview objective, other threads to the email communication. Equally, being more personally engaged with participants enables the researcher to create a comfortable and friendly context for interviewing. As the rest of the chapter will demonstrate, the initial objective of interviewing that was behind the email communication immediately calls for the development of a personal relationship that, in turn, progressively becomes the essential condition for completing the qualitative interview to a high standard.

Between Interviewing and Conversing: The Importance of Reassurance

The online interviewer's ability to listen, reassure and develop sensitivity is crucial in preserving a personal relationship with the interviewee (Mann and Stewart 2000). With no clear-cut directions on how to proceed, these interactive skills are progressively acquired and developed during the interview process, which is constantly endangered by the online context.

First, the lack of physical presence means that understanding and perceptions of others have to be negotiated by text (Markham 2004): the simple gestures of nodding, agreeing or eye interrogation are, for instance, not possible through email. Such conversational elements must nevertheless be translated into a text-based context and have to be adjusted to each interviewee, in order to maintain the quality of the first contacts with each participant or, in some cases, to work towards better personal communication. Moreover, as each participant has her or his own style of communicating, the researcher needs to adapt her or his personal online style accordingly. The use of emoticons, for instance, generally palliating for the absence of conversational cues (Crystal 2001), may or may not be appropriate according to the interviewee. In this research project, the exaggeration of punctuation, capitalization as well as verbal descriptions and paralanguage were generally good indicators of the tone adopted and proposed by interviewees.[2]

Second, every answer sent by interviewees is embedded in a personal life context that escapes the interviewer, although it permeates the email communication. Busy days at work, a baby ill the previous night or, yet, a depressive mood, all impact on the answer provided. Preparing a new question therefore means being receptive to the interviewee's lifeworld. As shown in the following interview extracts, in some cases I only sent a supportive email while postponing the next question for a few days. In other cases, I simply had to wait for the interviewee to resume the interaction when the work or family life situation was stabilized.

Extracts 2: Apprehending the Offline Context in Email Interaction

Amy, 36 years old, email 13:
```
Sorry this is so brief . . . having a hard time right now.
```
Joëlle:
```
Hello Amy, I hope you are feeling better this morning . . . Again,
take your time to reply, don't feel obliged to answer directly.
Your answers are very precious of course but time is not an issue
in this interview.
```
Amy, email 15:
```
Hi Joelle, I'm feeling a bit better this morning thank you. It's
a hard time for me . . . my depression is bad, made worse by
variuos other problems . . .
```

Emily 22 years old, email 14:
```
Hi Joelle Sorry to take so long to get back to you — am in
the middle of Finals, but have a few days off at the moment . . .
hope that is ok — sorry that it has been so long and so brief
Emily
```
Joëlle:
```
No problem for the delay. Continuing on your interest in health
issues, . . . That's all for today. Good luck for your exams. Joëlle
```

Charlotte, 39 years old, email 16:
```
Hi Joelle — many apologies for not replying sooner. Stephanie
[Charlotte's young daughter] has just cut 3 teeth in as many
weeks, and has yet another cough which is keeping us all awake,
so the brain hasn't been up to much.
```
Joëlle:
```
Hi Charlotte, Thanks for your answer. I was indeed thinking that
your daughter kept you busy these last weeks!
```
Charlotte, email 18:
```
Stephanie is now on antibiotics, so hopefully she'll bounce back
soon. This is the most ill she's been so it's been a bit
stressful.
```

Listening to those invisible elements of the conversation and interpreting them in the context of a text-based environment, while essential to preserving the online relationship, is, however, not sufficient to ensure the interview rapport. Because of the loss of observational communication signs and physical presence, participants on the research project frequently called to be reassured on the evolution of the relationship and on the 'quality' of their participation in the interview, whether explicitly or implicitly. The interview situation, and what it implies in terms of the developing relationship between the researcher and participant indeed needs to be regularly reformulated in order to reassure the participants. By contrast, some participants, feeling confident within the interview context, needed to escape the formal interview rapport to find elements of the interpersonal relationship.

Extracts 3: Reassurance – On the Interview Process and Being 'There'

Kathleen, 50 years old, email 4:
> I hope this is the sort of information you want tell me if you want anything different

Jane, 53 years old, email 2:
> Hope you aren't bored with all this! If so you don't need to email back! With best wishes Jane

Joëlle:
> Hi Jane, I'm not bored with emails . . . Feel free to answer what you want, the way you want, just a few words, a long email, several emails ...

Caroline 29 years old, email 6:
> I think that covers everything you asked about. How is everything else going with your project? And how are you? I look forward to hearing from you. Regards Caroline x

Joëlle:
> Hi Caroline, Thanks for your answer. I'm fine, thank you! I came back on Tuesday from France . . .

Jane, 53 years old, email 14:
> I look up information on nutrition on the Internet . . . Is the food in the UK similar to that in Belgium is there anything in Belgium that you cant get over here? Tomorrow is Friday again, what do you find to do at the weekends in London? Best wishes Jane

Joëlle:
> Hi Jane . . . To answer your questions . . . What you can't get here is good chocolate and beers!!! . . . Ok, my turn to ask questions!

These interview extracts illustrate the precariousness of the email relationship within an interview situation. The strength of the research rapport crucially depends on an agreed, although implicit and negotiable, understanding of the relationship objectives, requiring from the researcher the ability to balance the communication between the interests of interviewing and those of maintaining a personal and intimate relationship with respondents. Reassurance plays a key role in this process. On the one hand, the interview being, after all, the initial pretext to developing an email relationship, it appears indispensable to reassure participants on the interview progress: more than in a face-to-face situation, the interviewee needs and looks for signs of encouragement in order to pursue the interview exchange. On the other hand, the lack of physical contact means the participants need to be reassured of the presence of the researcher, of his or her personally being 'there'. The interview's progress, to be consistent, also depends on the existence of an interpersonal exchange. In other words, as moments of informality are likely to occur, returns from informal conversation to a formal style of interview are needed for the process to move forward, and vice-versa. Email communication is then constructed as a continuous alternation between an informal and a formal style in answering the question, between interviewing and conversing.

Installing a context of trust and preserving a relationship demands a long-term involvement both from the interviewer and from the interviewee. Paradoxically, allowing time and space for the relationship to exist and develop, as well as to let the in-depth quality of the interview emerge, may be the main threat to the email communication. How many email exchanges it takes to establish a relationship and to produce the required data, and how long the process would lasts, emerge as matters to be handled in the process of email interviewing. This is discussed next.

The Temporal Dimension of Email Interview Interaction

Both a prerequisite and a consequence of the online interaction, the temporal dimension of the email communication is a key feature for ensuring the interview relationship. The three months I initially allocated to conduct interviews extended to a one year period of email interaction. While part of this one year period was aimed at gaining access online, most of the interviewing time was committed to establishing relationships with the respondents and to maintaining their interest in the research topic and in being interviewed.

The period of interviewing inevitably varies from one interviewee to another, as asynchronous communication enables participants to answer at a convenient personal time, meaning that they can choose to reply instantaneously or let three or four weeks go by before answering. Moreover, the style of answering also implies more or less email exchanges: a yes/no answer to a question is generally followed by new questions, hence new emails, aimed at developing the initial answers. At the other extreme, some interviewees expand at length on the topic discussed, requiring more 'listening' than 'enquiring'. In the project, the shortest email interview lasted two weeks while the longest was conducted over a whole year, the number of emails exchanged for a single interview varying from ten to more than forty.

Managing the Long-time Interview: Sharing Agendas

When conducting an email interview over an extended period of time, the principal challenge that the online interviewer faces is to preserve the respondent's interest in the research. A respondent's initial excitement at participating in an interview may disappear after the first few email exchanges. The role of the researcher is then to keep asking questions that are pertinent to the participant's experience, inviting him or her to elaborate in order to produce consistent data and to reach relevant core issues. The process of sharing the same interview agenda is, however, not simple to achieve. Generating exchanges relevant to the research topic is necessarily progressive, developed over the duration and requires the online researcher's patience and repetitive adjustments to participants' experiences, revealed by fragments.

In this project some participants wrote long emails and lengthily elaborated on their experiences from the start, whereas others answered only concisely. The length of answers received, however, is not a clear indicator of the intensity of the relationship and the expected quality of interview data, as a long email answer does not necessary reflect a well-established relationship. Indeed, after two or three at-length emails, some interviewees tended to close the discussion, while repetitive and short email answers supported the personal email communication relationship and progressively reached the stage of producing in-depth data. The challenge is therefore not so much in generating long email answers as in maintaining interviewee's interest in the interview process and in the topic discussed.

Besides the risk of participants losing interest in the research, the asynchronicity of email interviewing also means that respondents may forget to reply to questions, particularly when they have professional or family responsibilities. Inattentive participants simply tended to leave a pending question for reply at the bottom of their mailbox. In such a situation, while it is tempting to declare the participant has given up the interview, patience and humour are certainly the key qualities for the email interviewer. Many reminders were sent to absent respondents. These generally prompted friendly apologies and a resumption of the interview process. Similarly, likely absences on my side were notified to participants in order to avoid breaking the ongoing rapport.

Extracts 4: Sending Reminders, Notifying Absences

Joëlle:
```
Dear Peter, I don't know if you have received my last question
. . . As you are usually prompt to answer and I haven't received
```

your answer, I prefer to send it again! Best regards.
Joelle

Peter, 58 years old, email 32:

Dear Joelle, I did receive your last email and put it in the
folder; fatal mistake.

Joëlle:

Hi Elizabeth . . . I'm contacting you about the interview, I know
that I'm insistent! . . . Just let me know if you still want to
participate.

Elizabeth, 36 years old, email 10:

Hi there sorry not been in touch I had a lovely Easter but hard
work with the kids but then I was looking forward to getting them
back to school when my youngest came down with Chicken Pox!!! He
was off school for two weeks then my eldest came down with them!!!
AARRGGHH!!

Joëlle to David, 65 years old:

Hi David . . . I'll be away for the next 3 weeks from tomorrow. I'll
be reading my emails from time to time but won't probably be able
to continue the interview during this period. I'll answer to you
at the end of April then … Have a nice Easter time. Regards Joëlle

Finally, a significant risk of long-term interviewing is participants terminating
the process of replying to questions and reminders. Asynchronous email communication makes the whole research study dependent on, and vulnerable to,
the commitment of interviewees who can easily disappear from the project. In
this study, some participants dropped out after several email exchanges.
Withdrawals were sometimes overtly justified and explained, for instance by
interviewees being submerged by personal and/or professional duties and
unable to pursue the interview. In such cases, one or two emails can help to conclude the interview, without ending it abruptly. By contrast, for the researcher,
unexplained absences may be difficult to deal with, as well as to accept (Mann
and Stewart 2000; Bampton and Cowton 2002). The dilemma is not only to
decide whether or not to include the unfinished but rich interview material in
the final set of data, but also to be left not knowing the reason for the withdrawal. More importantly, withdrawals uncover one of the limits of email interviews: the achievement of the interview by email does not depend only on the
online presence of the interviewee. Whereas all participants were email users
and, at the start, email was a promising way of communication, the few withdrawals I experienced illustrate that email cannot be regarded as the most
appropriate mean of interviewing simply on the grounds that participants are
users of email and the Internet. This also emphasizes the complementarities
between the online and the offline modes of interviewing: the online interviewer must be sensitive to the appropriateness of the online communication

with each participant, and ready to turn to an offline mode of interviewing, if required.

Timing the Interview to Produce Qualitative Data

If time can be a threat to the online interview situation, it is also its principal ally. The production of in-depth qualitative data gathered via email can, in fact, be successful only if the interview process involves several email exchanges that engage interviewers with interviewees for an extended period of online communication. The timing of the interview is therefore crucial and requires from the researcher the ability to manage the interview rapport over the duration of the process.

It is first of all important to give a tempo to the interview process, based on the freshly established relationship. In this study, in order to embed the interview in a shared and evolving time frame, each question–answer exchange was accompanied by personal information: family, holidays, work, even the progress of the research, were generally discussed at the beginning or the end of an email message. Whereas this type of information is aimed at setting the rhythm of the relationship and helps the maintenance of a close rapport with the respondent, it enables, in turn, increasingly dense and personally orientated questions to be dealt with, albeit with sensitivity and caution (Mann and Stewart 2000). The intimacy progressively shared with several interviewees allowed me to deepen my knowledge of some sensitive aspects of their experience, only briefly mentioned in one of the first emails, but developed at length towards the end of the interview. Though I was unsure of how to handle the question at the start of the interview, the topic could be discussed freely towards the end of the exchange. For example, after conversing for some weeks, Caroline and I both felt comfortable enough to discuss Caroline's depression: I in asking the question, Caroline in elaborating on her experience. After communicating about the previous few days, Caroline at first expressed some doubts about how to talk about her depression, then started writing and detailing her experience at length, uncovering one of the crucial aspects of our interview.

Extract 6: Deepening the Relationship, Handling Sensitive Questions

Email exchanges 10 to 12 with Caroline 29 years old.

Joëlle:

> Hi Caroline! Back in London . . . I arrived on Sunday and was quite desperate when the plane landed in the mist! I spent my last Saturday in Marseille, climbing, near the see, on white cliffs and in t-shirt . . . I always need two days of acclimatization when I come back! . . .
>
> Now, my second question regarding your depression: can you just develop how it helped you? . . .

Caroline:

```
Hiya Joëlle, It's great to hear that you have had such a good time
over Christmas, It must have been lovely to be with your boyfriend
again. I bet you really miss him when you're working so far apart.
I bet it was a real shcok to get back to this English weather
thoug. Brrrrrr. I had quite a nice break, thanks for asking. Did
quite a bit of walking in the hills . . .
    Not sure how best to approach this answer. I dont want to bother
you with too much detail that may be irrelevant to your research
. . . Hmmm — well . . . So there you go :)
```

The long period of email interviewing also proves to be fruitful in terms of the collection of qualitative data as it involves repeated interactions and, consequently, enables closer reflection on some interview issues. While continuously re-reading the interview text, the researcher can return to some issues, choose to develop them further with the interviewee, or to put them into perspective in the light of new elements of the interview conversation. The asynchronicity of the communication is the key to the reflection process: both the researcher and the respondent can take time to answer, maybe re-discussing previous exchanges and trying to elaborate ideas expressed earlier. While in a synchronous interview the interaction and the sharing of experiences is framed by the researcher's and participants' online presence, email interviewing over a long-term period based on repeated interaction enables the capture of moments of the participants' lifeworld. Email communication also means the participant can intervene whenever she or he wants, independently of questions sent by the researcher. Some interviewees used this process, for instance, by sending articles or relating facts relevant to our conversation, independently of the question asked. A change in respondent's health condition, a newly visited web site, or advice recently drawn from discussion groups, provide occasions to develop new or previously discussed issues. This dynamic interaction between the lived moment and the question asked is even prolonged by some participants who, after the end of the interview, still contribute by sending articles, talking about their new experiences, or sharing personal reflections.

Extracts 6: Additional Interviewees' Insights to the Interview Exchange

Christine 29 years old, email 14:

```
This article was in my Sunday paper and I thought it may be of
interest for your project.
```

Sonia, 56 years old, email 5:

```
Just a little extra towards my input to your research. I am
writing this at home and not at work. Just to let you know that
I had a look at music therapy today . . .
```

Peter, 58 years old, 'after-interview' email:
```
This article was recommended to you by a friend:  . . . Best wishes
from Peter.

PS Hope you work is making good progress.
```

Time is thus essential when interviewing online. Markham (2004) describes synchronous online interviewing as taking twice as long as face-to-face interviews. Illingworth (2001) insists on the need for successive stages of interviewing to deepen the understanding of respondents' answers. One of the pilot interviews I engaged in at the beginning of the project, for instance, was concluded after the whole set of data was gathered. At first a practical constraint on the research agenda, time becomes a fundamental element of online interviewing. First, the time frame influences the intimacy and the depth of the data, as seen in Caroline's example. Second, while elements of the offline world cannot be physically observed, they can nevertheless be part of the online communication: not only words and wording are important in revealing personal experience, but also the timing process is essential in the inclusion and perception of offline contextual elements within the email communication. In other words, preserving personal contact and prolonging the interview situation are both essential factors in the production of in-depth data in email interviewing.

Conclusion

Caroline, 29 years old, last email:
```
Joëlle, Hello :) I dont think I have anything to add, but will
mail you if I think of anything. Must confess to feeling rather
sad that you have nothing else to ask. Was nice to receive your
e-mails, even if I was terribly slow at replying (would have been
better this year — promise :) ) Anyway — I hope all goes well with
you. Speak to you soon All the best. Caroline
```

After ten, twenty, forty email exchanges, the interview suddenly finishes and, with it, the routine of impatiently waiting for and receiving emails, reading respondents' experiences, formulating answers and new questions, and, for the duration of an interview, entering the living spaces of interviewees through email text. The empty interview mailbox then reminds the researcher that the established relationship was first and foremost a research relationship with the precise objective of conducting an interview.

This chapter has reviewed some of the practical dilemmas of conducting an interview by email and the methodological opportunities of engaging online with interview respondents. The centrality of the research relationship is reinforced in an online context where the key to a successful qualitative interview is the maintenance of rapport over time. The email interview is also a reflexive process where the repetitive exchanges of emails allow the researcher and the respondent to be flexible, not only in the practical terms of replying to messages, but also in the time for reflection before expressing questions and/or answers.

As a contribution to the debate on the capabilities of CMC, and particularly email, in developing the rapport essential to pursuing qualitative research, this chapter not only demonstrates the feasibility of creating personal rapport online but also highlights a method for collecting rich, in-depth interview data.

Notes

1. Ellipses (. . .) indicate deleted text. All interviewees' names have been changed for the sake of anonymity. Text in brackets stands for references to a person or contextual situation. Interview extracts are reproduced as originally received. Grammar and spelling errors have been left untouched.
2. Examples of paralanguage are hehehe for laughter, lol for 'lots of laugh', etc. (Mann and Stewart 2000: 134).

–4–

From Online to Offline and Back: Moving from Online to Offline Relationships with Research Informants

Shani Orgad

Since its early days, the field of CMC research has been overwhelmed by a tendency to rely merely on 'virtual methodologies', that is, studying Internet-based phenomena through methodologies implemented by and through the Internet (Bakardjieva & Smith 2001: 69). Even when studies combined offline methodologies such as interviews with Internet users (for example, Correll 1995; Turkle 1996), almost no attention was given to the implications of moving from online to offline with research informants and of triangulating the two kinds of interactions and the data they generated.[1] This chapter seeks to address this gap in the literature, by stressing the significance of combining online and offline interactions with informants when studying Internet use contexts and considering some methodological aspects implicated in this approach. To explore these methodological issues I draw on an empirical study which involved a move from online correspondence with patients who participate in interactive breast cancer web sites as part of the experience of their illness and recovery, to face-to-face interviews.

The chapter starts by discussing the strengths, as well as the potential risks, of choosing a methodology that combines online and offline interactions with informants. It then moves on to exploring in detail the empirical process that a move from online to offline might entail. Drawing on the experience of my study, this section discusses two key stages of the empirical process: first, establishing a relationship with informants online, and second, moving with informants from online to offline. The next section reflects on the differences and the similarities between the online and offline interactions with informants, considering both the informant's and the researcher's positions. Finally, the remainder of the chapter focuses on the implications of the move from online to offline interactions with informants for epistemology, analysis and the actual context being studied.

Capturing Both Sides of the Screen: Why Combine Online and Offline Interactions with Informants?

Generally speaking, triangulation of methods increases the validity of interpretation. Extending researcher–informant relationships that emerged online into an offline context could be seen as a way of contextualizing and adding authenticity to the findings obtained online (Hine 2000: 48). For instance, in her study of an electronic lesbian bar, Correll (1995) used face-to-face meetings in addition to online interaction she conducted with her informants, in order to substantiate what the informants told her in their online interactions about their offline lives. Turkle (1996: 324) too, reflects on the significance of conducting face-to-face in-depth interviews with her online informants, as a way to further 'explore an individual's life history and tease out the roles technology has played'. Turkle (1996) even goes as far as including findings only on those online informants whom she also met in person, a methodological decision she justifies by her concern with the relationship between users' experiences in online reality and real life. Bakardjieva & Smith (2001) take a similar approach in studying computer networking of domestic users. They stress the need to capture 'developments on both sides of the screen', that is 'on the screen' and 'off the screen', in order to investigate both the real-life contexts and actions of users and 'their exploits in cyberspace' (Bakardjieva & Smith (2001: 69).[2]

Another significant point in justifying the need to conduct offline interaction with informants when studying an Internet context is highlighted by Paccagnella (1997: 4): 'Obtaining information about someone's off-line life through on-line means of communications . . . is always a hazardous, uncertain procedure, not simply because of the risk of being deliberately deceived but also because in such cases the medium itself increases the lack of *ethnographic context*.'

Indeed, in interpreting what people say online about their offline lives, the researcher might lack an ethnographic immersion in the context about which these statements are being made (Hine 2000). Bruckman (2002: 3) spells out this claim: 'It's important to remember that all "Internet research" takes place in an embedded social context. To understand Internet-based phenomena, you need to understand that broader context. Consequently, most "online research" really also should have an offline component.' At the same time, in stressing the significance of access to users' offline contexts, we run the risk of implying that online interactions are not as authentic as offline ones, nor is the information the researcher generates from them. As Hine (2000: 49) argues: 'The point for the ethnographer is not to bring some external criterion for judging whether it is safe to believe what informants say, but rather to come to understand how it is that informants judge authenticity.'

So conducting offline interactions with informants should not be driven by the assumption that the offline interaction would reveal more authentic or more accurate information than that generated by online interaction. Rather, the rationale for combining offline and online interactions with informants should be grounded in the research context and its goals. The researcher should ask him or herself: would the offline interactions with informants reveal something significant about their experience of Internet use that could not be obtained online? In what ways might offline interaction with informants enhance the interpretation of the data obtained through online interaction? What is being risked in moving from online to offline with informants?

Notwithstanding the potential contribution of triangulating data generated from both online and offline interactions, as Hine (2000) points out, there is also an associated risk. Since most participants in online spaces have never met face-to-face, in instigating face-to-face interactions with them researchers might place themselves in an asymmetric position, using more varied means of communication to understand informants than those used by the informants themselves. Rather than adding authenticity, researchers might thus actually threaten their experiential understanding of the informants' online world.

Bearing in mind this caution and the potential benefit of combining online and offline interactions with informants, in what follows I discuss in more detail opportunities and challenges involved in the methodological shift from online to offline with informants. To go about this task I draw on my own study, in which capturing both sides of the screen (that is, interacting both online and offline with informants) was crucial for making sense of the context of Internet use that was studied. The aim of the study was to inquire into the meanings of Internet use in the lives of women with breast cancer. Patients' use of the Internet is deeply embedded in their everyday experience of chronic illness. Therefore, to make sense of their perception of their Internet use, it was necessary to immerse myself in the context in which they actually used the Internet. It was clear that if we are to understand patients' online context, we have to have knowledge of their offline contexts – that is, of the everyday life aspects of their coping with breast cancer.

The opposite is also fundamental: to make sense of patients' experience of breast cancer, we need to get to grips with their online engagement as a significant part of their experience of coping with their illness. In short, at the heart of this inquiry are the connections between users' online and offline experiences, how patients' online participation affects their life offline, and vice versa, how their offline world shapes their online experience.

Methodologically speaking, this focus boiled down to an acknowledgment of the significance of gaining access to both offline and online environments of the users. The study required a methodology that would sensitively capture the multi-faceted nature of users' experience and encompass 'both sides of the screen', that is, combine onscreen and offscreen methods.

Employing both online and offline methods of studying breast cancer patients' Internet use meant that the researcher had to engage in both online and offline inter-actions with her informants. Consequently, the researcher's experience becomes an inevitable part of the story that is being told: the empirical process itself, and the particular relationships that emerge between the researcher and her informants (both online and offline), entail substantial meanings inextricably related to the actual phenomenon being studied. For instance, the online interaction of partici-pants with me as a researcher reveals much about what influences their willingness to disclose their personal experience of breast cancer to fellow sufferes online (for example, anonymity). This required a constant effort to be sensitive to, and highly reflexive of, my own research experience and to consequently allow meaningful room for what emerged from my own experience when accounting for users' expe-rience of the Internet. More generally, I suggest, a move from online to offline with informants requires the researcher to be reflexive of the ways in which his or her own empirical experience enlightens the Internet context that is being studied.

Establishing Relationships Online

Given that the concern of the study was users' online experience, I started my investigation online. I began by lurking over a period of several months in breast-cancer-related online spaces. This preliminary stage was crucial in order to famil-iarize myself with the nature of patients' CMC. In particular, as the context of the CMC being studied was highly personal and sensitive, it was vital to gain famil-iarity with the culture and discourses of breast cancer patients' online spaces.

Although this point of departure was absolutely necessary, it was obviously insufficient on its own. There remained the need to obtain users' constructions of their experience of Internet use. The target constituency was defined as women who suffer from breast cancer, or suffered in the past and who used the Internet in the context of their illness. Since this definition focuses on the actual use of the Internet as the key factor, the natural place to recruit informants was online.

In order to obtain users' constructions of their experience, I posted messages on online breast cancer message boards on health-related web sites, inviting women to share with me their experience of using the Internet in the context of their illness. In addition, I directly emailed women who provided their email addresses with the message they posted on those boards, or on personal homepages devoted to the telling of the story of their illness. Following the notes I posted and the per-sonal emails I sent, I received eighty-three replies in total. Some of these replies consisted of rich accounts that I could use straightforwardly as data for analysis. However, many informants initially replied very briefly, sometimes expressing their suspicion of my true intentions. For instance, one of the respondents sent me an email that started by saying:

Tell me, is this research for an organisation that wishes to use the Internet to promote products to cancer patients? Also, I should be interested to know if you have had breast cancer yourself? (email 9).

Trust: An Essential Component in Building Online Relationships

To maintain the interaction with informants and encourage them to collaborate and share their experience with me, it was necessary to build a certain degree of trust. There is a real challenge in building rapport online. Trust, a fragile commodity, as Dasgupta remarks (1988: 50, cited in Silverstone 1999: 117), seems ever more fragile in a disembodied, anonymous and textual setting. Harrington and Bielby (1995) go as far as arguing that the conditions for people to trust one another are absent in computer-mediated settings. Even if we do not accept that extreme a claim, we cannot ignore the potential obstacles that anonymity and disembodiment pose in attempting to arrive at a relationship of trust with other people online. It was therefore not surprising that in the emails women wrote me in response to my online message, they tended to 'bombard' me with questions, such as: 'Where are you? On what site did you find me?' (email 10), 'what are you using the information for? Is this a classroom type project, or something you are undertaking on your own? Where do you live? What school are you attending?' (email 19). Notably, such questions were often raised despite the fact that I provided the answers in my initial online message (for example, the purpose and the kind of the research, my academic institution, my geographical location). It might have been informants' unconscious (or conscious) attempt to corroborate my identity and the sincerity of my intentions.

Building trust with informants online was even thornier given the sensitive context of the communication, that is, the request for informants to share with a stranger a highly intimate and personal experience. How can trust be established online, despite these obstacles? There are no recipes as to how to go about this endeavour. However, drawing on my experience, I wish to suggest a few insights into possible ways to address the challenges of building rapport and establishing trust with informants online.

First, it is often suggested that using the researcher's academic email account for to interact with informants works to promote informants' trust in the researcher's real identity and genuine intentions.[3] By contrast, in my case, my academic email address highlighted that I was a 'stranger', that I have entered breast-cancer-related online forums not as a fellow sufferer who wants to share her experience of illness, but rather as a social science researcher who seeks to recruit participants for her academic study. Participants could have easily regarded my motivation as insignificant, or even considered my research as an unfair use of their suffering. Nevertheless, it was ethically important to identify my interests and intentions upfront. I therefore did use my academic email address. In phrasing my recruitment online message, I made every effort to show sensitivity to the painful situation in which readers of the message might be, in a way that would not be threatening and would motivate the reader to reply.

A second aspect that was highly central in establishing a trust relationship with informants involved the temporal dimension of our interactions. Prompt replies to informants' emails proved very significant as a way of demonstrating my serious engagement in the project, and my commitment to listen to their stories.[4] More generally, since the aim was to study enduring practices through which online spaces become meaningful to patients, it was important to maintain long-term relationships with informants, avoiding an instrumental style of interaction that revolves around a short topic-focused email exchange. This implied, among other issues, the need to keep a finger on the pulse and remember to send messages at significant moments in users' lives such as surgery, an important appointment with their doctor, or personal events such as birthdays. A key incentive the researcher can give informants is care, attention and genuine interest in their lives and experiences, even if they are not directly related to the research topic.

Another incentive I used, that constituted a significant milestone in the establishment of trust with my online informants, was sending them academic papers that I wrote in relation to the research project. I introduced this incentive in the very beginning of our online correspondence, promising them to send a paper that I would produce, once it was completed. Receiving the promised paper was 'proof' that I had fulfilled my part in our online contract. What is more, seeing their personal experience being transposed into an academic context, produced, I think, a certain reassurance and, consequently, appreciation of my seriousness as a researcher. Another positive influence was that the paper was sent as a hard copy via snail mail. Incorporating an offline component into our online relationship enhanced the 'realness' of our relationship beyond its primary online setting.

The Risk of 'Going Native'

In my experience, it proved extremely difficult to strike a balance between being attentive and empathetic to informants on the one hand, while maintaining distance and appropriate researcher–informant relationship on the other. Once a certain degree of trust had been gained, informants would often treat me as a close friend, disclosing very personal issues, and sending email messages on a highly frequent basis:

> I just know we will be friends for life through our meeting on the internet. (email 27)

It was thus crucial to act in such a way that would enable me to maintain a certain distance, and allow me to keep a critical approach to things informants said. For example, although informants very early on wrote messages in a very colloquial manner, throughout my whole correspondence with them, even when we became closer, I continued writing with a certain degree of formality. I avoided sharing personal issues with my informants, unless they explicitly asked me about them, and even then I did it in a quite formal way. It is significant that the researcher avoids losing the necessary distance from informants also for practical reasons. In the beginning of my project, I used to spend a couple of hours a day replying to informants' emails.

Building trust on a long-term basis was certainly a prerequisite for shifting the relationship with informants from online to offline. Informants with whom I failed to establish appropriate trust online, often because long-term relationships were not achieved, were naturally the ones most reluctant to meet me later for a face-to-face interview. Informants with whom I maintained a certain level of correspondence, even a year after the period of our active exchange, were usually happy to meet face-to-face. The next section explores in more detail the actual move from online to offline with informants, illuminating the challenges and opportunities it entailed.

Moving from Online to Offline

Having completed the first stage of harvesting informants' accounts online, the next stage involved shifting this relationship offline. Geared towards mapping and understanding respondents' lifeworld frameworks, and more specifically the relationship between their Internet use and their situation of chronic illness, the main offscreen method employed in this study was qualitative interviewing. I contacted fifteen of the women with whom I had maintained correspondence asking if they would meet me for a face-to-face interview to follow up their written story in greater depth.[5]

Some women expressed their agreement immediately and the correspondence that followed concerned the technical arrangement of the date and venue of the interview. Others were more ambivalent, mostly stating that they did not feel they had anything new to tell that they did not already tell in their online accounts. To 'crack' their ambivalence and persuade them to participate in a face-to-face interview, I had to engage in a gentle and sensitive process of negotiation. It took the exchange of several emails to persuade them that a face-to-face interview would be extremely significant, even if they were to repeat what they had already told me.

As I mentioned earlier, the ambivalence regarding meeting face-to-face came mainly from respondents with whom our online relationship was relatively new (one to two months), and who arguably did not trust me enough to smoothly move into offline interaction. They never expressed explicit distrust in my genuine motivation and interest in their experience, however they did make implicit comments about the significance of my study, or, more generally, about an offline meeting with a stranger from an online context:

```
I am a bit leary of meeting people I've just met on the
Internet. I would be willing to answer any further questions you
may have online. (email 30)
```

The lesson learnt is that 'instant rapport' is no more common online than offline. Contractual relationships between researcher and informants have to be built gradually, allowing trust to be established over time.

Another challenge embedded in recruiting interviewees from online spaces should be taken into account. While many online participants are only 'lurkers' who do not participate in interactive online activities such as posting messages on bulletin boards, when we recruit informants online our access is necessarily limited only to those who *do* post messages on bulletin boards (and who are therefore 'visible'). However, the aim should be to capture the multifaceted nature of Internet use and account also for the kind of work that users do 'behind the screen', such as lurking, for example. There are substantial interpretative processes, practices and things in which users are engaged online that do not occur on an observable representational level, and yet entail significant meanings for users. To overcome this bias, one method which I employed in my study was to recruit some interviewees by snowballing. Initial contacts with women whom I met online were exploited in order to recruit as interviewees acquaintances who participated online but not necessarily in interactive forums. This enabled access to an appropriate range of users involved to varying degrees in different kinds of uses of the Internet in relation to their illness.

The actual procedure of the face-to-face interviews primarily involved issues of the 'traditional' kind (for example, dilemmas around the setting of the interview, aspects of the course of the interview and its management). These issues are of course methodologically significant, however I will not dwell on them here. Rather, I focus on some distinctive aspects that are implicated in the move from online relationships with the informants (mainly through email) to face-to-face interviews. I suggest that although this move from online to offline is a methodological issue, it has substantial implications beyond this context.

A note of clarification is in order: in discussing the move from online to offline relationships with informants I rely mainly on the experience of my study, which involved shifting from asynchronous online mode of interaction (email correspondence) to face-to-face in-depth interviews. Arguably, a different empirical design could involve different kinds of online interaction (for example, synchronous interaction via Internet Relay Chat or IRC) as well as other forms of offline interaction (for example, focus groups). While I try to go beyond the scope of my study, and make more general observations regarding the move from online to offline with informants, the reader should nevertheless bear in mind the specific design of the study described, and its implications for the transition from online to offline.

Continuities and Discontinuities between the Online and the Offline

Moving relationships from online to face-to-face generally proved to be a smooth transition.[6] The first aspect in which there was often a meaningful difference between the online and the offline interactions with informants was their level of articulacy. In some cases, informants who were highly fluent and articulate in their email accounts were sometimes inarticulate and even incoherent in their face-to-face interviews. One respondent, for example, in our online interactions was very open and willing to disclose her experience:

> . . . if you want the graphic details of chemo, etc, let me know
> — I'm not shy . . . if you need more [information], let me know
> . . . [I will be away, but] I am taking my laptop with me so I
> will have access to my email each day. (email 2)

Her email account was very detailed and included far more information than what I had asked for in my online recruitment message. By contrast, in her face-to-face interview she was quite hesitant. She insisted on maintaining a question-and-answer format, rather than telling her story flowingly, as she did online. Gaps between informants' level of articulacy online and offline occurred also in the opposite direction. Informants who were not so articulate in their online writing, and whose email accounts were short and quite limited in terms of the insights they provided into the informant's experience of Internet use, often were surprising in their richness and their high level of expression in face-to-face interviews. In other cases the level of articulacy of informants' online accounts was generally consistent with that of their face-to-face accounts.

Closely related to the issue of informants' level of articulacy, the second aspect in which there was often a gap between online and offline interactions was informants' openness and collaboration. Most notable is the case of Amy (false name), an informant who in our email correspondence was quite guarded and reluctant to participate in the research (which was paradoxical in itself, given the fact that she responded to the online recruitment message in the first place). In her first response to my online recruitment message, she started her email saying: 'I think there is not much to tell' (email 1a). She followed with a relatively short account of her experience of Internet use in relation to her illness. When I later approached her, asking to meet for a face-to-face interview, she responded:

> Since I really have no vested interest in your project (no
> offense) I will meet you only if it is convenient. (email 1c)

I stressed that the interview would take place only at her full convenience. However, Amy maintained her reluctant attitude, and the more our email correspondence progressed towards the actual arrangement of the face-to-face interview, the less I was convinced the latter was actually going to take place. I arrived at the interview with a lot of anxiety about the way it would flow. To my great surprise, Amy was highly collaborative and extremely talkative and open. The interview lasted almost two hours, while I remained silent most of the time, listening to Amy sharing her story of using the Internet in the context of her illness.[7]

The third gap involved the kind of language used. In both their online and offline accounts, informants sometimes used expressions or abbreviation with which I was unfamiliar. The asynchronous element of the online interaction (which was email based) allowed me the time to check the meaning in order to be able to make sense of the informant's account and to respond accordingly. Spending extensive time in breast cancer online forums was crucial in order to get familiar with the 'local' language and be able to make sense of informants' accounts. For example, I came to learn that 'BCANs' stands for a specific online board, which is quite popular among breast cancer patients (http://www.bcans.org), or that 'BC ladies' commonly refers to breast cancer patients who are veteran participants on breast cancer interactive forums. In this sense, the online interactions with inform- ants served as very useful preparation for the face-to-face interviews. They fur- nished me with a basic familiarity with the interviewee's argot, an aspect that appeared crucial, particularly given the specific medical jargon with which patients become very familiar during the course of their illness and treatment. Despite this preparation, in the face-to-face interviews there were still quite a few instances where I was not familiar with the jargon the interviewee used. In partic- ular, since face-to-face interviews revealed much more about the contexts of informants' everyday lives than emerged in their email accounts, certain expres- sions that were used in the face-to-face interviews were completely new to me. For example, in her face-to-face interview Georgia (false name) discussed the experi- ence of anonymity in corresponding online with fellow sufferers:

> it's easier to pull your heart when you know you will never gonna have to run into them at the AMP. (interview 7)

'AMP', the name of a local supermarket chain in New York, was a term I was not familiar with and thus did not understand during the interview. This kind of word, which relates to informants' everyday social and cultural contexts, would usually arise in the face-to-face interviews, rather than in informants' email messages. Decisions about whether to interrupt the interviewee and ask for clarifications of terms I did not understand during the interview were made ad hoc, according to how crucial it was to understand the specific term on the spot. In the case of 'AMP', for example, I decided not to interrupt the interview and checked the meaning of the term only when transcribing the material later.

Level of articulacy, openness and collaboration and the use of language are all aspects related to the informant. However, in significant ways they affect the researcher. The transition from a disembodied, anonymous and written interaction to an embodied and oral interaction with the informant introduces significant challenges, as much as opportunities, to the researcher. One such challenge concerns the use of information that was obtained from the online interaction in the face-to-face interaction. On the one hand, the online interaction constitutes a significant context for the face-to-face meeting. The researcher can draw on the information obtained in the online interaction as a useful background to connect to the informant, in the 'here and now' of the face-to-face interview. In my study, I often used the online exchanges as probes to take the interviewees back further, by linking to things they raised in their written online accounts. Referring to things that were said in email correspondence was an instructive way of stimulating the interviewee's memory and encouraging her to elaborate on her experience. By the same token, the researcher can refer to issues that remained undeveloped, contradictory, unclear, or that were completely omitted during the online interaction, to stimulate the interviewee to explore them during the face-to-face interview. For example, one of my informants mentioned very briefly in her email account that she used to exchange her experience with other fellow sufferers online. Since the issue of experience exchange seemed highly central in the CMC of breast cancer patients, I used our face-to-face interview to ask her to develop this aspect. I realized that online, informants tended to describe very briefly or completely omit subjects that they thought trivial or insignificant. They often tried to construct their account according to what they thought would suit my research interests. In this respect, the face-to-face interviews were crucial: they enabled me to explore many issues, such as the exchange of experience, which remained undeveloped in informants' email accounts.

On the other hand, the researcher should be very cautious and sensitive when using elements from the online interaction with informants in the face-to-face interview. First, there is a danger of reproducing the same information rather than gaining new insights. Second, there is also a risk in that the online interaction could prejudice our perception of the informant. Having corresponded with most of my informants at least a year before having met them, inevitably I had a certain 'picture' of who each informant was, and how the face-to-face interview would proceed. As I already discussed earlier, there were many surprises. Researchers should try to eschew as much as possible the inevitable prejudice they have following the online interaction with informants. It is important not to let the impression we have from the online interaction determine the offline interaction. In a sense, I suggest, there is much to be gained in treating the face-to-face interaction as a *tabula rasa*.

Another related issue concerns the researcher's degree of control over the interaction. Both researcher and informant have less control over the offline interview than over the online interaction. The disembodied, anonymous and asynchronous character of email correspondence allows a relatively high degree of control over the interaction, in so far as both sides can plan what they want to say, write and rewrite it, in their own pace and their own time. By contrast, the face-to-face interview is much 'messier'. For instance, I sometimes asked questions that interviewees did not quite understand, and had to rephrase them a couple of times to clarify myself. Online, I was able to send informants just the final version of my questions. For the researcher, this implies a need to prepare a very good topic guide for the face-to-face interview, and ideally conduct pilot interviews to simulate the face-to-face interaction. At the same time, there is an opportunity in having less control over the interaction: it enables researchers to move away a little from their own agenda, allowing issues that they had not necessarily thought of, to emerge. My research took several substantial conceptual and thematic turns following the data obtained in the face-to-face interviews (a point on which I expand elsewhere).[8] The limited control I had over the face-to-face interactions (compared to the online correspondence) proved actually fruitful in so far as it opened up the agenda of the research to new ideas that otherwise would not have been raised.

From Online to Offline and Back: Methodology and Beyond

Beyond its methodological significance, the move from online to offline interactions with informants also has epistemological, contextual and analytical implications. From an epistemological point of view, the transition from online to offline forces us to reflect on the ways that, as researchers, we come to know our informants both online and offline. The face-to-face interviews with my informants made me realize that my ways of knowing my informants were biased toward the *textual*. As long as the interactions with my informants remained at an online level (through email correspondence), making sense of users' experience relied on informants' textual self-presentation. Having done the face-to-face interviews, and reflecting back on the online interactions, forced me to acknowledge that my ways of knowing offline are biased toward the *visual*, and embedded in *embodied* ways of expression. Combining online and offline interactions with informants, enhances the ways in which researchers are positioned in relation to their informants, and the ways they comes to know them. As a consequence, arguably, the analysis that is being produced is enriched.

The transition from online to offline relationships also has contextual significance for understanding the experience of Internet use under scrutiny. In my study, perhaps the most pertinent issue that emerged from shifting research relationships from online to face-to-face is recognition of the complexity of the relationship between the lives of the users and the use they make of the Internet. Generally speaking, informants' email accounts produced a somewhat limited understanding of their online experience. 'The Internet' is described in these accounts in a fairly 'reifying' view: either in emancipatory ways, as 'a miracle', and 'dazzling', empowering or in a reductive tone, as nothing but another source of information about cancer.

Alternatively, the face-to-face *oral* accounts referred to the experience of using the Internet more implicitly. The face-to-face accounts depict the role of the Internet in informants' lives in more subtle ways. They were primarily stories about oneself, rather than the Internet, and so the experience of using the Internet is embedded in the story, most of the time in implicit ways. In this respect, the meetings with the informants and their face-to-face accounts provided a much more complex and rich picture of the relationship between their lives and the use they make of the Internet as both technology and text.

In short, the knowledge we generate, and the story we tell as researchers about the context we study, whether based on online interactions, offline interactions, or both, is crucially constructed by the means and the kind of interaction in which we engage. Moving from online to offline relationships with informants must therefore require us to be reflexive about the ways of knowing our informants, and how they shape our understanding of their experience of Internet use.

On a more general note, the empirical experience of this study, of moving from online to offline relationships with informants, teaches us about the complex connections between 'online' and 'offline'. The consequences of the shift from online to offline were indeterminate: as has been shown, in some cases informants were more collaborative and articulate online, in some cases it was rather the move to offline interaction that encouraged them to open up and be more talkative. Reflecting on the move from online to offline endorses our thinking about the indeterminacy of the Internet and the complexity of the relationship between online and offline experiences.

The move from online to offline interaction with informants is also an interesting intellectual exercise, in so far as it reverses the order in which we usually consider the relation between face-to-face interaction and CMC.[9] Usually when CMC contexts and practices are studied, by both dystopians and utopians, the implicit (and sometimes explicit) question is what has been lost in the move from face-to-face to online, or how this loss is being compensated for. Starting our research by building relationships with informants online, and then moving to offline, challenges this way of thinking: we could easily decry the many things we have lost in the move from online to offline, and think of face-to-face interaction as a form of communication which is rather limited. In the move from online to offline interaction with informants, the researcher loses some things and gains others.

The move from online to offline challenges another central assumption in CMC research. As Slater (2002a) observes, the relationship between online and offline is often interpreted as the relationship between phenomenon and context. Hence 'the offline is treated as that which makes sense of, or explains, the online' (544).

Moving from online to offline helps us, as Slater urges, to break down this dualism and see how each configures the other. The online interaction with informants and the information obtained in that interaction help us make sense of the offline interaction with them. In my study, the email correspondence with my informants served as a significant background, to contextualize what informants said in their interviews. Equally, the face-to-face interviews, and the accounts they generated, provided the context within which users' online experience was to be understood.

Breaking down dualistic thinking about offline as the context and online as the phenomenon has, of course, implications for the analysis of the data. How do we treat data obtained online and offline? Are the two sets of data comparable and, if so, how? One challenge that faces the researcher, as Hine (2000: 50) highlights, is 'a translation task between the authenticity standards of two different discourses', that is online and offline. To my knowledge, relatively little has been written about analysis which combines online and offline data, and future research should certainly fill this gap in the literature. In treating online and offline data, we should be informed by a recognition of the distinct character of online and offline interactions, and of the consequent texts they produce, while at the same time accounting for the inextricable connections between the two.

In conclusion, the discussion of the methodological move from online to offline relationships with informants, has underscored how methodology informs theory, in particular, how the integration of online and offline methods is interlinked with the conceptual concern with breaking down the dichotomous separation between the 'online' and the 'offline'. By no means do I suggest, however, that engaging in both online and offline interaction with informants is always necessary. The decision whether to conduct offline interactions with informants or restrict research only to online interaction, depends on the research focus, the approach it takes and the actual Internet context that is being studied. The intention of this chapter was to provide researchers with some counsel to help them make appropriate decisions, and guide them as to what they might face in pursuing those decisions.

Notes

1. More recently, scholars have begun to tackle this issue. See, for example, Kendall (2002) and LeBesco (2004).
2. Ironically, while Bakardjieva and Smith (2001) stress the need to capture both sides of the screen, the methodological design of their study involves only offline interactions with their informants. The only 'online' component of their research procedure included what they call 'a tour of the "computer space" constituted by internet-use practices' (Bakardjieva and Smith 2001: 70), which meant an investigation of the traces of Internet use that were deliberately saved in respondents' computers.

3. Even in interactions that are not email-based (for example, IRCs) the researcher can refer informants to an academic email address so they can write to it and authenticate his or her identity.

4. Prompt replies proved significant especially in the beginning of our online relationship, when informants naturally 'tested' me and the sincerity of my intentions. Many of the informants were online for many hours each day (some due to their illness, which confined them to their homes), so as soon as I sent replies to their emails, they would send another message, to keep the relationship 'alive'.

5. The particular women whom I approached were selected according to specific criteria; however, it is beyond the scope of this chapter to elaborate on those criteria.

6. Neice (2000), for example, reflects on a similar experience in his study of users' perception of social esteem gained through network experience.

7. Amy was definitely an extreme example; with other informants differences between their openness and collaboration online and offline were also present, but in more subtle ways.

8. I discuss in detail the conceptual and thematic turns that my research has taken following the move from online to offline in Chapter 3 of my PhD thesis, 'The use of the Internet in the Lives of Women with Breast Cancer: Narration and Storytelling Online and Offline', London School of Economics, University of London, July 2004.

9. In making this proposition, I draw loosely on an idea suggested by Ron Rice, in a presentation given at a doctoral consortium that took place in September 2002, at the University of Haifa, titled: 'Computer-Mediated Communication, the Internet, and Social Aspects thereof'.

–5–

Researching the Online Sex Work Community

Teela Sanders

This chapter reflects on an ethnography of the sex industry that utilized the Internet to help in understanding the social organization of prostitution in Britain. The aims of this chapter are threefold. First, using this study as a case example, I illustrate the opportunities that the Internet presents for researchers who seek to understand secretive, illicit social activities and access groups who are hard to locate and engage. Second, I outline some of the ethical and methodological challenges posed by recruiting from the Internet and the complexities of creating online and offline relationships with informants. Third, in the context of the sensitive topic of sex work, I demonstrate how research questions dictate the usefulness of the Internet as a site for understanding the deep meaning of social interactions. Therefore a combination of online and offline methods may be appropriate to achieve levels of acceptance and rapport with respondents and consequently the data necessary to write about other people's behaviour.

Fieldwork, Sex Work and Computer-mediated Communication

I conducted a ten month ethnography of the social organization of the sex industry in Britain (Sanders, 2004b), in which I observed indoor sex markets (licensed saunas, brothels, escort agencies, working premises and women who worked from home) as well as street prostitution. Face-to-face interviews were conducted with fifty-five sex workers and I spoke with over two hundred women involved in the sex industry, some of whom were owners, managers and receptionists. In order to move away from the issues of child sexual exploitation, trafficking and pimping, the sample was selected on the following criteria: women had to be aged 18 years and over, hold British citizenship and describe their involvement in prostitution as 'voluntary'.

The aim of the study was to understand the activity of selling sex for money as a form of work and prostitution as a type of occupation. The hypothesis was that sex workers would experience several other types of occupational hazards in addition to the violence and sexual health issues already documented in the literature. By exploring different types of occupational hazards I found that sex workers rationally responded to managing risk by creating calculated strategies. It was necessary to explore the impact of computer-mediated communication on the organization of sex economies in order fully to understand different aspects of risks and responses.

The Internet, as a fieldwork site and recruitment tool, featured in this ethnography in three ways. First, I became aware that some entrepreneurial sex workers had abandoned traditional forms of advertising in favour of using the Internet to market their business, conforming to Singh's (2001) description of women using the Internet as a tool compared to the popular male usage of the Internet as a play technology. Sex workers are a specific female occupational group who are utilizing new technologies as a tool to make money by creating web sites to promote and organize their business. At a minimum, sex workers' web sites display the types of sexual services on offer, often with a photograph gallery, menu of services and a price list. Appointments are organized with clients via email and women rely on the web to make their business cost-effective, efficient and safe. Notable features are reviews of the service written by customers. These 'field reports' are graphic descriptions of the commercial sex exchange and reveal that a 'virtual community' exists where sellers and buyers of commercial sex communicate and negotiate business (for a description of 'cyberpunting' see Sharp and Earle 2003).

My second observation site was a small number of web sites specifically for male patrons and female sex workers of the sex industry in Britain. Although, as Fox and Roberts (1999) summarize, the concept of a virtual community is contested, a sociological analysis of these specific web sites for patrons of the sex industry reveals similar social rules and interactions to those that happen in real-life groups. Durkin and Bryant (1995) explain how the innovation of technology provides new outlets to pursue sexual deviance and the appearance of what they term 'computer erotica' provides information for those seeking to engage in activities that are otherwise considered unacceptable.

Some web sites specifically target female sex workers and are tailored to address the issues raised by working in a somewhat dangerous, illegitimate occupation that is marginalized, criminalized and stigmatized. The content of web sites that are organized by women (most of whom are workers or organizers of sex establishments) for others working in the sex industry reflect what Rheingold (1993a) calls the 'gift economy'. Factual information is given freely while at the same time trivial banter on bulletin boards forms the social cement that unites members and highlights their commonality, despite an absence of geographical proximity. For instance, web sites offer chat rooms where sex workers exchange advice on how they keep safe, procedures for visiting men alone, and the use of third party protection and monitoring systems. These sites are particularly useful as a source of support and knowledge for women who do not have access to a 'real life' occupational community. One interviewee confirmed: 'I think it [the online sex work community] is brilliant. It is a great way of getting information to all the girls and information is power. Also we can email each other with telephone numbers and names of dodgy clients which is great because we don't get to meet often'.

CMC thus facilitates interaction between sex workers who are often isolated from colleagues and sometimes work in secrecy. Computer-supported cooperative work has been described by Wellman et al. (1996) as an important basis for virtual communities where physically dispersed workers can make social networks through a computer. These networks provide social support through emotional aid, group membership and specialist information. As Denzin (1999) describes through his analysis of an online self-help group, computers can be a medium of intimacy despite asynchronous communication and the likelihood of never actually meeting co-supporters. This is the case for sex workers who work alone and interact with colleagues only through the Internet. However, through sexual transactions this virtual community made up of buyers and sellers of commercial sex moves beyond the screen into real-life relationships.

The most popular site for both male clients and female sex workers, Punternet, has been in operation since January 1999 and describes itself as 'The Online Community for Patrons and Providers of Adult Personal Services in the UK' (http://www.punternet.com). This site was the main focus of my virtual observation and enabled me to view daily textual interactions between sex workers and clients. There is an abundance of information on this site: 24,441 sexual encounters ('field reports') are written by male clients and represent a monetary exchange of £2,924,299, an average of £121 spent on each transaction (as of 31 July 2003). The site is well organized through a set of rules that proscribe unacceptable topics and netiquette suggesting how clients and sex workers should correspond. The aim of the site is explained:

> This site was created to facilitate the exchange of information on prostitution in the UK. Here you will find information on where to find services, what to expect, legalities etc. You will be able to read reviews of encounters with working girls and submit your own 'field reports'. This web site aims to promote better understanding between customers and ladies in hopes that everyone may benefit, with less stressful, more enjoyable and mutually respectful visits.

Those who do not respect the values of the self-defined community, for instance by posting inflammatory messages, risk exclusion from accessing and contributing to the site. The web site also imposes expectations of proper real-life behaviour and there are sanctions for unacceptable conduct in a sexual transaction. In an interview, Cheryl, a 36–year-old escort, explained:

> The only bad experience I have had is when someone went out without paying me and that was because he could not get a hard on. But I had his phone number and my

security gave him a lot of hassle and so did the people on the message board as well. I put his email on the web site and they all gave him a hard time and he offered to give me the money.

This virtual community can be distinguished from other online networks where CMC facilitates only online relationships as the online sex work community challenges the boundaries between virtual and real relationships. Although some contributors never meet but interact only through online banter, the very nature of their mutual interest means that many sex workers and clients do meet to engage in a most intimate, albeit commercial, relationship. Forums such as message boards and a weekly live chat session encourage patrons to interact and ultimately find a mutual match between seller and buyer. Therefore much of the discussion online relates to real-life expectations and encounters.

The sex work community did not exist in a readily observable form before the Internet became a virtual meeting ground. Previously, buyers and sellers of sex communicated only on a private and individual basis whereas now, through CMC, these interactions have entered the public domain. Observing relationships between those who buy and those who sell sex has been practically impossible before the advent of CMC. The limited research on male clients in Western society highlights the difficulties of accessing the patrons of the sex industry. Through the Internet the researcher can now be privy to other aspects of sexual behaviour that have been hidden and largely clandestine. For some, the advent of new technologies has provided an outlet for a particular cultural condition, in this case sexual behaviour, that has always existed but without a communal, public declaration of identities. However, despite the popularity of sites such as PunterNet, they represent only one sector of the indoor sex markets and therefore exclude a large number of patrons. Several sex workers I interviewed continued to use traditional methods of advertising such as newspapers and cards in phone booths despite their costly inefficiency and increasing criminalization (also see Swirsky and Jenkins 2000). These women rejected the Internet as a business tool because they considered it an unknown entity and a threat to their secrecy. For the purposes of my study this highlighted an important distinction between sex workers who used the Internet and those who did not, in terms of the intricate organization of the indoor sex markets.

For those who do use it, one particular web site appears to have provided a meeting ground where both parties can test each other out and check credibility and suitability from the safety of a computer screen. Indeed both sex workers and clients who occasionally meet for a commercial exchange revealed to me that some form of friendship can continue between visits through email contact. As a researcher, the online/offline reality imposed by the very nature of selling and buying sex was a predicament that was raised early on as I explored the possible place of the Internet in my ethnography. In the same way that sex workers and clients inevitably transfer their relationship from online to real encounters, questions relating to risks and management strategies led me to move beyond the screen to face-to-face relationships. As Hine (2000: 64) explains: 'cyberspace is not to be thought of as a space detached from any connections to "real life" and face-to-face interaction. It has rich and complex connections with the contexts in which it is used'. As I will discuss below, the third use I made of the Internet was to recruit sex workers for in-depth interviews.

Observation and Ethics

This ethnography involved physically spending time with sex workers 'in the field', as well as being 'in the virtual field' where commercial sex was advertised, discussed, selected and negotiated online between clients, sex workers and owners of establishments. Initially I catalogued sex workers' web sites and used a content analysis method to establish common features of marketing. However, for the most part, I took on the role of a 'lurker', where I observed interactions on the message boards without revealing my presence or intentions. I decided against disclosing my identity as it could potentially alter the behaviour of the participants, fracture the strength of the shared community and probably provoke hostility. It was also clear to me from reading threads on the message board that participants recognized that 'outsiders' were regularly observing the site and that interactions and possibly commercial encounters were being monitored by professionals such as the police, journalists and, of course, researchers.

The ethics of covert non-participant observation through the Internet has been debated vigorously since the mid-1990s and continues to be an unresolved issue for researchers. In the light of these issues, Marx (1998: 172) comments 'conventional principles offer no criteria for deciding if a given means of data collection is ethically acceptable'. Reid (1996) argues that if researchers will not come to any harm by revealing their identity online, then they should ask permission from those who contribute to and organize web sites. However, the negative repercussions of revealing one's professional identity and contact details can be unknown in the largely male-dominated, aggressive and anonymous world of cyberspace (Spender 1995).

Marx (1998) applies traditional ethical research practice to the virtual arena promoting the basic rights to respect, dignity and privacy of contributors. The notion of privacy is problematic when discussed in the context of a medium that is accessible to all and where contributors recognize that the ever present 'electronic eye' (Lyon 1994) surveys the public forums to which they subscribe (for a discussion of 'situated privacy' see Hine and Eve 1998). The web is a public domain and those who post information realize that it is not private in the traditional sense of a personal conversation but accessible for anyone to read. Joinson (Chapter 2 in this volume) explains how people may be willing to reveal more about themselves online than in real life situations. Indeed, the attraction of self-disclosure in an anonymous environment is one of the reasons why the sex work community web sites appears to be so popular. Those who engage in commercial sexual activities are generally considered to be breaking acceptable social values and as a sanction they risk stigma, embarrassment and even criminalization (McClintock 1993; Scambler and Scambler 1997). Such anti-prostitution sentiment drives those who purchase or sell sex to reveal their activities and personal feelings anonymously through a medium that is uncensored and readily available to the general public.

Therefore, non-participatory observation as a method to understand social interactions may not be as ethically controversial as actually taking data (that is, quotations) from CMC without the permission of individuals. As Fox and Roberts (1999: 651, original emphases) point out, there is a difference between information 'that is publicly *accessible* and that which is publicly *disseminated*'. In defence, the nature of CMC on web sites such as PunterNet is usually anonymous, and due to the characteristics of the sex industry, most patrons use pseudonyms to protect their personal identity. Because no information can be personally identified, using material observed online without direct permission meets the criteria of protecting individuals from harm set out by Marx (1998). For some of these reasons, regulatory bodies such as university ethics committees often exempt researchers from the limitations of formalized informed consent (S. King 1996).

Establishing Bona Fide Status

A central question of this study motivated by my findings in 'real life' was to understand the nature of sex workers' professional working identities in contrast to their private identities. Sex workers devise many different strategies to separate their home and work life, and one of these techniques is to create an identity that enables them to act into the prostitute role (see Sanders 2004a). Nowhere was this dichotomy of selves more apparent than online, where sex workers promote their working character as a marketing technique and correspond with clients to disclose their professional persona. Generally, as an occupational rule, sex workers construct boundaries to prevent their personal self from entering into their professional world.

To understand both the professional and personal identity of sex workers and the place of the Internet in sustaining these identities it seemed appropriate to combine online contact with offline, face-to-face relationships as the most effective way to captivate the essence of this 'double life'. As Orgad (Chapter 4 in this volume) explains, for some research questions it is important to capture both sides of the screen to fully understand the experiences of others. Using this rationale, I decided to mirror the snowball sampling method that had been successful in saunas and escort agencies. I emailed twenty sex workers who had been recommended by other sources, to ask if they would be involved in my project. Five sex workers agreed to face-to-face interviews, two agreed to take part in email interviews, six did not respond, four refused and three refused with hostility. Both the positive and negative responses to my request reveal important insights into the conduct of research on the Internet, especially with sensitive subjects.

Recruiting hard to reach populations through a snowball sampling method has been established as a most productive technique (Kaplan, Korf and Sterk 1987; Hendricks, Blanken and Adriaans 1992; Faugier and Sargeant 1997; Atkinson and Flint 2001). However, the low response rate and reactions to my request indicate that transferring a methodological procedure from a traditional context to the virtual environment is not necessarily effective. One refusal revealed the complexity of establishing credibility as a researcher when contacting people online. After I had sent an email to a recommended sex worker asking if she was prepared to be involved in the project, an unknown informer alerted me to a discussion that was taking place on the PunterNet message board. The sex worker had posted my message on the bulletin board asking others if they thought my request was legitimate. The unknown informer kindly summarized the debate:

```
Both male and female respondents were distrustful of your request,
and usually quite rude about it. Comments were on the lines of:
1) Why hadn't you done more to authenticate your identity, such
as giving the name of your supervisor, or a university phone
number; 2) how would Mr X have passed you on to a named individual
— not the sort of thing he would do; 3) this kind of research was
in any case exploitative, in the sense that Miss Y would have no
control over the use made of her testimony. The general verdict
was that your request was full of holes.
```

Mr X had genuinely recommended the sex worker as a possible interviewee, yet the chain referral that snowball sampling depends upon was weak, leaving the potential informant suspicious. In hindsight, it was a mistake not to provide details that could further substantiate my identity. Emailing from an official university address either was not considered enough evidence that I was a bona fide researcher or was overlooked. Equally, supplying only a mobile telephone number and not an official university contact was also not considered acceptable.

Negative reactions from potential respondents are part of everyday experience for the ethnographer, and refusals to participate in a study are sometimes more prevalent than acceptances: see Miller (1995) and Sharpe (2000) for a discussion of the difficulties of accessing prostitution. However, what makes this research experience different is that it is rare for the ethnographer to be privy to such 'in-house' discussions about their requests. These open discussions on the Internet can help researchers to understand the impact of asking people to take part in research and subsequently to redesign methods and sampling appropriately.

For instance, this experience reminds us that academic researchers are not the only professional group that pursues data and informants via the Internet. Access to groups can be undermined by suspicions of unethical practice, in addition to the overload of electronic surveys and research requests that email users experience. The unknown informer politely explained that the online discussion concluded that I was probably a journalist and therefore untrustworthy:

> There is a regular theme of distrust towards researchers, par-
> ticularly journalists. There have been incidents of journalists
> posing as would-be working girls. The perception is that jour-
> nalists play up to a public judgement that prostitution is a
> sordid, shameful and sick feature of society, a judgement deeply
> resented by the sex work community.

Again, hindsight suggests that the furtive nature of some CMC mean that researchers must do much more to establish their bona fide status than they would perhaps in offline situations. Hubbard (1999) already advises the kind of reassurances needed by informants, such as sex workers, who are involved in secretive and sensitive activities. Trying to access female prostitution, Hubbard (1999: 233) learned that gatekeepers and sex workers comply with researchers only if they understand that the research will be undertaken using the following four principles: that the research will produce knowledge to help reduce stigma surrounding prostitution; that the researcher has an insight into reality; a recognition that prostitution is a legitimate form of work; and a belief that health and safety risks should be minimized. My intentions to demonstrate these qualities did not come soon enough for respondents who needed reassurance before engaging in any type of dialogue.

The discussion on the message board about my request revealed much about the sensitive nature of the researcher–respondent relationship, the general suspicion towards researchers and the weaknesses of snowballing as a recruitment tactic. It also exposed the shared identity of the sex work community and the substance of the relationships sex workers and clients create online. As the unknown informer commented:

> Prostitutes and their customers engage in direct dialogue over the
> whole range of their shared experience. There is a sense of shared
> values and sympathies. The solidarity and trust between them is
> such that Miss Y would sooner expose her private email to public
> discussion by this group than check you out for herself.

Positive responses from five sex workers who agreed to be interviewed face-to-face also reveal some methodological issues relating to using the Internet to gather high quality and accurate data. Before agreeing, these respondents asked questions about who I was, the nature of my research, the type of questions they would be asked and my personal opinions regarding prostitution. They later described how they had confirmed who I was either through typing my name into a search engine or indeed checking with the university.

One incident revealed that not only do researchers have the responsibility to establish legitimacy with respondents but also they must check that the person who is responding to emails is the person they want to answer their questions. In the context of this ethnography that sought to understand women's experiences, emotions and thoughts about sex work, it was essential that sex workers answered the questions and not other people on their behalf. One of the interviewees, Natasha, is a successful sex worker who charges a significant amount of money for her services. In a similar way that a client would arrange a meeting, I contacted Natasha on her work email address and explained that she had been recommended as a useful informant. She agreed to take part with enthusiasm, and the interview took place in a rented apartment she used only for work, over several hours. During the interview Natasha revealed that she was computer illiterate and that her husband organizes that side of the business, as well as security, housekeeping and accounting. Unbeknown to me, it was Natasha's husband who was responding to my emails just as he emails all of her clients and screens them for credibility.

Rapport and Trust

The valuable exchanges that can be made between the researcher and informant in a 'real-life' situation can often be missed if relationships exist only online. Referring back to my attempts to recruit sex workers through email, it is interesting to note that despite offering the same information to potential interviewees in online and face-to-face situations, very few sex workers I actually spoke with expressed initial suspicions about my status or intentions. My actual presence in the recruitment and negotiation stage clearly seemed to be important for the type of respondents I was targeting and the nature of the inquiry.

Although it has been argued that email interviewing can overcome some of the interpersonal problems associated with face-to-face interviewing because of its 'user-friendly' approach (see Selwyn and Robson 1998) and because concepts such as race, gender, age and sexuality do not influence the researcher–respondent relationship as they may in real life (Spender 1995), there are still significant disadvantages. Even when I had convinced sex workers online to take part in the study, the structured email interviews did not produce the detailed, rich data that I acquired through face-to-face questioning. When questions were emailed and respondents replied in written text, the essence of the inquiry was often misunderstood or answers would diverge to other subjects. It was difficult to maintain the flow of dialogue with interviewees online, and because of the asynchronous nature of email contact, the lack of spontaneity meant that it was difficult to probe and threads were easily lost. This could have been simply due to a lack of experience and an unrefined technique on the part of the researcher. However, it felt uncomfortable and clinical to ask intimate questions about sexual behaviour and living a secret 'deviant' lifestyle to someone I had not met and, more importantly, who had not met me.

This was in stark contrast to the relationships I created with sex workers I came to know in their 'real-life' environments. Spending ten months in the company of sex workers, in both their work and home surroundings, not only allowed me to observe their daily routines but also placed me in a position to understand their life circumstances, emotions and predicaments. I was able to 'get close' to some individuals, not only because I established myself as a bona fide researcher from a legitimate institution, but primarily as a woman interested in finding out how other women live, without making judgements or imposing morality on their actions. In real life, the essence of my relationships with sex workers, and therefore the basis on which they revealed their lives and emotions, was built on trust and a mutual exchange of information and respect.

The relationship between the female researcher and respondent, either online or offline, must be understood by reflecting on the intersubjectivity experienced in the interview. In trying to establish a 'non-hierarchical relationship' (Oakley 1981: 55), to reduce social distance and build on shared gender socialization and critical life experiences, the Internet may present an added barrier. Although the concept of the 'non-hierarchical relationship' has been problematized (for a review see Tang 2002), and gender and personal 'knowing' may not necessarily lead to empowerment or equality between a female interviewer and respondent, differences in power and status can actually be highlighted through CMC. When researching the nature of how women sell sex and manage the risks associated with prostitution the physical proximity of face-to-face interaction reduced the distance present because of the researcher and respondent occupying different positions of power. The virtual arena did not appear to provide the same opportunities to come to know someone well enough to write about the intricacies of their lives.

The multilayered and fluid nature of power and knowledge that flows between the interviewer and interviewee gains different dynamics when the relationship is contained in an online environment. As Finch (1984) notes, the place where the interview takes place can significantly alter the nature and quality of the relationship and information given. Indeed, my physical presence with sex workers in their place of work produced opportunities to ask specific questions that arose out of everyday events. For instance, speaking to one sex worker shortly after she experienced a condom break during sex with a client was a natural occurrence that facilitated questions about the emotional, psychological and physical risks associated with the intimacies of exchanging sex for money. Asking the same questions online, without a specific context or incident, did not have the same results in terms of detailed explanations from women that enabled me to understand their experiences. The dynamics of the online environment can reduce the chance of intimacy and understanding between interviewer and interviewee.

The non-verbal communications that are passed when one person comes to know another in their own environment are often unacknowledged. E. King (1996) explores the use of the self in qualitative interviewing and notes how non-verbal communication such as active listening is essential for effective interviewing. Indeed, the questions that were asked in this study were of the most intimate nature, and therefore may have been inappropriate in an online context where mutuality, warmth and honesty, much of which is exchanged intuitively and non-verbally, is lost. After several interview sessions with Astrid, she decided that she felt comfortable enough to invite me to meet her family and also to observe a sexual interaction with a client 'to see just how clinical it is'. These opportunities could not have been explored in a relationship contained in a virtual arena, even in an online relationship that produced high quality textual data.

Establishing rapport and trust with informants is at the heart of ethnographic work, especially with informants who occupy very different positions from the researcher. If researchers are to understand how people live and interact in their own social groups and environment, they must manoeuvre themselves into a position whereby they can invest themselves and show how they are worthy of receiving intimate details about how others live. Perhaps creating trustful relationships is possible solely through online communication if the research design is attentive to the specific sensitivities created by the virtual arena. My experience indicates that rather than dabble with the Internet as an addition to traditional 'real-life' methodological procedures, if the Internet is made the priority research site and online relationships are afforded the time required to create quality alliances (see Kivits, Chapter 3 in this volume) then fruitful data can be collected. However, with specific reference to understanding sensitive activities such as sexual behaviour, gathering accurate and high quality data only through online relationships is perhaps beyond the capabilities of qualitative methods. Avoiding 'real-life' ethnography would also be a missed opportunity for the researcher to experience a precious and privileged relationship.

Conclusion: Lessons Learnt

This chapter establishes the Internet as a valuable field site to explore a range of different social interactions and behaviours, especially secretive, illicit and sometimes illegal aspects of social activities. The Internet provides a unique window into underground cultures that are otherwise difficult to access. The widespread nature of CMC provides an abundance of data on human interactions that occur in virtual spaces. For the ethnographer, research questions can be designed, hypotheses tested, data collected and queries clarified without having to leave the safety of their office.

The opportunities created by the Internet as a resource and fieldwork site appear to make the work of a qualitative researcher more efficient and focused. However, the Internet as a research tool, data source or recruitment site brings with it ethical and methodological challenges that can make qualitative work more complicated. First, it is not simply a matter of transferring tried and tested methods from 'real-life' environments to the Internet. In this chapter I have described how snowball sampling online presents different issues to those normally apparent in offline research. Qualitative research methods must be sensitively adapted to online research relationships and consider specific issues that are borne out of both the type of questions and the type of social behaviour at the centre of the research design. Traditional methods for understanding how people live can be appropriate online, but often the principles of such methods need to be applied sensitively in order to achieve a different form of practice in the virtual arena. As Hine (2000) suggests, ethnography can be adapted to the specific conditions of this form of social activity. Too often, whether as a result of the way that social scientists learn qualitative methods, or due to lack of actual experience of 'doing ethnography' in the field, the principles of ethnography as a method of data collection are applied without astute attention to how such principles will react with the social conditions to which they are applied.

Ethnography and the methods associated with it are live activities that change in accordance with the human interaction and environs they are placed in. In this chapter I have demonstrated how using one system to recruit participants was successful in a physical face-to-face situation but was not as effective when directly transferred to a virtual site. The virtual and often anonymous nature of Internet communication means that researchers must establish their bona fide status and the boundaries of the study more carefully than they might in a face-to-face situation. The consequences of revealing a researcher's own identity to certain groups online may have unexpected implications for individuals and institutions and this must be considered carefully in the process of deciding how or if to gain informed consent.

Finally, this research experience illustrates that the advantages of the virtual arena – anonymity, privacy, access, heightened self-disclosure, fluidity of time and space – did not allow some types of data to be observed and understood. As Durkin and Bryant (1995: 197) note, the prognosis for computer sex research is that there is scope for systematic research using CMC as a vehicle for understanding the social meaning of electronic erotica and sexual behaviour. However, this must be approached with caution because specific questions about sex, sexuality, emotions and multiple identities in professional and private spheres may only be fully explored in a face-to-face situation. In many situations, interactions online can only be fully understood as extensions of wider social relations and lifestyles. Therefore, combining online and offline qualitative methods may be the most plausible and satisfying approach for the ethnographer who seeks to understand the intricacies of how other groups live. In the context of the sex work community, the Internet is an appropriate and useful tool where the virtual can be used to access 'real life', and in time 'real life' can explain the virtual.

–6–

Ethnographic Presence in a Nebulous Setting

Jason Rutter and Gregory W. H. Smith

In this chapter we examine some methodological and ethical aspects of our first venture into the developing realm of online ethnography, reviewing our specific ethnographic experiences in light of some of the more general concerns of ethnographic researchers. Our focus in this chapter is upon 'presence' and 'absence' as they are recast by online ethnography and yet resonate with the concerns of ethnographers in more traditional settings. We have chosen to organize our chapter following a conventional structure shaped by the ethnographic practicalities of getting into research settings, getting along with members of the setting and getting out of the setting (Goffman 1989). We also comment on some ethical issues raised by the research. First, we give a brief overview of the basic conceptions that informed the project.

Research Aims and Setting

Our approach to ethnographic work was shaped in part by our prior research experience. Jason Rutter had just completed a study of live stand-up comedy acts using transcribed audio and videotaped data (Rutter 1997, 2000). Gregory Smith (2001) had used observant participation and semi-structured interviewing to analyse the public harassment of runners. In both these studies we drew upon some standard interactionist and ethnomethodological conceptions. We planned to use interview and observational methods to describe and analyse the everyday activities and experiences of newsgroup members. We were interested in examining the 'native's point of view' and in constructing 'thick descriptions' (Geertz 1973) of the lifeworlds of newsgroup members. In particular, we were struck by the opportunity to capture on computer file all the messages transmitted over a given period – to ground our analytic observations in the details of message exchange.

Our original research design involved a comparison of general newsgroups offered by four Internet Service Providers with a significant presence in the North West of England. We sought to analyse the nuts and bolts of sociability practices in newsgroups, seeking to discover how sociability is discursively constructed in a text-based environment. We conceived our research as pitched at the processual, social organizational level 'underneath' the more generalized debates about the characteristics of virtual communities (Rheingold 1993a; Doheny-Farina 1996; Fernback 1999). Since the project was designed to focus on sociability practices, we envisaged it as primarily a piece of analytic ethnography, informed by the approaches of Goffman's sociology of the interaction order (G. W. H. Smith 1999; Fine and Smith 2000) and conversation analysis (Sacks 1992). Broader concerns with online selves, virtual communities and the general features of CMC were seen as secondary matters that close study of the messages themselves might possibly illuminate.

The comparative element of the original research design receded as one ISP, which we shall call 'RumCom', and in particular one of its newsgroups, 'RumCom.local', became the centre of our inquiries. Our selection of RumCom.local arose from our early appreciation of the rich culture it manifested. There was a high flow of messages – we archived some 17,000 messages over a five month period in 1998 – and ample evidence of liveliness. The messages contained much teasing, joking and argument along with the seeking and giving of information and advice. We soon came to know the 'characters' in the group, their foibles and hobbyhorses. A number of prominent posters had web pages from which we could glean more information about their identity and interests. We seemed to have stumbled upon a flourishing virtual community (howsoever that may be defined) that presented us with fertile ground for a study of sociability practices. Our decision to concentrate our efforts on this single newsgroup was confirmed when we attended an organized social gathering convened for RumCom.local posters ('RumRendezvous'). Initially apprehensive about how the open admission of our research purposes might be taken, we were gratified to be received by the assembled RumCommers with only minimal scepticism. Leaving the gathering late on a Saturday night we felt like anthropologists who had just discovered their 'tribe', their 'people'.

We should not have been surprised. In a manner similar to the virtual communities examined by Rheingold (1993a) and Baym (1995a), RumCom.local has a reputation for 'friendliness'. In interview one poster put it this way:

> Demon dot Local, I mean you go in there, you're [laughs] within your first few posts you're likely to be flamed. People that come into RumCom dot Local are made welcome. So the hand of friendship is offered there, which in other newsgroups quite often until you become established people will ignore you or be downright rude to you. The ethos of dot Local, you know, it's like going into your local pub, does seem to be true in that respect . . . it's just the fact that it is quite a friendly place. It's an easy place for a newbie to step into and know they're not going to be particularly flamed.

The unofficial frequently asked questions (FAQs) web site welcomes readers to 'the wonderful world of RumCom' and continues:

> You see, that's what RumCom is – a community, not just another ISP. Through the world of RumCom.local (although there are other RumCom based newsgroups for general discussion, RumCom.local is the most popular) people can talk; get to know each other; discuss problems, current issues and bizarre facts of life; even have heated discussions and arguments – within limits of course <g>.

Interestingly, it was an enthusiastic subscriber, not a member of RumCom staff, who maintained this page. A similar example of the supportive blurring of the division between ISP staff and customers was found in RumCom's list of newsgroup definitions, compiled and updated by a subscriber who undertook the task on a voluntary basis. The 'friendliness' of RumCom.local seemed to extend to the ISP itself. The staff of RumCom, including the most senior members of the company, were not remote from their customers: they were accessible at the end of the phone or an email and have been known to attend the organized social gatherings (RumRendezvous) of RumCommers. Contrasting RumCom practice with that of a much bigger and better-known ISP, one interviewee noted, 'I don't think the ordinary punter normally could get through to the managing director of AOL.'

These features of the culture of RumCom are tied in with its history. The company was founded in 1994. Its administrative headquarters is on a small island off the Scottish coast. A significant proportion of the ISP's early customers were people from the island who wished to support local enterprise, or were from mainland Britain and intrigued by its remote location. However, it began to grow rapidly in the mid-1990s, in part due to its very competitive pricing system. For a time it held an advantageous market position because its in-house software allowed emails to be read offline and thus not incur the telephone costs that were charged for local calls in the UK. One of the developers of the software had extensive experience of bulletin board systems. This programmer was also responsible for implementing the acceptable use policy and dealing with complaints. Through this key staff member the assumptions informing bulletin boards were carried forward into RumCom newsgroups. He was also responsible for securing closure of the newsgroups to non-RumCom subscribers. The relative seclusion of the newsgroup from the wider Internet further helped the cultivation of a friendly ethos on RumCom.local: the technology rules out 'hit and run' flaming from the outside. History, culture, seclusion and acceptable use policy all contributed to a distinctive culture and the acknowledged friendliness of RumCom.local. Consequently one of our first research questions was to ask how this friendliness was manifested at the message-by-message level (Rutter and Smith 1999).

Getting into the Research Setting

By definition online ethnography describes places that are not spaces. Disembodied persons people these places. Such facts are the fuel of the cyberpunk imagination. For the ethnographer they create a more mundane dilemma: there is no obvious place to 'go' to carry out fieldwork. Rather, data collection seems more a matter of deskwork than fieldwork – getting the seat of your pants worn but not exactly dirty since online ethnographers tend to work in their own office, not the dusty archives and grimy bureaus in which Robert Park urged his students to labour. In this respect online ethnography is surely a researcher's dream. It does not involve leaving the comforts of your office desk; there are no complex access privileges to negotiate; field data can be easily recorded and saved for later analysis; large amounts of information can be collected quickly and inexpensively. A techno-savvy researcher can even automate most of the process of data collection with the right software and artificially semi-intelligent 'bots'. Doubtless Malinowski or Whyte would have been appalled by the ease with which the online version of their craft can be done.

We were attempting naturalistic research (studying people in their natural settings) although because of the nature of our topic (the communicative practices that make for sociability in a virtual community) we did not practise participant observation, at least, not as it is conventionally understood. We veered more to the 'observer' than to the 'participant' pole. RumCom.local messages were objects of technical interest to us, to be noted and stored in a database. We did not encounter them as newsgroup members might, as messages of relevance and interest for the information and views they contain, or as statements that might even warrant a response. Our focus centred on what RumCommers found interesting, relevant and worthy of response. So while we audited the messages in accordance with the demands of carrying out a piece of sociological research, RumCom posters wove their message-reading and postings into the fabric of their daily lives. The husband and wife with their own village shop told how they dialled in to read and post messages in the lulls in the rhythm of their working day. A housewife composed many of her postings mid-morning after the children had gone to school or in the late evening after they had gone to bed. A recently divorced man (and by far the heaviest poster in the period we intensively studied) told how entire evenings from getting home from work at 5.30 p.m. until going to bed around 2 a.m. might be spent reading messages and composing replies. RumCommers monitored and responded to messages in the daily round of their everyday activities. For them, message reading and response embedded in a multitude of real-world activities, and this frame was very different from the frame in which we as researchers collected, read and analysed the messages.

Furthermore, the electronic storage of newsgroup messages and the asynchronous nature of newsgroup communication meant that everyone involved in the newsgroup stood in a different temporal relationship to the messages, based upon their local exposure to them. The messages had no 'natural' link to the time and space in which they were created, only to the times and spaces in which they were consumed. The ordering, timing and association with other messages was not uniformly constructed within the newsgroup and the virtual space created for it by the participants, but in their own everyday use of these texts. On the face of it our collection and analysis of newsgroup messages has more in common with the methodology of unobtrusive measures (Webb et al. 1966) than participant observation. Yet we did observe, and we did in a limited way participate and make ourselves known to RumCom subscribers and staff, hence our deployment of 'presence and absence' to describe the peculiar way in which we were 'there' but also 'not there' in studying this virtual community. We did not hide, but we did not go out of our way to make ourselves conspicuous either.

Our research experiences have also led us to problematize the conventional notion of a 'research setting'. We took as our research setting the social network around RumCom.local, not a social group or subculture or geographically defined locale. Our decision to focus on a newsgroup was in keeping with studies of other newsgroups, MUDs, MOOs and similar multi-user environments (for example, Baym 1995a; Mnookin 1996; Markham 1998). However, an alternative methodology could be devised which pivoted around individuals rather than a network. Such a methodology would seek, in a biographical manner, to focus on the individual's use of the Internet, and might involve the ethnographer travelling with people through newsgroups, IRC, meets, email and so on. Such a surfing strategy would permit ethnographic examination that was non-site bound, or at least multi-sited or trans-sited in its scope.

All this suggests to us now that as online ethnographers we need to be very cautious about the *where* that we are studying. Defining the field, conceptualizing how the research setting was to be constituted, turned out to be an issue never far away from the routine ethnographic work. Like a telephone call, the place inhabited by the RumCom.local newsgroup is defined only by acts of interaction and communication. There is no 'place' in the virtual beyond the metaphor. For the virtual ethnographer this repositions the notion of place or setting from geographical zone to assemblage of forms of conduct. Consequently, the definition of the research setting becomes not a starting point but a primary research question requiring careful and continuous examination by the virtual ethnographer throughout fieldwork.

Getting Along in the Setting

Our data collection did involve real places outside the office and real research activities beyond databasing RumCom.local messages. We visited the homes of a number of RumCommers in order to interview them. We attended four RumRendezvous in a variety of locations in the UK. These meetings were held over a Saturday and Sunday and offered an opportunity for those who had met only online to test their assumptions face-to-face. We took notes after these meetings and compared them to the accounts lodged on the newsgroup and on personal web sites in the days that followed. We drank coffee with RumCommers, ate meals and got drunk with them, sat on their furniture or floors and slept in their homes. No great privations to be sure – certainly nothing on the scale of those faced by anthropologists – but we 'went out' (Molotch 1994) rather than adopt the supposedly easier task of just watching our computer screens. Like other ethnographers, we had many reasons to be grateful to the generosity of our informants. We used our ordinary skills of sociability in order to study sociability practices. A web site to disseminate research findings was set up (but was never used when we realized it would compromise our assurances of anonymity and confidentiality).

We adopted overt roles as researchers in all our dealings with RumCommers. These dealings mainly concerned arrangements in connection with interviews and RumRendezvous meetings. In our self-presentations we endeavoured to be innocuous in appearance and attitude. There was a slightly age-graded division of labour when interviewing. The less old in years of the two of us (and more computer literate) (JR) interviewed younger RumCommers. The other (GS) became skilled at disguising his lack of computing knowledge; he interviewed many of the older RumCommers, who tended to be less preoccupied with technical concerns. In fact the level of technical knowledge needed to address the sociological questions that concerned us was not high. We cultivated the role of unobtrusive, interested outsiders seeking to learn about the history and ways of RumCom. Our participation was 'minimal' and 'restrained' (Emerson 1981: 368) and we seldom posted to the group.

Our major method of data collection was the messages that were placed in a database for ease of retrieval. This proved a valuable resource since many RumCommers did not have a clear recollection of threads, even the ones they had actively participated in themselves. We constructed a simple questionnaire that gave us some very basic demographic information but which more importantly led to an interview in a substantial proportion of cases. Phone and face-to-face interviews were carried out mainly in the second half of 1998 to find out how people became involved in computing and the Internet and what they got out of participating in RumCom. We managed to interview about 18 per cent of the total number of active posters on RumCom.local, including several of the heavier posters. Interviews were taped and transcribed. One of us visited the administrative headquarters on a Scottish island, a visit that also permitted interviews with some of RumCom.local's longest established members. The managing director supplied organizational data. These were the data-gathering activities that, along with the RumRendezvous in which we participated, helped establish a conventional ethnographic presence.

'Passing' or acceptance by those we were studying rarely proved much of an issue for us. For most of the time to most posters and readers of RumCom.local, we were invisible. The social acceptability of 'lurking' and the optionality of participation was one factor. Our primary 'researcher as lurker' role was also aided by the accommodative character of the interaction order: 'it may be possible to pass as a member without actually performing as a competent insider (owing to the politeness or face-saving graces of members, for example)' (Emerson 1981: 363). The social composition of RumRendezvous was sufficiently heterogeneous in age, gender and class terms for no one to stand out (our first meeting was attended by a range of people from 18 to 80 years of age). Among the conduct we took as tests of passing, we noted that some RumCommers teased us and joked and argued with us (the body piercings of one of the researchers attracted comment on occasion). We were 'let into' group and individual secrets. Personal likes and dislikes, candid judgements of character flaws or confidences about 'inappropriate relationships' were given to us, usually when the tape was turned off. Further, it was not uncommon for RumCommers to offer to share personal histories of the newsgroup with us. They would present views of the RumCom context and report interaction that took place outside the highly public forum of the newsgroup in small get-togethers on Internet Relay Chat or in personal emails and phone calls. (This, once again, adds a further layer of confusion to definitions of place when approaching a newsgroup-based community.) Of course, we were seeing a biased sample, for those who did not accept our project (or us) simply did not cooperate or contribute to our research work.

Our participation in the activities of RumCom.local was limited and circumscribed. It was driven by a wish to answer questions that could not easily be obtained in the more public forum of newsgroup interchanges. We also wanted to add some depth beyond what we could discover through the analysis of messages. We felt that our online ethnography had to do more than merely observe and collect textual data (but see Mason (1999) for the argument that full immersion in the setting investigated in *its own medium only* is what distinguishes virtual ethnography from other kinds). Different kinds of research questions will of course generate different degrees of participation for the online ethnographer. Our concern with the discursive construction of convivial sociability placed relatively small demands on the kinds of data that can best be obtained by participant observation. Nevertheless, on one occasion our face-to-face acquaintance with some posters proved fateful. We sent out questionnaires to posters who figured in our database. While these were administered individually via email, some posters decided to air their misgivings about certain of our questions by posting direct to RumCom.local. Our bona fides were queried in a very public forum. We were 'rescued' by established RumCommers whom we had met earlier in the year, who replied to the effect, 'These guys are OK'. Without the trust that the face-to-face meeting had helped to secure, it seems unlikely that anyone would have leapt to our defence.

Getting Out of the Setting

Although our visibility reduced after our fieldwork year, we do not consider that we have left the field yet. Perhaps it is because we are still grappling with where we were when we were in RumCom.local that we could not create a sense of closure about having left it. However, unlike leaving a physical site, our contacts with RumCom remain active: the tools that facilitated our presence in the virtual environment still reside on our desktops. Sporadically they come back to life when we dip back into RumCom.local to update ourselves or just out of curiosity to look at what is going on there now. On occasion we receive emails inviting us to new RumRendezvous or requests for information about how the project progressed. Our web pages still reside on the RumCom server with the RumCom screen saver we built as a thank you to our virtual hosts and photographs taken of us at RumRendezvous still reside on RumCommers' homepages. Every now and again we run into RumCommers in different parts of the Internet – and occasionally in the offline world.

We recognize that members of a studied group may have mixed feelings about reports published about their activities. As noted, we have been reluctant to publish our initial papers on a web site for reasons of confidentiality. There is the question of 'host verification' that we have yet to work through. Issues of presence also arise at the stage of leaving the field. To pose the question sharply, what does withdrawal amount to when you have never been fully 'there'?

Ethical Aspects of Online Ethnography

The negotiation of absence and presence is an important ethical issue, not just in online ethnography but also in its more conventional variety. In the field the ethnographer may make considerable efforts to mask and make redundant the research role. Those around are encouraged to 'forget' that the ethnographer is in the setting as a researcher, and to begin instead to see him or her as a person. For the online ethnographer the problem is transfigured: how to be seen as a person or a researcher when you cannot be seen at all? Once again the idea of visibility proved to be central. Whereas in a physical environment the ethnographer's physical presence can act as a reminder of the presence of an agent, 'net presence' (Agre 1994) turns out to be a very nebulous thing. While we can accept the general rule that practising ethnographers should declare their research identity in the field and be reasonably open about their research agenda,[1] the play of absence and presence has specific implications for online research.

It is very difficult for the online ethnographer to maintain a stable presence in a virtual environment when people cannot see that you are there. This is made worse with the constantly changing composition of many virtual environments as new people arrive and others leave – mostly unannounced. Ethically, how are we supposed to negotiate informed consent? Do we opt for maintaining the letter of the law with regular postings that announce our research identities and our presence as researchers or do we, after a general announcement of our presence, slip into a more naturalistic mode?

The former carries with it the risk that the researcher alienates regular users of their online environment whereas the latter, advocated by Ward (1999), means that it becomes 'the participants' responsibility to read the message'. Surely, when we suggest to members of a community, whether online or physical, that they have a responsibility to help us with our research, we are treading on very thin ethical ice? The compromise we opted for was the adoption of a specifically non-personal email address, ethno-research@rumcom.co.uk, and mention of our research in our signature. Ironically, as discussed above, the most effective tool for gaining trust and negotiating consent was not any of our online activities but our self-presentations in the non-virtual venues of RumRendezvous meetings and face-to-face interviews. (As a result of this attendance we found that our pictures would appear with those of other RumCommers on web pages and that people would recognize our postings.) In the incident mentioned in the previous section, we found that those whom we had met face-to-face vouched for our credibility to those with whom we were not acquainted non-virtually.

Further ethical issues exist when approaching notions of what kind of 'space' online ethnography takes place in. For example, how public is the interaction that goes on within Internet newsgroups? Often a very naive perspective is taken on this problem, with authors arguing that online interaction in MUDs, newsgroups and on listservs is public in an absolute sense that has little need for qualification. For example Paccagnella (1997) quotes Sheizaf Rafaeli:

> We view public discourse on CMC as just that: public. Analysis of such content, where individuals', institutions' and lists' identities are shielded, is not subject to 'Human Subject' restraints. Such study is more akin to the study of tombstone epitaphs, graffiti, or letters to the editor. Personal? – Yes. Private? – No

This statement is an oversimplification. Just because talk takes place in public it does not mean that that talk *is* public. Surely there must be some distinction between what is said among friends in a café, pub or public arena and the talk of politicians or celebrities to open meetings or interviewers; between social chitchat and the form of pre-composed statement that Rafaeli draws comparison with? So too is such a distinction maintained in online interactions. Those involved have a recognition that their words and actions are viewable by others but this does not mean that everything that goes on in the groups is essentially public discourse and as such ethically available to the online researcher. Distinctions are made within the community-like networks between core members, newbis, the occasional contributor and, indeed, the online ethnographer. Not all these people are addressed in the same way, gain the same response rate to their posting or have the same status within the list (Baym 1995a). As we have suggested elsewhere (Rutter & Smith 1999) just because newsgroup interaction is transparent it does not mean that certain postings are not directed to specific individuals. Newsgroups like those we looked at may, broadly speaking, be public spaces but they are bounded so that people can leave (or effectively be expelled) from the group and encroachments (spam, off-topic contributions) are thoroughly frowned upon.

Further, even if we accept the discourse of online interaction as public, what right does that give us as researchers to appropriate that talk and do with it what we will? Do we have the same right to report that X is regular topic of conversation as we do the personal contents of a posting sent to a newsgroup in error rather than emailed to a confidant(e)? We suggest not. However, the decisions that need to be made are to be done so topically and contextually and they are essentially reliant on the researcher's sensitivity towards the environment (virtual or otherwise) that they are exploring. The interaction that goes on within newsgroups may be largely virtual but the ramifications of unethical disclosure are real and inescapable.

If we are uncertain as to the public/private status of the sites of our online ethnography, how can we begin to approach the ethics of identity and anonymity within our work? Unlike many other online ethnographers, we chose to make anonymous not only individuals but also the ISPs that hosted the newsgroups we looked at.[2] Concurring with Paccagnella (1997) we saw that '[c]hanging not only real names, but also aliases or pseudonyms (where used) proves the respect of the researchers for the social reality of cyberspace.' This we did at an early stage of the research and offered this promise of anonymity to people involved in our research as we assured them of our good intentions and commitment to good research practice. However, what we discovered is that RumCommers generally did not share our concerns for confidentiality. When interviewed, many expressed disappointment that they would not be personally identified by our publications. While we are sympathetic to these sentiments and remain extremely grateful to the research participation of a number of RumCommers who deepened our understanding of the newsgroup, our commitment to norms of confidentiality embedded in disciplinary ethical codes was always going to override these expressions of a desire for recognition.

Conclusion

We have tried in this chapter to avoid sweeping generalizations about how virtual ethnography should be undertaken. Instead we have reviewed a selection of issues our first extended ethnographic exploration of an online world raised. Many are doubtless already very familiar to ethnographers of other domains of social life. We suspect that the methodological issues we explore in this chapter are not unique to research conducted on, or using, the Internet. They would seem to apply to other communities that do not primarily manage their existence through face-to-face encounter, whether these be play-by-post gaming communities, chat networks supported by the newest generation of mobile telephones or even what Wilson and Peterson (2002) describe as those emerging communication technologies that have yet to find their way into people's everyday lives.

The online ethnographer faces the issue of 'being there' while also, in a non-trivial sense, 'not being there'. Corresponding membership issues arise in determining who can be said to be central to the research site under study and who peripheral. These issues often arise when seeking to ascertain the status of 'lurkers' who may be informed and knowledgeable about a particular segment of online activity but hidden from view. For example, Kanayama's (2003) study of an email community of older Japanese Internet users recognizes that lurkers, invisible to other participants as well as the researcher, represent a threat to the validity of some of the study's findings. Yet it is all too easy to fall into the trap of believing that every issue encountered in virtual methodology is the product of, and unique to the technologies employed in the area under study. If anything, what lurkers represent is the broader problem of establishing the boundaries of an ethnographic field and understanding. Who is local, who belongs and how that identification is displayed, where are the lines between this group and others to be meaningfully drawn? These are issues that have long troubled ethnography (see, for example, Gluckman 1964; and Sharrock 1974).

We suggest that the epicentre of the troubles considered in this chapter is the apparent gulf between the virtual ethnographer's research sites and the long-established, clearly defined social arenas wherein canonical conceptions of anthropological fieldwork were developed. Exploring beliefs and practices facilitated by rapidly changing technologies, the archaeology of which can involve going back all the way to the late 1980s, means that researchers may find themselves not only studying but also participating in the development of new and emergent methods of constructing identity, community and interaction. Nevertheless, we are wary of those who in the face of all this novelty and change would call for abandonment of the well-founded analytic attitudes and investigative stances associated with ethnography.

Certainly, the online position of the ethnography makes its practice more precarious than in traditional environments. Yet it is this very difference that underlines the conventional necessity for spending time within the setting in order to explore the culture within it. In online ethnography there is often an assumption that the researcher is not going into a culture that is substantially different from their own or that the organization of the culture can be rapidly assimilated through a few brief visits or even the automatic collection of data. Online ethnography may look deceptively easy to do but there are very good reasons for insisting on the application of traditional standards of ethnographic conduct and criteria of adequacy. We appreciate that ethnography has been in crisis in recent decades and many of its core assumptions have been challenged (Wittel 2000). If ethnography is successfully to illuminate online worlds, then an adaptive approach (Hine 2000) that seeks to address the distinctive features of those worlds has much to recommend it. In such an adaptive approach core ethnographic attitudes and stances are brought to bear on the materials at hand. Among these attitudes and stances, immersion – sustained presence in the culture by the ethnographer – seems indispensable, even where that presence is nominally accomplished through conventional markers of absence.

Notes

1. See Bulmer (1982) for an argument about circumstances where such openness is not a valuable approach.
2. This distinction between organization and individuals is used here as one of convenience. Especially in the case of RumCom major figures in the running of the ISP would contribute to the newsgroup threads and attend RumRendezvous. Conversely, subscribers would demonstrate great allegiance to the ISP, defending it against complaints, referring to staff by their first names and taking an active interest in the health of the key figures.

–7–

Centring the Links: Understanding Cybernetic Patterns of Co-Production, Circulation and Consumption

Maximilian C. Forte

The visual stillness of a web site, static as it appears on the screen, can be an entirely deceptive optical effect that fails adequately to represent the depth and extent of social ties, networking and exchange that leads to its construction. Cultural practice, revealed partly by the embedding and projection of particular visual symbolism on a web site, might also be lost on the 'average visitor' if we are to believe that web surfers are often simply 'speed clickers'. On the other hand, 'speed clicking' within a combine of related web sites might provide an effective impressionistic method for getting at the symbolic or ideological environment which can be observed by reading between the web sites. What lies between web sites is ostensibly undefined and possibly unintended, a kind of meaning suspended in the electronic equivalent of ether, a distillation of compounded impressions of images and ideas. What lies between web sites and what may also make a surface appearance on a given site, is also the product of actual patterns of exchange, information distribution, dialogue and revision that went into the construction of web sites whose only overt relation is a categorical one, that is, 'Society > Ethnicity > Indigenous Peoples > Caribbean' (as one would find in the Open Directory Project at http://www.dmoz.org).

The purpose of my chapter is to explore the social and cultural 'constructed-ness' of web sites, that is to say the patterns and processes of cultural practice that bring together individuals into online groups of producers, promoters and infor-mation consumers. There seems to be a prevailing concern in social scientific research about the Internet with synchronous modes of communication (typically chat) or more dynamic forms of asynchronous communication (such as email), with less attention paid to web site development and research using web pages. I address this oversight using the case of a group of nested (that is, tightly intercon-nected) web sites that come together in the *Caribbean Amerindian Centrelink* (CAC), already more than five years in existence at the time of writing.

This case study will be presented primarily as a descriptive ethnography with relevance to theory and concept (re)building where virtual anthropology is concerned. The CAC is itself a site and a combine of related sites that involved co-production by both researchers and 'informants', centred on the aboriginal peoples of the Caribbean and their current revival efforts. While the CAC has no offline physical existence as such, that is, it is not housed in a headquarters, it can exist only as an extension of offline research and activism. The revival dimension, or ethnic resurgence, is a critical ethnographic factor here, for the actors concerned have turned to the Internet precisely as a means of challenging scholarly and wider public perception of the 'facts' of an aboriginal Caribbean presence, as often denied or dismissed as it is lately celebrated. I provide methodological suggestions concerning appropriate research designs that stem from participation in web site co-production for particular constituencies, while evaluating diverse indicators of usage/consumption. I look at dynamic social and cultural aspects surrounding the web sites in question from the angles of producers, distributors and consumers. In particular, I devote some attention to the research-oriented webmaster as a broker, the problems caused by what I call 'broker overload', and the resultant strains on research relationships. I also consider the impact and transformations that ensue from introducing a networked artificial intelligence entity into a web site – an animated talking head that can field questions and engage in conversation on its own – and how one can research the resulting interactions and the effects that they produce. The main theme underpinning this chapter is that even a seemingly 'static' display such as a web site may well in fact be the product of intense social organization, brokerage and exchange, revealing quite a different story from what might appear on the seemingly placid surface of a site. Web sites do not just tell stories; they contain stories within them about themselves.

Some Social and Cultural Bases of Online Exchange

The meaning that lies in between web sites, that is, not necessarily made explicit on any one member of a collection of related sites, is thus shaped by offline social and cultural contexts, processes and agents. The principal social and cultural context surrounding the online productions studied in the following sections stems from two distinct yet related constituencies that shape the parameters for online patterns of production, circulation and consumption of web-based information resources. Both constituencies proclaim themselves to be engaged in some form of 'cultural revitalization' or 'restoration'. One of these constituencies consists of newly reorganized communal organizations within the Caribbean, such as the Santa Rosa Carib Community in Arima, Trinidad. Another constituency comprises recently founded Taino organizations based in the United States, populated by individuals who have 'rediscovered' and articulated their self-identity as Taino (Forte 2002).

The current resurgence of aboriginal identities and traditions and the wider recognition that these are receiving within the Caribbean itself is marked by state support and recognition for bodies such as Trinidad's Carib Community. At the regional level we can also witness the formation of the Caribbean Organization of Indigenous Peoples and the emergence of an array of new Taino organizations composed by Puerto Ricans in the United States. There is already considerable evidence to suggest that the growth and development of Amerindian identity and traditions in one territory is significantly aided and shaped by Amerindian cultural revitalization efforts in other territories. It is from these quarters and out of these processes that a challenge to established perspectives on 'Amerindian extinction' in the Caribbean has been mounted and then disseminated almost unchallenged on the Internet. The central importance of the Internet to these processes of seeking recognition, obtaining support from researchers and furthering the revitalization of aboriginal identities and traditions, is that the Internet allows relatively marginalized groups to recover a history and identity that colonialism, in large part, helped to erase or distort, and which dominant social science helped to inscribe. As Cisler (1998) observed: 'One of the strongest reasons for having a presence on the Internet is to provide information from a viewpoint that may not have found a voice in the mainstream media'.

The bulk of my research on the Caribs of Trinidad was conducted 'on the ground' (that is, offline) yet with online extensions. In the case of Taino groups, my research solely involved online participation and observation. At the beginning of my fieldwork with the Caribs of Trinidad, my would-be informants made it clear to me that they expected researchers to be of some assistance to them, to not just 'come and take'. It seemed to me that helping them to get online would be a way of furthering their aims for greater recognition both locally and internationally, while I as a researcher could gain valuable insights into how they wish to represent themselves to others. Accordingly I acted as a direct contributor and 'co-constructor' in the preparation of web sites on behalf of my informants. This activity itself led me further afield, that is, to create other web sites as a research resource about the Caribbean, and these sites became a means of interacting with other researchers. Emerging from these previous efforts, I founded the Caribbean Amerindian Centrelink. Apart from being a tool of participant observation, all of these online activities became a platform for furthering my offline field research goals. This involved observing the outcomes of what going online did for the Caribs of Trinidad, whose web sites received several thousand visitors early on. In addition to an increased level of interest in the Santa Rosa Carib Community, from local journalists and students, Trinidadian expatriates, general Internet users, and other academic researchers, there has also been an emergence of new web sites on the Caribs or sites that have begun to mention them.

The visible results of these social processes and cultural practice can be discerned on many of the web sites linked to by the CAC (Forte 2002). To summarize, there is a recurring iconography that is meant to immediately evoke long-term roots of current expressions of indigeneity, that is, symbols derived from ancient artefacts, feathered headdresses, photographs of monuments and landmarks, and so forth. The online presence of members of a community depicts rituals and gatherings, with members shown in what is described as 'full native regalia' in the case of several Taino community web sites. In textual terms, as I have described at length elsewhere (Forte 2002), there is the recurring appearance of word lists, maps of chiefdoms, extracts from early colonial chronicles, petroglyphs and legends, all combined in an effort to attest to the veracity of a continuing aboriginal legacy in the Caribbean. These emphases represent an index of the kinds of interests vested in the production and consumption of web-based information resources.

Co-production: Making One Centre among Many Links

In 1998, while building web sites for the host community at the centre of my dissertation fieldwork, the Santa Rosa Carib Community of Arima, Trinidad (Forte 2003), I envisioned one central platform that researchers, activists and interested members of the general public could consult and utilize rather than having to wade through seemingly endless, sometimes obscure, search results that varied by the search engine used. The CAC was initially created as a mere gateway site without any original content. I soon started to use this venue for posting some of my own writing, and these materials began to attract the interest of other researchers. Having drawn some of these researchers into web site content production, we eventually reformulated and relaunched the CAC. The CAC has since evolved into an Internet-based information resource that specializes in research, publication and cataloguing of Internet sites centred on the indigenous peoples of the wider Caribbean Basin as well as helping to build wider networks of discussion among scholars and activists. In addition, it also led to the founding of *Kacike: The Journal of Caribbean Amerindian History and Anthropology*, a peer-reviewed electronic journal that is managed and edited by some of the leading international scholars in this field of study. The two sites are now, to a certain extent, siblings, that is, the CAC leads to *Kacike*, while the latter also hosts a plain text mirror of the CAC.

The Caribbean Amerindian Centrelink, as its name implies, is a central link to a wide range of web sites that either focus upon or shed light upon the Native peoples of the Caribbean and Circum-Caribbean. This is the type of entity that has been termed a 'web sphere' by Foot and Schneider (2002: 226; also see Chapter 11 in this volume): 'a hyperlinked set of dynamically defined digital resources spanning multiple web sites deemed relevant or related to a central theme or "object"'. A web sphere includes both producers and users and, in fact, the role specializations that presumably distinguish the two are often intertwined in practice. The intention behind the CAC acting as a link site, a specialized directory, is to enable deeper content organization of the web, guided by the notion that web sites ought to self-organize rather than behave as dispersed atoms awaiting a higher order unity imposed by disinterested agencies such as Google or Yahoo! The CAC also endeavours to provide a venue for communication and mutual awareness among Caribbean indigenous peoples. It presents a variety of research, including histories, news and articles about Native Caribbean peoples, educational resources, online surveys and discussions of problems and prospects for Caribbean Amerindians and their descendants. It aims to provide content and build community at the same time. The CAC is also engaged in research information outreach. It publishes both non-refereed papers by individuals in *Issues in Caribbean Amerindian Studies*, and peer-reviewed scholarly papers in *Kacike: The Journal of Caribbean Amerindian History and Anthropology*. In addition the CAC distributes a free monthly electronic newsletter that is also posted on-site. Lastly, the CAC also owns and operates its own electronic discussion list, uniting scholars, activists and interested parties in one forum.

Co-production, as a concept, has been utilized independently by a range of authors writing in different contexts. In the work of Foot and Schneider (2002: 227, 229), inspired in part by anthropological writings on multi-sited ethnography, the basic definition of co-production is 'to produce jointly', a process that in practice can involve joint production by disparate actors. This concept of co-production echoes work on the distributed nature of cognition. Foot and Schneider include hyperlinking, with or without active consent on the part of the linked-to, as an expression of co-production in itself. Writing in a different context, Rogers (1996) speaks of 'co-production' as a process of multiple actors creating a cultural repertoire that can then be drawn upon by singular actors.

In the case of the CAC we are dealing with distributed authorship in a manner resembling some postmodern writings on the decentralization of the author, with elements of both of the above treatments of the term 'co-production'. Essentially we are dealing with multiple interests invested in the production of information resources, not necessarily characterized by a single-minded unity, but sharing at least some goals in common. The process of co-production in this case is often more deliberate and overt than hyperlinking, that is, through actual discussion and coordinated efforts. Users can enter, even force their way into the production process: initially angry emails demanding that certain resources be provided, or other links be amended, have sometimes been transformed into productive dialogues resulting in the creation of new information resources provided by the CAC. At least one former CAC editor entered this process precisely in this manner, starting with an initial indignant email. Given that pressure from users can sometimes be intense and demands worded in a manner that is sometimes unfriendly or impolite, CAC editors such as myself have grown tired of the abrasion, resulting in new site policy statements asking users to refrain from issuing edicts, decrees or ultimata in their messages.

Transforming Research: Creative Observation and Field Creation

I experienced a transformation in my role as ethnographer through online research and communication practice, especially with respect to my role as an author or as an independent agent. One of these transformations has to do with what I call *creative observation*, which presupposes the *creation of a field* – for example, a web resource – that others can then join as participants and/or observers (Forte 2003). This is almost the reverse of traditional offline fieldwork, where one goes to find a community to research, one that pre-exists the ethnographer's research project and which the ethnographer seeks to join through the mode of participant observation. In the case of field creation and creative observation, the researcher produces an information platform in advance of any interaction that could be of ethnographic value. In producing a web site, one becomes the gatekeeper to that site and may find oneself in the role of key informant to others in answering repeated questions on one's research topic, one's background, motivations and interests or on other aspects of one's web site. Questions, in other words, are no longer predominantly one-way, as they are in the case of the traditional ethnographer asking questions and seeking answers from informants. In this type of online creative observation, one is providing a set of research data that then itself generates further online data that one may study.

Yet, how does one create a site that others wish to interact with regularly, that establishes a seemingly central presence in a particular field,[1] and that enables the generation of relationships? I cannot produce a recipe book of ingredients and cooking methods here with respect to creating such a site. However, I can summarize what I think are some of the main elements needed in constructing a platform that generates regular transactions that lead to building relationships. I refer to those elements in these terms: usability, validity, institutionality, incorporationism, mutuality and linkage.

By 'usability' I mean that users have to find one's site especially compelling and noteworthy, a resource worthy of repeated consultations, having use value, inviting ever deepening investigation, and one that facilitates if not compels users to be drawn in closer and closer. One is able to gauge the degree of user-perceived usability not only through murky statistical site tracking devices, but also by inviting users to fill in on-site survey questionnaires and by analysing emails received. All of these methods are employed by the CAC. It is also a measure of how the production process attempts to cultivate consumption frequencies.

By 'validity' I mean that the information that one presents is credible, referenced, reasonable, cogently explained and illustrated, and not merely cobbled together for the sake of having something on a screen. As much 'heat' as one may draw from select respondents and users, aiming for a balanced coverage of views is still widely respected as something that demonstrates one's 'objectivity' and thus seriousness and reliability as an information provider. It also helps to ensure that one remains accessible to the widest body of public feedback and interaction, without pre-discriminating against users, although inevitably this will happen in extreme cases.

The notion of 'institutionality' arises from my experiences where positively impressed users somehow believed that the CAC was also an offline institution, with a physical headquarters, that is, an entity that was established, organized and operated by professionals. In other words, the CAC possessed a certain symbolic capital, suggesting to users the background presence of actual capital. Essentially, this stems from building one's site so that it projects and achieves credibility. This can be achieved by a wide variety of means, including clearly identifying the site creators and editors; branding; using effective visual design; trading in some of the offline currency of prestige and authority (as unfortunate and self-gratifying as these terms are); and providing 'proof' of respectability and reputability in the form of certain traces, for example in the case of the CAC, user traffic statistics, FAQs that indicate a frequency of interaction, links to one's site from a wide array of sites belonging to respected institutions, a history of the site (thereby adding temporal depth), and a cosmopolitan editorial board (CAC editors having been, at different times, located in institutions across the United States, Canada, France, Australia, New Zealand, Colombia, the Dominican Republic, Guyana and Trinidad & Tobago).

By 'incorporationism' I mean that a site has to achieve pre-eminence in a particular field, by claiming and demonstrating itself to be the ultimate, central, and most comprehensive resource of its kind in a given field, especially if the field is a novel or specialized one that can permit such an accomplishment. Everyone who shares an interest in the site's field of expertise has to be compelled to come to the site.

'Mutuality', or what web design newsletters often call 'stickiness', involves creating a site that makes users come back repeatedly – and most of this can be done by providing 'free stuff'. In the case of the CAC, users have free access to research material and digitized books with expired copyrights; there is a free monthly newsletter for subscribers; even news and email accounts are provided. CAC editors have also been known to act as mentors for students engaged in research projects related to their interests. I refer to all of these as mutuality in the sense that it is not a case of an ethnographer merely taking from an informant, but of creating value and making knowledge freely available.

'Linkage' is a vital element: I refer here, in the case of the CAC, to actual links of the hyperlink sort, as well as to a programme of offering awards, producing reviews of web sites that one lists in one's site, and the creation of a webring. Having said this, I must disagree with assertions that 'hyperlinks are an impoverished and one-dimensional way to represent and express social ties' (Wittel 2000). Hyperlinks can have multiple layers of meaning and they can also be of a wide variety (see Park and Thelwall, Chapter 12 in this volume). They can be the sites of intense contestation and can be as emblematic of social relationships as a handshake, an exchange of gifts, an embrace, an invitation to a birthday party or a 'thumbs up' offered in praise. In my experience, owners of sites linked from the CAC are acutely concerned with where their links are placed, with informing us of updated links, demanding that we link to them, angrily protesting that we linked to certain sites and that we remove those links, and so forth.

Broker Overload: Reaching the Limits of Co-production

Working with diverse constituencies (scholars, activists, students, other interested members of the public) and under the pressure of competing demands on time, can very easily lend itself to an unmanageable situation that can also be reflected in the character of a web site. This is a syndrome that I refer to as 'broker overload' and aside from some of the features listed above it can include too many requests for information and advice; flaming and counter-flaming when mediation fails; and unequal distribution of work tasks among brokers. In this case, the brokers are the editors and contributors to the CAC, working between different clienteles (that is, host communities on the ground) and audiences (other scholars, activists and web surfers), engaged in a selection and interpretation of cultural materials while reworking meanings and symbols to suit what is deemed to be intelligible and welcomed by diverse audiences.[2]

Broker overload can be manifested on a web site in a wide variety of possible manifestations, although the presence of any of these perceived 'deficiencies' in a site does not necessarily imply broker overload, nor should one assume that broker overload necessarily has these particular manifestations. In the case of the CAC, which maintains a specialized directory of sites, broker overload can have manifestations that include the following: the presence of 'broken links' left undetected and thus unamended; few or no new sites added for periods of months; the inability to immediately process requests to add new sites or correct information already listed; a slowdown in the production and circulation of electronic newsletters; long periods of silence before responding to requests for information sent via email; and the inability to undertake the creation of new features for a given site. In this sense, apparent stasis can itself betray underlying social processes such as broker overload, rather than simple apathy or lack of attention. In the case of the CAC, periods of stasis have been rendered visible, for example, by the fact that each page shows the date of the last update. When updates are frequent and regular the number of visitors actually increases markedly. When updates are infrequent (that is, once every four months), it is not uncommon for visitors to lodge complaints via email, or to be very pointed in their messages about broken links.

When repetitive work tasks become too sizeable and burdensome for the limits of human labour, what would one normally expect to happen? Automation is one possible consequence. In the case of the CAC, automation on a number of fronts, attests silently to a history of broker overload. The presence of a page of frequently asked (and answered) questions clearly shows that some questions have been received in such volume and with such repetition that it became necessary to develop stock replies. The other noteworthy feature of FAQs is that they can also hint at a 'user model': by suggesting that *these* are the questions that have been *frequently* asked, then we can come to at least an impressionistic overview of the common denominator among the various interests of users, that is, the audience, the constituency, or the consuming public of a web site. We thus have a rudimentary profile not just of the clientele but also of the various pressures and demands for information that have been exerted on the further revision and reconstruction of a web site.

Automation can take on a much more graphic, to some even shocking, form. The CAC is assisted in its question-and-answer tasks by ANACAONA, the acronym for a robot that mirrors the name of a legendary Taino heroine from the early colonial history of Hispaniola. ANACAONA stands for 'Anything About Caribbean Aboriginals from an Online Networked Assistant', and it/she makes its/her presence felt by a live talking face, with animated expressions and a voice that is used to speak with visitors. The robot's software is based on Dr Richard Wallace's Artificial Intelligence Markup Language (see Wallace n.d.), coupled with the animation work of a company called Oddcast, the two technologies bridged by yet another enterprise called Pandorabots.[3] In existence for a little over a year at the time of writing, the results of this form of automation have been mixed at best, distressing at worst. Most users find that ANACAONA either does not have the information they desire (the robot requires training, which itself adds to broker overload since, in the extreme, the robot may require a data volume equalling that of a doctoral programme), or does not understand or answer their questions (even the most minor typographic error causes it to 'misunderstand' or stray into other subjects). From my own calculations, ANACAONA successfully answered 80 per cent or more of questions on Amerindian issues posed in any one conversation for less than 30 per cent of recorded conversations. In some cases the robot actually possessed the knowledge but was 'confused' by grammar or spelling, or its programmed 'drive' to ask its own questions.

What disturbed some visitors, causing one of the few rare instances of email seething with anger and indignation to be directed against the editors of the CAC, was the manner in which the robot's acronym echoes the name of the historical

Anacaona.[4] The claim made against the CAC was that we were disrespecting and denigrating Taino traditions by appropriating the name of a 'sacred' figure, one that should never be parodied by a mere chatterbot, whatever its intended uses. Attempts to make the handful of complainants understand that we did not intend for the two to be confused, that the robot does not attempt to portray itself as either a Taino or as the voice of the historical Anacaona, met with little success. On occasion, the robot is still engaged by users who complain of 'her' non-Amerindian facial features, 'her' name, or the fact that 'she' is unable to recall events of her past life as Anacaona, the historical Taino leader. Depending on one's perspective, this could be a disturbing sign, within a technologically mediated society, of the increased inability of individuals to discern the difference in meaning and character between the socio-historical human and the techno-artificial device, a blurring of the lines between humans and machines that seems to be emerging at least in North American popular culture as glimpsed by the emergence and re-articulation of cyborg and other post-human fantasies/dystopias (Gray 2001).

Even the more problematic social and interpersonal consequences of site automation can themselves generate more constructive causal forces. A seemingly trivial issue concerning the name of a robot can act as a foil for crystallizing and redefining contemporary Taino identities. Anacaona, an historical figure that is known only through early Spanish colonial chronicles, becomes transformed into a legendary icon of aboriginal resistance and then is further redefined as a 'sacred' and even 'divine' entity whose memory and name must be shrouded within a veil of deference. The fact that the word Anacaona is reputed to simply mean 'golden flower' and is listed as any of a number of nouns in surviving lists of Taino lexical items, added to the fact that everything from the names of restaurants, resorts, travel agencies, artistic troupes and musical bands have adopted the name, only seemed to sharpen the critiques of the naming of the CAC robot. By indirect and unintended means therefore, the CAC facilitated the articulation of Taino identity, even if by paradoxical means in making itself the target of the criticisms of the constituents it seeks to serve.

Site automation can have other constructive consequences as well, these more intentional than the facets just discussed. From one perspective, there is a middle road between a site that is static and one that is dynamic, and that is the automatic. From a different point of view, the automatic is simply a false dynamism, the routine reproduction of static values within unchanging parameters whose constant recycling can project an aura of activity and change while masking the fixity of its underlying 'intelligence'. Either way, how can the presence of a robot be constructive then? On the one hand, where humans fail to respond, there is an agent that is available *all the time* and that can potentially answer most of the routine questions in a manner that stimulates users into believing that they are actually chatting with a thinking entity (the vast majority of logged conversations reveal that users converse with the robot as if it were human, even probing deeply personal questions and engaging in discursive sexual intercourse with the robot). The impersonal nature of chatting with a robot has had one striking consequence: the robot receives several hundred more queries in a single month than are received by the combined human editors of the CAC in an entire year. Being overtly non-human coupled with the anonymity of online chatting *seems* to have facilitated users to disclose more about themselves, to sustain conversations without fear of becoming a nuisance, and to ask many more frank questions without concern for being judged on the quality of the questions. The robot is itself merely a talking version of a very large FAQ, with one distinct advantage: it has a human-like face and a human voice, masking mechanical impersonality with programmed personality. It can freely be flirted with and insulted; in turn, it can make sexual comments of its own, fight back, or quickly lead the user into new subjects for discussion. This is a degree of 'interpersonal' discourse that simply does not occur between CAC editors and members of its public on an everyday basis. ANACAONA is a 'distortion' in the CAC's co-production network, involving different sets of authors and interests and generating different types of consumption patterns.

Cyber-cultural Patterns of Circulation

The fact that the CAC brings together numerous web sites into one directory, numerous webmasters into one discussion and email list, and several researchers into particular online publications, can serve to at least simulate a sense of collectivity, and indirectly perhaps, a *sense* of centrality. One of these senses of collectivity, especially among webmasters who have produced content that is then linked and highlighted by the CAC, involves the question of *common interests* in Caribbean indigenous issues. The second sense of collective orientations sometimes involves *related content* (essays on Taino or Carib history and culture, information on archaeological sites, language resources; sometimes sites will appropriate content from other sites). Third, to some extent the various sites *share perspectives* (exemplified by a shared idiom for discussing and presenting Caribbean indigenous issues). A fourth facet relates to *shared symbols* in terms of images that are often recycled from one site to another (petroglyphic icons, depictions of shamanic objects, animal figures seen as sacred symbols in Amerindian cosmologies). The fifth consists of *boundaries* (formed for example by sites crossreferencing each other for users, by use of hyperlinks and 'webrings' and through the granting of awards). A sixth involves *mutual advantage* (the legitimacy of each site bolstered by the fact that other such sites exist as well, thus rendering any one site less of a 'one-click wonder'). The seventh consists of *regular exchange* (electronic newsletters, email petitions, mailing lists, listservs, newsgroups, message boards, chat rooms and individual email messages). Taken together, these processes of exchange and cross-referencing, even competition, result in 'co-production' on a large scale, without a single centre of authority, but rather an authority found between the various web sites.

Instrumental expressions of circulation can be found in the form of newsletters, participation in lists, webrings, reciprocal links, advertisements, and even the appropriation and sharing of content across sites. What these devices point to, I would argue, is something more than just the mechanics of online communication. What we are in fact dealing with here are the expressions of a wider and more profound social interaction. A web site in this case is both a medium and forum where people bring the offline into the online, with the hope of producing a new 'effect' that can then be taken offline and generate new realities on the ground, such as wider recognition of an aboriginal presence in the Caribbean.

The circulation of online information resources is an expression of a deeper cultural practice that stems from offline roots, at least in the case of this ethnography. The need for research support to assist in the articulation of indigenous self-representations, in the face of hostile authorities, indifferent neighbours or sceptical scholars, forms one of the bases for the dissemination of particular ideas as found on specific web sites. Circulation in this instance is not of the ordinary commodity kind; rather, it is the result of clear-cut ideational investments and labour. Sites are circulated (that is, via reciprocal links) for their particular use value as determined by specific ideational interests. The formulation and expression of these interests also determines, in part, observable patterns of consumption of these information resources.

Patterns of Consumption

Understanding patterns of consumption in this case is not a straightforward task given that it is impossible for the producers of web resources to have anything other than select glimpses of the many unspoken, distant, practical or imaginative ways that one's resources have been used. Understanding who the consumers of a site may be involves tracking patterns of usage which do not necessarily follow the expectations shaped by the producers and those who try to mediate the circulation of information resources online.

The fact that a site is ultimately 'open' means that it can possibly attract any of a number of unintended constituents. At the start of the venture, I did not expect that primary and secondary school students would be one of the most persistent constituencies in asking for information of a broad character. Catering to this audience has introduced certain 'distortions' into the production process. With the need to provide a balance of perspectives and a diversity of subject areas, new content was generated specifically in the form of reference materials (such as encyclopedia articles) and teaching resources (for example, lesson plans). This younger audience is one of ANACAONA's primary users as well and given the fact that some of 'her' responses to insults were initially quite 'foul mouthed', a lengthy process of sanitization and retraining was undertaken. Our fear was that a robot, intended for an adult audience, could attract protests of abusive behaviour, hardly the way a resource such as the CAC would wish to be seen. How it is seen in fact is an ongoing process: the presence of a visitor feedback questionnaire on the site is evidence of the fact that we are searching for answers to this question, a self-conscious display of uncertainty that actually encourages further cycles of co-production.

Conclusion

A web site can mask the fact of its own construction, in an iterative process, as a joint venture between multiple interests and actors. There are no automatic results of the ways in which fellow producers, brokers and consumers feed back into the production process. Clearly the CAC emerged from a specific offline social and cultural context, designed to meet the needs and interests of its most immediate partners and intended beneficiaries. The online context, however, introduces its own qualitative transformations – one may control what the audience sees, but one is obviously not able to control what it wishes to see. Likewise, consumers may try to exercise pressure on producers in modifying or diversifying their products, but it is not necessarily the case that an independent agency such as the CAC, which ultimately is not directly answerable to any 'higher authority', will respond to the many, often contradictory, demands which are put to it. Both production and consumption are subject to ongoing negotiation, a process of sometimes intense negotiation that is seemingly belied by the ostensibly unperturbed static surface of a web site.

Notes

1. The Caribbean Amerindian Centrelink has been rated by Alexa as the number one site among all sites on Caribbean indigenous peoples, as listed in the Open Directory Project at http://www.dmoz.org (accessed 3 November 2004). The rankings are based on the volume of traffic. In fifth place is the CAC's offspring site, Kacike.
2. For more discussion of cultural brokerage, see Antoun (1989) and Peace (1998).
3. The web site for Pandorabots can be found at http://www.pandorabots.com (accessed 3 November 2004), and the site for Oddcast is available at http://www.oddcast.com (accessed 3 November 2004). The URL for the

A.L.I.C.E. Foundation, which hosts versions of the software that constitutes the CAC's Anacaona robot, has shifted recently, but may most likely be found at http://www.alicebot.org.

4. One study that has been done on negative personal reactions to 'chatterbots', that I would recommend for those interested in more discussion of this subject, is by De Angeli, Johnson and Coventry (n.d.)

Part II

Research Sites and Strategies

Research Sites and Strategies: Introduction

Christine Hine

Defining contexts for social research

Among the uncertainties which new media have introduced into the social research process is where to go to in order to carry out a study. Given that we now see the Internet as a cultural context in its own right, it seems clear that we can view that context as a place in which to carry out social research. The success of ethnographers in claiming the Internet as a field site attests to acceptance that the Internet is a form of social space. At the same time, however, it has become apparent that mediated communications can only provisionally be bracketed off as objects of study for social researchers. Uses of the Internet, the telephone, the mass media and the printed word permeate face-to-face social settings, and disrupt any easy assumptions about the boundedness of social life.

For many social researchers, then, the definition of the site for an investigation is not a straightforward issue. As the case studies in Part I showed, the decision whether to conduct research relationships online or offline is situated in the demands of a specific research goal. In Part II we address this concern in more depth, exploring some different ways of defining the field site and exploring socially significant aspects of its organization. The Internet has frequently been understood by social scientists as providing a new space for social interaction and for the development of social formations, and innovation in research methods is needed to address these new spaces. However, this does not mean that the traditional sites of research into everyday life become irrelevant. Where to begin, when to stop and how to combine research into online and offline contexts are the problems which Part II addresses.

The Internet can also challenge us to break down the distinction between qualitative and quantitative methods. The traces which online activities leave provide a valuable resource to social researchers who wish to understand both what people do online and what significance these actions have. The sheer amount of traces that online activities can leave, and that the researcher can amass, tend to lead even hardened (or softened) qualitative researchers towards more quantitative methods for summarizing data and exploring patterns. The chapters in this part employ both qualitative and quantitative methods in their exploration of how to define a research site and how to visualise and analyse it.

Case Studies in the Exploration of Research Sites

The first two chapters in this part examine diametrically opposed approaches to the spatiality of online interactions. Martin Dodge explores the role of mapping in developing an understanding of online spatiality, and illustrates some research strategies that this perspective on the geography of online connections suggests. He demonstrates that mapping provides some provocative ways to conceptualize research sites and explore interactions. These methods exploit the visibility and traceability of online activity in order to provide ways for researchers to develop and explore hypotheses about the shape of social interactions facilitated by the Internet.

In stark contrast to Dodge's treatment of the online as a distinctive and spatially complex sphere of social action, Hugh Mackay asserts the importance of understanding new media use within traditional contexts. Mackay begins with the location of the home, and argues that understanding online interactions can usefully build on existing traditions of media use ethnography. He makes the case that informants have an integrated approach to online and offline activity which does not carve out the 'online' as a relevant social sphere. Methodological approaches which value participant perspectives can usefully therefore start, not in online spaces, but in the home.

A third perspective on the spatiality of research methods is provided by Mário J. L. Guimarães Jr, who proposes that we follow our informants and their social networks. Here it becomes apparent that the relevant contexts to study are defined not by particular software applications, but by the ways in which a specific social network chooses to combine various forms of communication. In his ethnography of an online graphical environment Guimarães shows the importance of gaining access to and appreciating the organization of participants' social networks. In similar vein to Mackay, Guimarães argues for the ethnographer's sensitivity to the specificities of the setting as a means to progressively define the field site. The two case studies come to dramatically different conclusions, but build upon similar principles.

The distributed and hyperlinked structure of the World Wide Web provides a distinctive challenge for the definition of research sites. Steven M. Schneider & Kirsten A. Foot propose the concept of the 'web sphere' as the unit of analysis, as a way to examine the formations that arise when multiple web sites on a given theme are created. The notion of the web sphere emphasizes the importance of emergent social structures in online settings. While they might be triggered in response to offline events, such as an election campaign or national disaster, web spheres develop a structure and set of meanings all of their own which can be treated by the researcher as a site for social research.

Han Woo Park & Mike Thelwall argue that quantitative studies of hyperlinking can usefully help us to explore the development of social structure and meaning across the web, particularly when combined with qualitative investigations of what the act of making a hyperlink means to a web author. Anne Beaulieu also explores the complex ways in which online spaces emerge, through her ethnographic exploration of data-sharing infrastructures in science. While the field site here is scientific research, the methodological guidelines are applicable to any work or leisure domain where computer-mediated communication is routinely used. She demonstrates the value of following connectivity, by observing the traces left by 'use' and 'linking', and once again stresses the importance of developing a sensitivity to the way spaces develop and a critical perspective on the meaning of hyperlinks.

The chapters by Park & Thelwall, by Schneider & Foot and by Beaulieu focus on process, exploring the dynamics which produce the web rather than treating it as simply found space. This theme of the online context as a culturally shaped space unites the chapters in this part, prompting a range of methodological solutions which allow researchers to explore the ways in which the social spaces of CMC are made and experienced.

Technologies, Sites and Strategies

The upshot of the case studies presented in Part II is that there is no clear recipe for defining and exploring a research site, particularly where the Internet is involved. Nonetheless, there are some themes which run through the chapters, and provide principles to inform research design in other areas:

- Appropriate sites for research are not obvious in advance, but are shaped through developing understandings of the ways in which people make use of available technologies as these intersect with our own research goals.
- Technologies are not research sites in themselves. If the aim is to investigate structures and processes of social meaning, it is a mistake to think that a given technological platform necessarily delivers a meaningfully bounded research site.
- It is not the case that all research sites, even ones which hope to address the use of the Internet as a social phenomenon, need to start online. Traditional contexts such as the home, the school and the workplace play a vital role in everyday social experience, and tried and tested strategies of social research have much to tell us about use of new media in these places.

- Mapping and archiving techniques and hyperlink analysis provide new means of visualising and exploring social situations. Online activities leave a myriad of traces, providing a valuable resource for researchers interested in exploring emergent social structures and connections.

−8−

The Role of Maps
in Virtual Research Methods

Martin Dodge

the map is a help provided to the imagination through the eyes.

Henri Abraham Chatelain, *Atlas Historique* (1705)

Mapping provides a uniquely powerful means to classify, represent and communicate information about places that are too large and too complex to be seen directly. Importantly, the places that maps are able to represent need not be limited to physical, geographical spaces like cities, rivers, mountain ranges and such like: maps can be used to represent online spaces of computer-mediated communication (Dodge and Kitchin 2001a, 2001b). This chapter makes the case for the use of maps as an addition to existing methods in virtual research.

Maps have long been useful in research into social phenomena. They provide a key technique in human geography of course, but they are also used in other disciplines such as archaeology, history and epidemiology, to store spatial information, to analyse data and generate ideas, to test hypotheses, and to present results in a compelling, visual form (Monmonier 1993). Mapping as a method of inquiry and knowledge creation also plays a role in the natural sciences, in disciplines such as astronomy and particle physics, and in the life sciences, as exemplified by the metaphoric and literal mapping of DNA by the Human Genome Project (Stephen S. Hall 1992).

The ability to create and use maps is one of the most basic means of human communication, at least as old as the invention of language and, arguably, as significant as the discovery of mathematics. The recorded history of cartography clearly demonstrates the practical utility of maps in all aspects of Western society, being most important for organising spatial knowledges, facilitating navigation and controlling territory (Thrower 1996). Some have gone further, to argue that mapping processes are culturally universal, evident across all human societies (for example, Blaut et al. 2003), although the visual forms of the resulting map artefacts are very diverse. At the same time maps are also rhetorically powerful graphic images that frame our understanding of the human and physical world, shaping our mental image of places, constructing our sense of spatiality. So in a very real sense maps make our world.

I begin by defining the nature of the map, discussing the theoretical basis of mapping processes and visualization. This is followed by a consideration of mapping in the context of research into the operation and structures of CMC by social scientists, where I advance reasons why mapping online space is useful but also challenging. I then set out a classification of contemporary mapping, showing how maps are used, before examining in some detail four exemplars. I conclude this chapter with a brief discussion of the limitations of mapping as a research methodology in terms of practical problems, ethics and ideology.

Maps and Visualization

Conventionally, maps are material artefacts that visually represent a geographical landscape using the cartographic norms of a planar view (that is, looking straight down from above) and a uniform reduction in scale. However, it is impossible neatly to define maps according to the type of phenomena mapped or the particular mode of presentation, or their medium of dissemination (Dorling and Fairbairn 1997). Maps have traditionally been used as static storage devices for spatial data and usually printed on paper, but now they are much more likely to be interactive tools displayed on a computer screen. Here I take a very broad definition, given by Harley and Woodward (1987: xvi), 'maps are graphic representations that facilitate a spatial understanding of things, concepts, conditions, processes, or events in the human world'. We currently live in a map-saturated world, surrounded by both conventional geographic maps and many other map-like spatial images and models (for example, animated satellite images, three-dimensional city models, magnetic resonance imaging (MRI) scans of the brain).

The development and diffusion of information and communication technologies (ICTs) since the early 1980s has profoundly affected the nature of cartographic mapping. Nowadays, the majority of maps are digital and only created 'on-demand' for temporary display on screens. The days of the unwieldy folded map sheet and heavy paper atlases are past, increasingly replaced by geographic information systems (GIS) and spatial databases. The web mapping portal MapQuest.com has already delivered more maps than any other publisher in the history of cartography (Peterson 2001). Cheap, powerful computer graphics on desktop personal computers (PCs) enables much more expressive and interactive digital cartography, such as animated maps, multimedia atlases and so-called geovisualization. Geovisualization draws on concepts from statistics for exploratory data analysis, envisaging highly interactive environments of linked, multiple representations (maps, two-dimensional charts, three-dimensional plots, tables).

As well as making maps more interactive, ICTs are also helping to give many more people access to cartography as map-makers themselves, be it via the 'map charting' options in spreadsheets to produce simple thematic maps, creating custom maps from an online mapping service, or desktop GIS such as ArcView or MapInfo. As more and more people bypass professional cartographers to make their own maps as and when required, it is likely that the diversity of map forms and usage will expand. Of course, the availability of 'point and click' mapping software is no guarantee that the maps produced will be appropriate and effective. Map-making still takes skill and thought, requiring considerable effort to make *good* maps.

The production of cartographic map artefacts and map-like visual images involves a whole series of mapping processes, from the initial selection of what to measure to the choice of the most appropriate scale of representation and projection, and the best visual symbology to use. The concept of 'map as process' is useful as a research methodology because it encourages particular ways of organized thinking to do with how to generalize reality, how to distil out inherent, meaningful spatial structure from the data, and how to show significant relationships between things in a legible fashion. Mapping provides a means to organize large amounts of, often multidimensional, information about a place in such a fashion as to facilitate human exploration and understanding. Yet, mapping is not just a set of techniques for information 'management', it also encompasses important social processes of knowledge construction. As scholars have come to realize, maps and culture are intimately entwined and inseparable (Harley 1989; Wood 1992). Mapping not only represents reality, but also has an active role in the social construction of that reality. Yet most people are not conscious of this when they use maps. Sparke (1998: 466) calls this the recursive proleptic effect of mapping, 'the way maps contribute to the construction of spaces that later they seem only to represent'. The power of maps comes from the fact that they are both a practical form of information processing and also a compelling form of rhetorical communication.

Mapping works, essentially, by helping people to see the unseen. This is achieved through the act of visualization, premised on the simple notion that humans can reason and learn more effectively in a visual environment than when using textual or numerical description. Maps provide graphical ideation which renders a place, a phenomenon or a process visible, enabling our most powerful information-processing abilities, those of the human eye–brain vision system, to be brought to bear. Visualization is thus a cognitive process of learning through the interaction with visual signs that make up the map and it differs from passive observation in that its purpose is to discover unknowns, rather than to see what is already known. Effective visualization in a research context reveals novel insights that are not apparent with other methods.

The power of mapping as visualization to elucidate meaningful patterns in complex data is well illustrated by some of the 'classics' of the pre-digital era like John Snow's 'cholera map' of 1854, Charles Joseph Minard's 'Napoleon map' of 1869 and Harry Beck's 'Tube diagram' of 1933 (see Tufte 1983; Garland 1994; Brody et al. 2000; Hadlaw 2003). Even though these examples are non-interactive, that is, they are static, two-dimensional images, hand-drawn on paper, they are nonetheless still powerful. They show the potential of visualization to provide new understanding and compelling means of communicating to a wide audience. Through their aesthetic visual form they also demonstrate the extent to which mapping can be a creative process in and of itself. The best visualizations go beyond merely representing to become a kind of cognitive shorthand for the actual places and processes themselves, illustrated well by the way in which Beck's celebrated diagrammatic design of the Underground provides such a powerful spatial template for the 'real' layout of London in the minds of many visitors and residents. The problem is that although Beck's map works well for underground movement, it can be confusing for surface navigation because it famously sacrifices geographic accuracy for topological clarity.

Conventional cartographic mapping is just one type of visualization and many other visualization techniques have been developed for handling large, complex datasets without gross simplification or unfathomable statistical models (for example, volumetric visualization in exploration geology, three-dimensional body imaging in medical diagnostics). Of course, there is a long history of visualization prior to computers and interactive graphics (for useful reviews, see Tufte 1983; Orford, Dorling and Harris 1998; Friendly and Denis 2003), but newer computer-based visualization techniques are particularly useful to researchers confronting poorly structured problems in information-rich environments – like a good deal of quantitative social science research on CMC.

Developments in the field of information visualization since the early 1990s have proved particularly fertile in creating navigable maps of information spaces (Card, Mackinlay and Schneiderman 1999). These maps are non-geographic, instead focusing on visualizing information structure using abstract projections, but interestingly they make explicit use of spatial metaphors (Couclelis 1998). The production of these novel types of maps of information has been termed spatialization (Skupin and Fabrikant 2003) and it often 'borrows' proven design concepts from cartography, for example the use of hill shading and contouring from terrain mapping to represent large text archives (Wise 1999).

Mapping the Spaces of Computer-mediated Communications

It may seem surprising, in the first place, that a worthwhile case can be made to use maps in social science research on CMC. This surprise is based on two false assumptions: first, that CMC has no meaningful spatial structures, is somehow divorced from geographic reality, and is thus 'unmappable'; and second, that maps can represent geographic phenomena only in relation to the surface of the earth. Both these assumptions are incorrect; maps are not just geographic and CMC has meaningful structures to be mapped (such as semantic similarity between content, affinity ties of differing strengths in online social networks, temporal usage patterns). The self-evident answer is that it *is* possible to map CMC – as many researcher have indeed done (see Dodge and Kitchin 2001b) – and several of the best examples are discussed later.

Given that it is possible, why might one actually want to invest time and effort to produce maps of CMC? Mapping is particularly useful for virtual research since so much of the 'terrain' of study, the social phenomena and the online places in which they occur, are composed of immaterial software (in essence they are just lines of code and database records) and are to a large degree invisible. Consequently, this 'terrain' can be hard to comprehend, and maps are an obvious tool to help make the virtual tangible. The processes of mapping can help make the virtual understandable to the researcher.

The extent and usage of CMC has grown very rapidly since the early 1990s. With so many distinct spaces and users online, cyberspace has become an enormous and often confusing entity that can be difficult to monitor and navigate through. Maps can help users, service providers and analysts comprehend the various spaces of online interaction and information, providing understanding and aiding navigation. Depending on their scale, some of the maps provide a powerful 'big picture' view, giving people a unique sense of a space difficult to understand from navigating alone.

Beyond the online spaces themselves, the adoption of CMC is having significant effects on social, cultural, political and economic aspects of everyday life (Dodge and Kitchin 2001a). Maps can help in understanding the implications by revealing the extent and interrelations of the changes occurring. Geographical mapping of the Internet is significant, as it can provide insights into who owns and controls the supporting infrastructure, and how and from where cyberspace is being produced (Dodge and Kitchin 2004). In addition, geographical maps are especially useful for public communications because they use a familiar template of countries and continents.

However, mapping CMC is a challenge. This is particularly the case because CMC is new and rapidly evolving, it is fluid, and it is diverse. It is not a single, homogenous and continuous phenomenon, but a myriad of rapidly evolving digital spaces, channels and media, each providing a distinct form of virtual interaction and communication. Many of the spaces of CMC are overlapping and interconnected, but often in ad hoc and unplanned ways, giving rise to complex rhizomatic structures that cannot easily be surveyed and mapped (Dodge and Kitchin 2001a).

Cyberspace offers places that at first often seem contiguous with geographic space, yet on further inspection it becomes clear that the space-time laws of physics have little meaning online. This is because the spaces of CMC are purely relational. They are not natural, but are solely the productions of their designers and, in many cases, users. They adopt the formal qualities of geographic (Euclidean) space only if explicitly programmed to do so, and indeed many media such as email have severely limited spatial qualities. The inherent spaces that do exist are often purely visual (objects have no weight or mass) and their spatial fixity is uncertain (spaces can appear and disappear in a moment, leaving no trace of their existence). Additionally, many online spaces violate two principal assumptions of modern (Western) cartography making them tough to map using conventional techniques. The first of these is that space is continuous, ordered and reciprocal. There are no sudden gaps or holes in the landscape, everything is somewhere, and the Euclidean notion of distance holds true, that is, the distance from *A* to *B* will be the same as from *B* to *A*. The second assumption is that the map is not the territory but a representation of it, that is, the territory has a separate, ongoing existence and meaning beyond the map. Yet parts of cyberspace are discontinuous, lacking linear organization and in some cases the map and the territory are conflated and cannot be separated (Dodge and Kitchin 2001a).

What are maps of CMC like? The diverse range of maps so far produced makes it hard to generalize. Just as there is not one true geographic map of a given place, so there are no definitive maps of CMC. Devising effective map representations for the structures of CMC when no obvious framework or intuitive metaphor exist has led to considerable creativity, with many visual forms, projection methods and models of interaction tried out. Many of the resulting maps, while novel and interesting, are not workable (that is, they are not effective visualizations). The wide range of CMC mapping is undertaken by a variety of different map-makers, including graphic designers, sociologists, artists, physicists, information scientists, librarians and interface engineers. Interestingly, almost none have been made by cartographers or geographers (although see the notable contributions discussed by Skupin and Fabrikant 2003).

Map Use in Virtual Research

One way to classify the nature of contemporary mapping is to focus on how maps are actually used to do work, for example in the different stages of an academic research project. MacEachren (1995) provides a useful conceptual device, the 'cartography cube', to do this (Figure 8.1), employing three axes to encapsulate the distinctive characteristics of contemporary map use. The first axis covers the scope of the user audience for the map (running from private maps, used only by their maker, through to published, widely distributed maps for public use); next is the degree to which the map offers interactivity in use (ranging from the low interactivity of traditional paper maps up to highly flexible map displays of GIS); the third axis is the so-called 'data relations' (a continuum running from revealing unknowns patterns to presenting known facts). Particular types of map use can thus be classified and placed within the cartography cube, and four examples are identified – explore, analyse, synthesize and present (Figure 8.1). These run roughly from the lower corner of the cube up to the other and the diagonal line they form can be thought of as marking the distinction between 'maps to foster *private visual thinking* early in the research process and those to facilitate *public visual communication* of research results' (MacEachren 1995: 3, original emphases). Some of the most interesting recent developments in mapping have been in the 'explore' usage – that is, highly interactive private maps for visual thinking,

In the course of a typical academic project, researchers may use maps in a number of different roles, from an initial 'scan' of raw data through to the creation of an 'eye-candy' map for the cover of the final report. In the 'explore' usage, maps

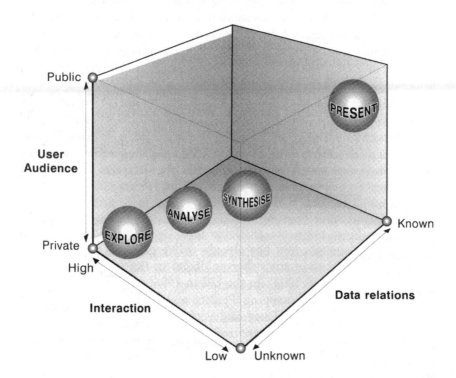

Figure 8.1 Alan MacEachren's 'cartography cube' conceptualisation of map use. This particular version is from Perkins (2003, p. 347). (Courtesy of Chris Perkins, Department of Geography, University of Manchester.)

can answer basic 'what is happening here?' type questions, by giving a visual inventory that can be quickly reviewed for interesting trends and anomalies (seeing the 'holes' in a map can be a good way to spot errors in data collection). The 'analysis' phase of research would use interactive maps to process and classify complex data, breaking it down in the hopes of revealing previously unknown patterns that could not be discerned from looking through the raw data. For example, scrolling through page after page of a web site user log would tell you little, whereas overlaying the pathways of individual user sessions onto a map of the hyperlink structure of content (so-called 'clickstream' visualization) might quickly show consistent patterns of site navigation. The 'synthesis' stage of research often requires evidence to be assembled to support particular hypotheses. Maps are useful tools here for marshalling together diverse data into a single visual explanation. Maps can facilitate visual explanation of observed patterns, for example through testing for the existence of spatial processes such as hierarchical clustering, small world networks, and distance decay functions. John Snow's 'cholera map' is often put forward as a prime example of maps as synthesizing tools (Brody et al. 2000). Towards the end of a research project, it is usually necessary to present results to external audiences and well-designed maps are an exemplary means of public communication. In a compact visual image, a good map can convey a huge amount of data in a legible, aesthetic and comprehensible fashion. Maps are rhetorically powerful ways to dramatize research results (Tufte 1983).

I now consider in detail four examples that illustrate the diversity of map use in research on CMC. The first two examples visualize aspects of the geographic structure of CMC at the level of Internet infrastructure and traffic flows. The last two examples are maps of online activities aimed to help researchers and potentially also users to understand the social structures of CMC spaces.

Envisioning Internet Geographies

The seemingly magical ability to surf around a virtual globe of information, moving from web site to web site at a single click, belies the scale and sophistication of the socio-technical assemblage of protocols, hardware, capital and labour that makes this possible. Despite the virtualized rhetoric, this assemblage remains embedded in real places and maps can help to reveal the intersections between cyberspace and geographic space. In CMC research, I believe that geography is still important, as knowledge of the physical location of virtual phenomena can tell you interesting things (such as which territorial jurisdiction it is in) and can also enable linkage to a large array of existing secondary data (for example socio-economic characteristics from censuses).

The 'where' and 'how' of the physical embeddedness of data networks and information flows are also important because of their uneven geographical distribution and the consequent socio-spatial implications in terms of access and inequalities, as

Return Receipt
Liverpool John Moores University
Learning and Information Services

Borrower ID: 21111114211113

Return Date: 24/10/2008

Return Time: 1:03 pm

Virtual methods :
1111012251789

rtual ethnography /
111008698597

Please keep your receipt

in case of dispute

starkly revealed in Figure 8.2. This is a global scale mapping of network infra-structure that contrasts the density of core Internet routers with the distribution of population. The maps are density surfaces, where the land is colour-coded so that higher densities are darker (in the original the colours range from white through to red). The map was produced by physics researchers based at the University of Notre Dame who are exploring the principles behind the topological structures of complex networks like the Internet (Yook, Jeong and Barabási 2002: 13,383).

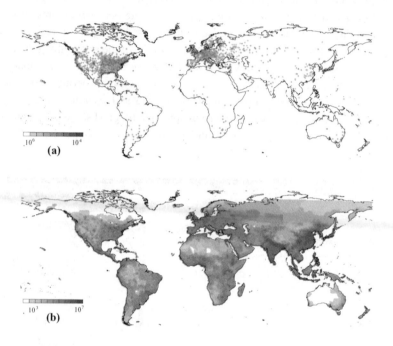

Figure 8.2 An example of how cartography can be used to visualise the uneven global distribution of the Internet: (top) map of the density of routers; (bottom) population density map. (Courtesy of Soon-Hyung Yook, Department of Physics, University of Notre Dame.) A colour version can be seen at http://www.cybergeography.org/atlas/geographic.html

In terms of the cartography cube, these maps are firmly in the 'present' usage category, being high in terms of public communication, high in terms of presenting known patterns and low in terms of interactivity. In design terms they are really quite conventional cartographic maps, using a geographic framework of conti-nental outlines to show univariate data. This type of world map is familiar to most people and can be easily produced using GIS software. It succinctly summarizes a large volume of data in an intuitive manner (imagine the same data presented as numeric values in a spreadsheet) and effectively demonstrates the potential of maps in virtual research for communicating complex patterns to a wide audience.

The maps in Figure 8.2 are non-interactive and the data present a static view of the Internet. Yet the Internet is obviously a dynamic environment, with continuously shifting patterns of usage. How can this be mapped? One way is to use software tools for measuring the Internet; these are called traceroutes and allow the active mapping of real-time data routing (Dodge 1999). Designed primarily for network engineers to 'debug' routing problems, they are also useful tools for researchers to probe the inner workings of the Internet. Traceroutes work by reporting the routes that data packets travel through the Internet to reach a given destination and the time taken to travel between each of the nodes along the route. They reveal the hidden complexity of data flows, showing how many nodes are involved (often more than twenty), the seamless crossing of oceans and national borders and the transfers through networks owned and operated by competing companies. They can also detail how geographically illogical some data routing is, following the cheapest paths rather than the shortest.

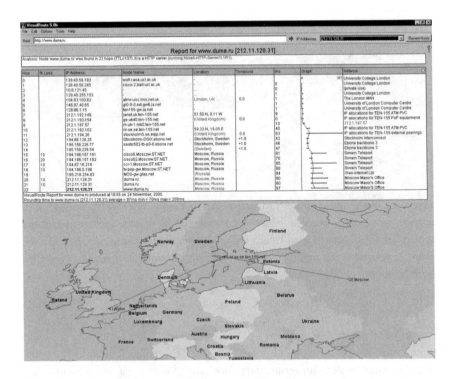

Figure 8.3 An example of geographic mapping of data pathways in real-time through the Internet using the VisualRoute traceroute utility (http://www.visualroute.com).

Figure 8.3 shows a screenshot of one particular traceroute program, called VisualRoute (http://www.visualroute.visualware.com), tracing the data pathway from my PC at University College London to the Russian Parliament web site in Moscow (http://www.duma.ru). Each line in the traceroute output represents a single 'hop' the data take across the Internet. The approximate locations (where known) of the routers are plotted on a simple map. Referring back to the cartography cube again, traceroutes are a good example of private, interactive mapping, aimed at revealing unknowns by actively 'exploring' routes through the Internet. Even though the map is crude in terms of cartographic design, traceroutes as a dynamic application show the potential for mapping as a research tool in exploratory analysis. Leaving the infrastructure level behind, mapping can expose the nature of online information archives and social interaction by exposing their latent structures in abstract, non-geographic visualization.

Mapping Social Cyberspaces

Understanding the formation of virtual groups and what is necessary for self-sustaining online communities has been a core element of social science research into CMC. A typical problem for researchers is how to gain a sense of the social nature of discussion spaces when conventional interfaces present only a hierarchical listing of text messages. There is growing body of work employing a wide variety of graphical techniques and visual metaphors to 'spatialize' online conversations (for example, Smith 1998; Donath, Karahalios and Viegas 1999; Fisher and Lueg 2003). Figure 8.4 shows a screenshot of PeopleGarden, a way of mapping social cyberspace that uses a quite novel visual metaphor (Xiong and Donath 1999).

PeopleGarden is an interactive map that spatializes web-based discussion boards in order to visually summarize overall patterns of social interaction over time. It was created by Rebecca Xiong as part of her graduate research at the Laboratory for Computer Science, MIT and deploys the visual metaphor of a flower to represent each participant, with petals being postings. Collections of flowers form a 'garden' to show the whole discussion space. Xiong says that she chose the flower metaphor because she liked 'the organic nature of a flower, and the suggestion that it changes over time, as users do' (Xiong and Donath 1999: 39). Thus the shapes of the flowers and the spatial structure of the whole 'garden' represent the nature of the online interaction and contrasting conversational styles of the participants. For example, if a PeopleGarden contained only a few small flowers, with sparse, faded petals, one could conclude that the discussion space is relatively lifeless.

The power of social mapping, such as PeopleGarden, is that it shows an overall structure not easily apparent from reading individual message postings. In a metaphoric sense these kinds of visualizations provide the missing 'up button' on the browser to allow people to get above the online conversations for a synoptic view of

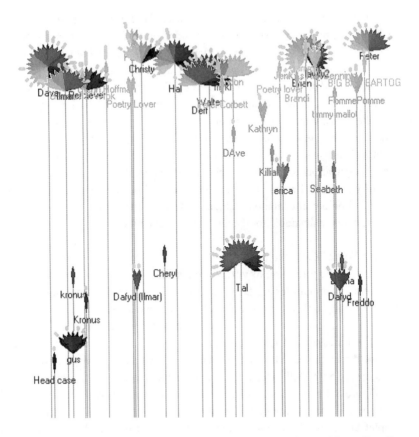

Figure 8.4 A screenshot of PeopleGarden, an interactive mapping tool for online discussion boards developed by Rebecca Xiong. A colour version can be seen at http://www.cybergeography.org/atlas/info_maps.html

the whole. On the cartography cube I would place the use of PeopleGarden and similar examples in the 'analyse' sphere as it provides a private map for researchers with a good degree of interactivity for use in revealing unknown data relations.

The final example I want to consider is an interactive tool for researchers to track and examine the activity patterns of users in three-dimensional virtual worlds, being developed by Katy Börner, Shashikant Penumarthy and colleagues at Indiana University (Börner and Penumarthy 2003). These spaces provide collaborative environments in which participants are represented as avatars and can interact with each other in real-time; they are used for games, community building, research and education primarily (see Damer 1998). They are one of the more interesting and novel CMC spaces for investigation by social scientists because of the navigable nature of their environments, the sense of presence engendered

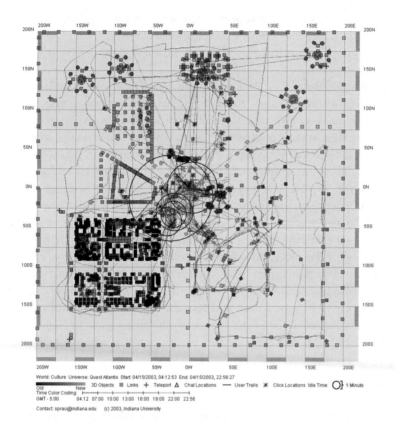

Figure 8.5 A map of all user activity in a three-dimension virtual world called Culture. (Courtesy of Shashikant Penumarthy and Katy Börner, Indiana University.) A colour version can be seen at http://www.cybergeography.org/atlas/muds_vw.html

through avatars and the scope for fostering virtual communities (Schroeder 2002; Snowdon, Churchill and Frécon 2003). The administrators of virtual worlds can log all interaction in the world by users (movement, actions, chatting), providing a potentially panoptic source of multidimensional social data.

While there have been a number of attempts to map out virtual worlds, these have mainly focused on 'physical' structures of the environments (Dodge and Kitchin 2001b; Bodum and Kjems 2002), whereas the work of Börner and Penumarthy is novel in its focus on the social and temporal dynamics of the worlds in relation to spatial environment. Figure 8.5 shows a screenshot of their tracking tool visualizing over nineteen hours of activity inside one particular virtual world called Culture (this an educational world, using the Active Worlds system). The map is dominated by the meandering paths of avatars (like pheromone trails), revealing where users went and when, and where they were talking. This degree of time-space tracking can be highly revealing when plotted on a map, but also potentially very invasive, particularly if the users are not made aware that this is occurring.

According to Börner and Penumarthy, the role of their social visualization is to serve three particular groups – end-users gain an overview map to ease navigation and raise awareness of what social activities are occurring, world designers acquire a guide for their work in constructing the environment and researchers can understand socio-temporal patterns, particularly in relation to group formation. According to the cartography cube, I would place the use of this tracking visualization in the 'explore' category for researchers and world designers as it is a private, interactive map revealing unknown patterns. If the tracking map was made available to participants in the virtual world then it would enter the 'synthesizing' category as it is more public and more about reinforcing existing knowledge.

Maps such as PeopleGarden and the virtual worlds tracker can give researchers useful new insights into particular social spaces. Another important question is how far these maps can be used by the participants of the spaces to augment or enhance their CMC experience? Will seeing a social mapping of the community help inform the social life of the community, helping it grow through additional feedback? Or might such maps actually be detrimental to community life?

Conclusion

Virtual research is still often about the exploration of online spaces, seeking to discover structures of information and patterns of social interaction. Maps are useful tools for any explorer (terrestrial or virtual), helping them to find their way and also explaining to others what they found. In essence, maps exploit the mind's ability to see complex relationships more readily in visual images, providing a clearer understanding of phenomena, reducing search time, and showing relationships that may otherwise not have been noticed. As a consequence, they form an integral part of how we understand and explain the world.

Although mapping is a potentially powerful research method for exploration, analysis, synthesis and presentation, it is not without its problems and I want to conclude this chapter by briefly outlining three types of limitations – practical, ethical and political. First, there are many practical issues to be faced and it is important to acknowledge the investment of time and effort necessary to make good maps. Map-making is now much easier to do, but it is not necessarily a quick fix. Like any chosen research technique, the potential of mapping has external practical constraints, including data quality and the level of user knowledge.

There are also issues to consider relating to the ethics and responsibility of researchers producing maps of CMC. The processes of data selection, generalization and classification and the numerous map design decisions mean that one can never remove the subjective element in map-making. As Monmonier (1993: 185) notes:

> any single map is but one of many cartographic views of a variable or a set of data. Because the statistical map is a rhetorical device as well as an analytical tool, ethics require that a single map not impose a deceptively erroneous or carelessly incomplete cartographic view of the data. Scholars must look carefully at their data, experiment with different representations, weigh both the requirements of the analysis and the likely perceptions of the reader, and consider presenting complementary views with multiple maps.

Further, these new forms of social mapping open up CMC to a new kind of surveillance, revealing interactions that were previously hidden in unused log files and databases. The act of mapping itself may constitute an invasion of privacy. If the appeal of some CMC spaces is their anonymity, then users may object to it being placed under wider scrutiny, even if individuals are unidentifiable. Here, public analysis may well represent an infringement of personal rights, especially if the individuals were not consulted beforehand. In some senses, these maps may work to shift the spaces they map from what their users consider semi-private spaces to public spaces, and thus the maps may actually change the nature of CMC itself. Thus, it is important to consider the ways, and the extent to which, maps of CMC are 'responsible artefacts', that do not destroy what they seek to represent or enhance.

Lastly, it should be recognized that mapping is also cultural process of creating, rather than merely revealing knowledge. All the sophisticated, interactive maps of network infrastructures and online social structures have politics just the same as any other form of cartographic text, and we must be alert to their ideological messages (Harpold 1999; Dodge and Kitchin 2000). Maps of CMC can prove to be very valuable, but at the same time they can never be value free.

New Connections, Familiar Settings: Issues in the Ethnographic Study of New Media Use at Home

Hugh Mackay

This chapter develops a rationale for researching the *context* of new media use and for examining the connections between online and offline interaction and activity. It then introduces my ethnographic project on the domestic consumption of mass media, to give a flavour of a research approach that seems useful for understanding uses of the Internet.

Internet ethnographers have generally studied online contexts: focusing on CMC, they have explored texts. One pragmatic reason for this might be because of the ease of recording data. As Hine states, the 'newsgroup as a record, an archive, is the ultimate field recorder' (Hine 2000: 22). While utterances are preserved, however, the experience of participating is not, and the social world that is explored is confined to the electronic data that has been recorded. This focus has provided us with a range of interesting accounts of virtual communication which have explored, inter alia the implications of virtual communication for identities and communities. Although commonly supplemented by online interviews, the corollary of this focus is that we learn relatively little about the *context* of Internet use – at work, home or elsewhere. The 'ultimate recorder' is a strength only in relation to the *text*. The *context* of use, though usually missed by online ethnographers, is something that can be explored by the in situ observation of users. My argument in this chapter is that doing so provides a more extended and richer account of Internet use, complementing the textual analysis and online interviews that characterize much Internet research.

Nor has the context of use been addressed by the range of critics of Internet communication (for example, Robins 1995) who assert the continuing salience of 'real-life' or local, physically bounded communities. In arguing against many of the claims that are made for virtual communities and the multiple and fluid identities that are facilitated by virtual communication, they argue that 'real-life' and physically based communities are richer and more complex and nuanced than virtual communities. The level of commitment, responsibility and intimacy involved in traditional communities is very different from a community which one can join with the click of a mouse. Such critical work, however, has tended to argue at a macro level, rather than being rooted in ethnographic or qualitative research on the context of use.

The ethnographic literature that locates Internet use in the cultural and spatial context of consumption is fairly limited. Notable is the work of Daniel Miller and Don Slater (2000) on the Internet in Trinidad, whose account is based on the notion that Internet use is best understood as a part of everyday, place-based, identity and activity. Their point of departure is that the Internet is neither some kind of place-less place, 'cyberspace', nor something *dis*connected from a particular place (Trinidad). They explicitly reject approaches to writing about the Internet as a space or place, somewhere *apart from* the rest of social life, a new social space that is characterized by a new set of social relations and practices (Slater 2002a). They found few instances of web site, email or chat being seen as a virtual experience, as opposed to a part of 'real' life. Those they observed failed to differentiate 'between, say, e-commerce and other commerce, playground chat and ICQ chat, religious instruction face-to-face or by email . . . in terms of any clear distinction between the "real" and the "virtual". Far more evident is the attempt to assimilate yet another medium in to various practices' (Miller and Slater 2000: 6).

Miller and Slater reject debates that distinguish between the real and the virtual, that compare the relative worth of each, that explore the implications of virtual communities for traditional communities, and that examine the Internet as utopia or dystopia. Instead, they emphasize how Trinidadians entered the networks of the Internet from a place and as Trinidadians. Indeed, expressions of national identity on the web are something that they found prevalent, in the form of personal home-pages that have assumed the role of national web pages. Detailing core national cultural characteristics (carnival, local recipes, Creole, etc.) these deploy national materials and symbols (flags, crests, maps, etc.) as they play an official-like role in promoting Trinidad.

Miller and Slater found a 'natural affinity' between Trinidadians and the Internet – with the Internet fitting, effortlessly, the music, shopping and leisure cultures, family and friendship patterns, and work and careers of Trinidadians – at home in Trinidad and extending across the Trinidadian diaspora. They found 'a series of "alignments" or "elective affinities" between Internet use and particular facets of what being Trinidadian was supposed to mean' (Miller and Slater 2000: 3). They found core Trinidadian values – national pride, cosmopolitanism, freedom and entrepreneurialism – prevalent in Trinidadians' use of the Internet. More specifi-cally, they identified how international nuclear families can enjoy routine, mundane and constant daily contact, and be involved in active parenting and mutual support despite their diasporic conditions. Trinis abroad can 'repair' aspects of Trini-ness, including 'liming' and 'ole talk'. 'Liming' is chatting, hanging around, exchanging banter, finding out what is happening: traditionally a practice of the street corner, it is now reproduced and practised on the Internet. 'The term "lime" is regarded as quintessentially Trini – both definitive of the place and definitive of its people' (Miller and Slater 2000: 89). Similarly one finds on the Internet 'ole talk' – endless talk about nothing in particular, stories, banter and ridicule invariably of a sexual nature.

Miller and Slater's work is important and distinctive because it focuses on the interconnections between, on the one hand, virtual communication, and on the other hand, local culture and everyday life. Perhaps counter-intuitively, they found that the global communications network of the Internet enhanced and strengthened local, indigenous culture, rather than functioning as a technology of homogenization. For the purposes of this chapter, the significant point is that their analysis contrasts clearly with that of virtual ethnographers, who have focused on online interaction and activity, and who give less attention to participants' offline lives and how Internet activity connects with these.

Somehow, decontextualizing use of the Internet exaggerates its significance for identities and everyday lives, and emphasizes the radical potentials and practices of Internet use. While not all Internet research extols the virtues of multiple and fluid identities, arguments or analyses that focus on extreme variants of Internet use are more likely to be generated by research that focuses on the electronic text. Much research on electronic communities has examined those who are heavier, rather than more ordinary or less committed, users. By contrast, focusing on Internet use in everyday life examines how Internet use connects and balances with other aspects of everyday life and identity. Examining the context of use, by definition, roots the research in everyday life, exploring how the potentials of the Internet are taken up and deployed in practice.

Using the Internet is a process of writing and reading texts and the task of the ethnographer is to understand these practices. Understanding the meaning of texts, however, is far from straightforward. It is difficult to isolate, in any simple sense, a single text for analysis, because of the interdiscursive nature of textual meaning (Bennett and Woollacott 1987). Every media text is mediated by other texts, so no text is bounded (Grossberg 1987). The text does not occupy a fixed position, but is always mobilized, placed or articulated with other texts in different ways. This raises the question of whether the text is dissolved into its readings. Barthes (1977), for example, argues that it becomes a text – as opposed to a 'work' – only when it is read. Rather than being fixed or stable, the text is continually re-created through the 'work' of reading. Indeed, it is argued that there is no text beyond the readings that are made of it – which leads Fiske (1989) to argue (about television viewing) that there is no such thing as either text or audience, only processes of viewing. Such a position points researchers in the direction of consumption activities – to examining the processes whereby meanings are generated through interaction with media texts.

The study of television audiences is a useful starting point for understanding Internet texts. There is a reasonably extensive and elaborated set of concepts that have been developed in television audience studies that offer rich possibilities for extending our understanding of Internet interaction. While this is not the place for a review of this literature (for that, see Morley 1992; Moores 1993), audience researchers have developed and applied analyses of domestic politics and power, particularly gender relations but also generational issues, for example about how conceptions of childhood and the role of parents inform practices to control children's television viewing. They have addressed, inter alia, household routines and temporal rhythms, and how these intersect with pleasures of consumption and styles of viewing and have explored the intersection of public and private in the domestic consumption of media texts.

It has commonly been argued that British cultural studies and audience studies (especially as developed in the journal *Screen*) have tended to focus on texts and readings – because researchers in the field have been drawn mainly from humanities, arts or literature backgrounds, and have been housed in such faculties (Murdock 1989). They have been criticized, consequently, for giving relatively little attention to production, and also to the context of use. The notable exception is the work of Stuart Hall (1980) on texts and reading, which was an intervention to counter the determinism of the 'effects' tradition of research on the impact of the mass media. In developing the notions of encoding and decoding, Hall addresses both text and context: his work has been highly influential in shaping subsequent research on television audiences.

Hall's argument is that texts are encoded by their producers and decoded, or read, by consumers: at both ends, symbolic 'work' is being done. All texts foreground some interpretations and marginalize others, in an attempt to establish a meaning. In any text, preferred readings (readings towards which the text directs its readers) are encoded. Decoding is a process of establishing a reading of a cultural artefact or phenomenon. Texts are not always decoded, or read, as intended: there are always possibilities for alternative, negotiated or oppositional readings. Decoding can differ from encoding for several reasons: first, because any text is to some extent polysemic, in other words, it can generate a number of possible meanings, although there always exists a 'preferred reading', and second, because of the possibilities of an aberrant decoding. Decoding is shaped by the reader's values, attitudes, tastes and ideological positions – the whole cultural framework that they have developed and use – so is not controlled and cannot be assumed, or in some cases even imagined, by the text's originators.

So Hall directs our attention away from the text, and in his later work criticizes the dominance of deconstructivism, and of power and politics being seen as exclusively matters of language (Stuart Hall 1992), in a way that connects with my critique of Internet studies in this chapter. David Morley, working with Hall at the University of Birmingham's Centre for Contemporary Cultural Studies, took up and applied Hall's ideas in his empirical research on *Nationwide*, a popular current affairs magazine programme. I shall describe Morley's work briefly, because the trajectory of his research embodies a set of concerns that together provide something of a framework for understanding Internet use. Morley identified the 'preferred readings' (Brunsdon and Morley 1978) that were encoded in the programme, and in a later study used focused interviews to explore audience responses to the programme. He categorized decodings in terms of 'dominant', 'negotiated' and 'oppositional' readings (Morley 1980). He connected these categories with the socio-economic class (managers, students, apprentices and trade unionists) of the twenty-nine viewing groups he convened.

From here Morley extended his concern with structures and divisions in society from class to gender. *Family Television* (Morley 1986) represents a further shift from text to context, with Morley addressing the meaning of domestic space for men and women. For Morley, practices of media consumption were to be read as signs of a cultural struggle between men and women in the domestic environment. For men, home is predominantly a site of leisure, whereas women are rarely 'off duty'. Morley found that men and women enjoyed very different forms of television viewing, with men more in control, and watching with fewer interruptions, while women routinely watched at the same time as undertaking housework, and took 'guilty pleasure' in their limited solo viewing. In this work Morley's concern is more with power relations in households, with his emphasis shifted from television to processes of interaction and patterns of leisure and labour in households.

Such a focus – on domestic politics and media use – was taken up and developed by Morley and others at Brunel University in the late 1980s and early 1990s in relation to ICTs, and home computers in particular. Their concern was with how ICTs were embedded in everyday culture, and how different families or household cultures mobilized the various technologies. To counter notions of technological determinism they explored the 'double life' of the technology, how it works in ways that conform to the intentions of its developers, but at the same time works behind their backs, in unanticipated ways. Examining how the technology was domesticated they analysed the consumption of technologies in terms of appropriation, objectification, incorporation and conversion. They explored gender relations and uses and control of household space, and the role of ICTs in articulating private and public spheres, and in disrupting domestic and national boundaries. Using the notion of the 'moral economy' of the household they examined how cultural resources and values are implicated in constructing the home.

The work of Miller and Slater, and Hall and Morley, provides a productive framework for identifying the Internet equivalent of television audience research, foregrounding situated sense-making by researching ethnographically the domestic *context* of use. In many ways, it is not easy to undertake research on media in households. Hine (2000) is somewhat discouraging, stating that 'since living within a household for an extended period is largely impractical, applications of ethnographic approaches to the media have involved some creative adaptations' (Hine 2000: 37). More positively, Morley (1992) argues that 'for the researcher to attempt to enter this "natural world" where communication is vague and meanings implicit, is inevitably to go skating on thin ice' (Morley 1992: 185). Like Morley, I would argue that research in households is more possible than Hine suggests, and that it should be attempted rather than dismissed. Access to the private sphere of household will always be a matter of degree – and one needs to take very serious account of observer impact – but ethnography in households is possible to some extent. Though relatively time-consuming and complex, it can usefully complement online ethnography.

There are many approaches to, and forms of, ethnography, but it is normally understood as involving participation 'in people's daily lives for an extended period of time, watching what happens, listening to what is said, asking questions; in fact collecting whatever data are available to throw light on the issues with which he or she is concerned' (Hammersley and Atkinson 1983: 2).

Usually ethnography is concerned with all aspects of social life, or all facets of a social setting. Broadly, the idea is for the researcher to be immersed in the setting, to generate an understanding of the context in which interaction is rooted. In its original social anthropological form (for example, Malinowski 1922) there was a notion that one could study holistically a physically and socially bounded community or society. Such a notion continued as the method came to be applied to Western society, notably in British community studies in the 1950s and 1960s. So a major strand of ethnography has been a concern with *holism* and, at the very least, it is hard to imagine ethnography without attention to *context.*

Now, of course, few would assert the possibility of physically or socially bounded communities or societies. The critique that was developed in the 1970s of the tradition of British community studies was a major contributor to this debate, which has been extended more recently in research on globalization. In other words, contested, shifting and unstable boundaries are a long-standing feature of communities, not something that arrived with the Internet. This has not prevented holistic forms of research: it has simply meant that researchers have been aware of, and some have focused precisely on, the fluid and dynamic boundaries of any community. The history of qualitative social research since the Chicago School in the 1930s is very much shaped by this agenda, with a commitment to identifying contextualized sense-making practices. The issue, in other words, is not that the Internet is a challenge to ethnography because it transgresses spatial boundaries, but that the boundary of any study will, to a degree, be defined arbitrarily.

My focus is the domestic arena, the home, a key site of personal relations, leisure activity and mediated interaction. Clearly this is a site with fluid boundaries. People come and go (on an hourly or daily basis, as well as over longer spans of the life cycle), and its boundaries are permeated also by the mass media which bring the public world into the private sphere of the household and – increasingly with the interactive capabilities of new media – facilitate our communication with outside, often far-flung, parts of the world.

In many ways the home is an arbitrary boundary for any research study. It has a certain pragmatic or utilitarian appeal, in that it is physically identifiable and locatable as a research site. To focus on leisure (for example) would be as valid an approach, examining domestic and public forms of leisure activity (as Morley 1992 argues). In the same vein, mass media consumption is not confined to the home, so a study could, quite usefully, include uses of radio in the car or television-viewing on big screens in pubs.

With this somewhat arbitrary and loose boundary, my study of uses of the mass media was of ten ordinary and diverse households in Wales (Mackay and Ivey 2004). It was concerned with the breadth of the mass media, including the Internet, and how these media were used in everyday life and how their use connected with daily rhythms and routines. Although limited in scope (ten households and twenty-six hours of fieldwork in each) and with a broad remit (the full breadth of the mass media), it provides an example of how Internet use might be researched. Ten households were selected to span a diversity of types and between them were users of a considerable diversity of mass media. They included childless adults, single parents, families with children and 'empty nesters'. Their adult members had a variety of working patterns (unemployed, working part-time, two working adults, one working adult and so on) and occupations, spanning a breadth of socio-economic positions. They used a variety of mass media: some had Internet access, some were avid game-players, some had digital television, and between them they read the breadth of the national press.

It was decided that a form of pragmatic sampling was the best strategy, contacting 'friends of friends' of the researcher. In other words, I asked friends to find suitable people, who I myself had not met, with the intermediary offering some vouchsafe for each party. This allowed some reassurance, or personal recommendation, but involved greater distance between the researcher and the research subjects than would be the case if they already knew one another.

At the outset our research subjects were contacted with a telephone call in which the aims of the project were discussed. The main purpose of this telephone call was to arrange an initial meeting at which their involvement could be explored further. Initial responses were varied, ranging from suspicion, through compliance, to enthusiasm and pleasure at having an opportunity to be associated with such a research project.

The next part of the strategy was to develop a relationship with each household's members. How this was done varied between households, but in all cases an initial visit was followed by a request for completion of a diary, recording one week's use of the full breadth of the mass media (newspapers, magazines, radio, television, computer games, the Internet) by each member of the household. The diaries were useful not only as a mapping of media use in the household, but also as a rationale for a subsequent visit that took place to collect and discuss the diary.

At all stages, and to progress from visitor to participant observer, the research relationship was crucial, with success dependent on being accepted. In one household the family pet seemed to perform the role of critical gatekeeper: the whole family stopped and waited while the dog checked out the researcher. His acceptance was received with relief, and a cup of tea followed. In other households, being accepted by the children seemed crucial: one parent was quite explicit that this was necessary. Developing common ground, on the basis of mutual interests or activities, was an important way of generating acceptability and relationships. From one household our researcher borrowed a martial arts video, with another he watched a cycle race at the weekend, and with a third he found himself cleaning out the gutters. Access varied between households, but in three of the ten households the researcher was invited to stay the night. To varying degrees, more relaxed contact developed and richer data were gathered as the research progressed. This progress was dependent on being seen as acceptable, generating trust, and on the researcher's presence becoming seen as more natural and less of an intrusion.

Semi-structured interviews – with open-ended, non-directive questioning – were undertaken with all household members on several occasions. This allowed us to explore topics in which we were interested and matters we had observed. It allowed some element of triangulation, checking the validity of what had been said or done. It was also a way of exploring the significance of media use through discussion, particularly in more elusive areas, and especially those relating to understanding the inherently private nature of much media use. At the heart of the research, however, was extended fieldwork: an average of twenty-six hours per household, in each of the ten households. This involved observing and participating in a breadth of household activities, including media use. Towards the end, some unarranged visits were made, demonstrating the high level of access that had become available.

We do not see our work as naturalism in any sense – as presenting some account of the world as it is – since what we observed and heard has been interpreted and represented (Geertz 1988). In a similar vein, we would acknowledge the impact of the observer on the setting, an effect we sought to minimize and to make due allowance for. Our fieldworker's age and gender, obviously, were highly significant to the conduct of the research. One outcome is that we gathered more extensive data on some households than others.

A frequent concern was the impact of the researcher on the setting: some research subjects in particular seemed to almost feel obliged to engage in some form of media consumption for the benefit of the researcher. Others ceased using media to talk with us. It was sometimes hard to judge what was normal behaviour, as routines are interrupted by more spontaneous actions. A major rationale for participant observation, not just semi-structured interviews, is that – to some extent – it allows the researcher to get beyond respondents' own account or rationalization of their activities and preferences. Our in situ observation over a reasonably extended period of time was intended to facilitate a more valid and reliable account. Finally, we undertook a little respondent validation, sending out what we had written about them and returning to the field to discuss this with our informants. This was one important way of checking the validity of what we had written.

Our study is unusual for its focus on the full breadth of the mass media. Having said that, 'the mass media' is not an easy category to define, and we did not include the telephone, which as a technology of mediated interaction makes it an interesting case to study. Our breadth of focus forced us to make some interesting comparisons between uses of the various media. Clearly some mass media are more open to observation or ethnography than others. For example, newspaper reading is an individual, private and relatively 'closed' activity. From observation alone it is hard to get much idea of an article's meaning or significance to its reader. Broadcasting, by contrast, is more 'public', and in some cases is accompanied by verbal interjections or comments from listeners or viewers. The Internet is nearer to the press in this respect, being a relatively 'private' activity. However, while this constrains the possibilities for research, its nature in this respect is nothing new for a mass medium.

Turning to the practicalities of our research of Internet use, we started with semi-structured interviews. Such discussions took place at intervals as the research progressed, and we undertook some observation of our research subjects using the Internet. At the beginning this was more of a demonstration of the sort of activity they engage in. We ran through their 'bookmarks' or 'history', to see what web sites they had been visiting, and they provided a commentary or explanation of what they had been doing. Clearly there is a considerable 'observer effect' in such activity, but some observation and recording of their Internet activity were undertaken. Given that our informants were relatively functional and limited users of the Internet, what we observed was fairly restricted in terms of the possibilities of Internet use, and our research remained fairly much on 'one side' of the screen. It would be interesting to complement such in situ fieldwork with online research of mediated communication and communities.

This is not the context to present our findings in any detail, but our report of our findings begins with a cameo of each of our ten households. This introduces the households' members' cultural tastes and uses of the mass media, rather like

Silverstone and Morley's (1990) 'ethnographic portraits'. We establish loosely some connections between cultural tastes and the lifestyle and social positioning of our households' members, touching on their consumption patterns to identify how they see themselves. Implicitly this draws on the work of Pierre Bourdieu (1984), who focuses on the socially constructed character of cultural preferences and tastes. Bourdieu's notion of the 'habitus' represents a framework through which people understand and respond to the social world: the habitus mediates between cultural practices and the objective position of a particular social group, and in our cameos we touch on the cultural capital and the processes of identification and differentiation that we found in our households.

In each cameo we detail the household's members, their occupations and ages, their physical location, the nature of their accommodation, its rooms, and how these are used. We say a little about the history and lifestyle of household members, their work, income, activities (together and separately), cultural tastes (and the ambience of their home) and how they see themselves (their identities). We describe briefly the breadth of media technologies in the household, where these are located, who they are used by, when, how and for what purpose. We refer to the temporal and spatial aspects of their use of the breadth of the mass media, identifying the various media forms that are implicated in household members' daily lives. Finally, exploring spaces of identification, we comment on our households' senses of Wales and Welsh identity, and report their views of the Welsh language and the Welsh mass media.

From the cameos, we proceed to describe our households' uses of each of the main mass media, and then analyse our findings in terms of temporal rhythms, domestic space, gender, spaces of identification and the Welsh language. Regarding Internet and computer use, perhaps unsurprisingly, we found a remarkable diversity of uses (and non-uses) in our households. Far from any one dominant or general use, we found that each household selected differently from the vast panoply of hardware and software that is available. Technological capability was also shaped by physical location, in that some households were able to subscribe to broadband or cable, or receive particular broadcasts, while others were not. Most of the uses that we found were of email and web sites, but thereafter there are few commonalities that could be identified.

Two overall findings are worth mentioning here. First, we found 'information searching', commonly to inform a consumption decision, to be a new form of domestic activity. Perfecting markets, this can be seen as empowering for consumers. It is certainly something that changes access to information, and transforms spaces of identification. Second, in every case of Internet use (four households) we found it a solitary activity and one located in a marginal room. Commonly it was in a spare room, and in no case did we find it in the living room. Of course this is rather more complex because, as the Internet becomes domesticated, social and spatial patternings in the home are transformed, with new activities and connections. However, it was remarkably unintegrated with 'public' domestic space, and clearly a 'lean forward' rather than 'lean back' activity: one requiring more focused, concentrated, active attention than the more relaxed nature of television viewing.

In the process of selecting from the available options, users adjusted and shaped their practices, and their understandings, perceptions and even identities. For example, the Internet was used as a means of sustaining family relations and identities, but at the same time, the technology provided access to new and wider resources and networks.

I shall just mention very briefly each of our ten households' Internet ownership and use. One household had a PC World set-up including a scanner, and used it to email their daughter in Canada and, occasionally, to make purchases online. In another it was used by the father and adult son to extend their working day in spatial and temporal terms, enabling them to work at home instead of being at work more: the son also used it for online purchasing of goods and services, for example a flight and hotel room in New York. In a third the Internet was used by both parents and their sixth-form son for work and occasional shopping. In the fourth it was used for web access and email, but not for games, even though they were big gamers. A further household had Internet access via their cable television but, despite the high-tech nature of the household (with a PlayStation 2 and multi-channel television, and using the EPG (electronic programme guide) to its full capability), they could not make it work so did not use it at all. Two households had computers unused in cupboards: one was a retired couple whose son had recommended its purchase, and it had been put away when a room was decorated, never to return; the other was a family with two young children, who had bought a package but found technical difficulties, so put it away and continued with their 'always-on' Sky. The final three households had no computer at all: they included the most affluent and the poorest households in our study.

Thus from even the most superficial account we can see a tremendous diversity of Internet use in our households. To understand the uses we encountered, we explored the intersection of Internet use with domestic life and cultural taste and with domestic rhythms and practices, and with other leisure activities.

To conclude, our research was based on diaries of media use, semi-structured interviews and participant observation in households. Clearly 'doing ethnography' means very different things in various contexts. Commonly, it is a very narrow definition of ethnography that has been used in studies of the mass media, hence it being referred to by one leading practitioner as 'an abused buzzword in our field' (Lull 1990: 242). Nonetheless, it is an increasingly popular research method, for both academic and industry research. Its strength is that it allows us to situate consumption practices, and to contextualize media use in everyday cultural life. For most participants, there can be little doubt that online activity is integrated with offline routines, practices and identities. People use the Internet for the same sorts of things as television: education, entertainment and information.

Clearly, using the Internet is very different from watching television: it allows for more participation, interactivity and even production. (Having said that, television is itself transforming in the direction of greater interactivity, more participation and more active audiences – with talk shows, docu-soaps and reality television, as well as interactive technologies, changing the nature of television.) With its many-to-many capability, the Internet challenges the producer–consumer relations that have characterized broadcasting. Internet texts are non-linear, so are qualitatively different from printed or broadcast media. Uses of the Internet are highly diverse, including chatrooms, bulletin boards, newsgroups, listservs, email and web sites. There is a huge choice and vast scale of data available. Crucially, the Internet facilitates new patterns of connection, new and global networks. While spatially dispersed networks and communities are nothing new, their scale and modus operandi – spatially and temporally – are transformed by the Internet.

Cultural life, however, is as yet only marginally shaped by the arrival of the Internet. Users of the Internet bring to their Internet use a set of dispositions and competencies that underlie and generate particular cultural practices. Locating Internet use in this context enables us to avoid rhetoric and analyses that refer to the Internet as something 'out there', something separate from everyday social life. Instead, and in a sense integrating notions of structure and agency, we can best understand the Internet by drawing on television audience research, developing and operationalizing techniques to study real-life, situated, domestic practices of Internet use. Such an approach can usefully complement online ethnography.

–10–

Doing Anthropology in Cyberspace: Fieldwork Boundaries and Social Environments

Mário J. L. Guimarães Jr

The quest for socio-anthropological methodological guidelines in cyberspace faces the very same problems as offline research: the massive diversity of human social experiences. In addition to that, the huge range of analytical themes and perspectives by which the online can be approached makes it virtually impossible to elaborate a methodology that could be employed widely in different online contexts. Nevertheless, it is always possible to compile some research tricks and empirical strategies that can be useful for the development of methodological approaches to deal with specific cases. At the end of the day, perhaps this chapter simply states something obvious for any ethnographer, that is, that the techniques to study any social group should be adapted to its own social and cultural context. The less obvious outcome of applying this basic principle to social groups that gather in cyberspace is to determine *what* exactly those contexts are about and how to draw their boundaries. In order to deal with these problems I put forward a way to circumscribe social groups in relation to the social and cultural bonds that tie them and not the spaces where they meet, whether physical places or cyberspace sites.

This chapter summarizes the methodological approaches and some of the theoretical framework employed in an ethnography of a sociability environment in cyberspace.[1] The environment studied is based on The Palace, a graphical platform where the user's presence is visually represented through avatars. These avatars can alter their appearance, exchange objects and emit sounds as well as wander inside a space whose architecture can be changed. The ethnography was done from an anthropology of performance perspective, seeking to capture the way in which the multimedia resources of Palace platform are appropriated and resignified by users through analysis of the interactions that take place inside it.

After describing briefly the Palace platform and its main features, I present two of the theoretical perspectives employed in my research. These are concerned with the approach adopted to consider the culture of the environment and with a critique of the concept of 'virtual community'. Subsequently, the outcome of this critique is presented: a theoretical and practical proposal to delimit fieldwork boundaries in cyberspace that takes into account the ways in which people construct and perceive their social environments. Some reflections about my process of getting access to these environments are then developed. The chapter finishes with a short reflection about the relationship between online and offline selves and its methodological implications, supported by the data from this ethnographic case.

The Fieldwork Site: The Palace

The research project was based on Brazilian contexts, and at the time the research project was undertaken (1998–9), The Palace was the prominent multimedia platform in Brazil.[2] The Palace was one of the first Internet-based multimedia sociability platforms to be widely used, being created in 1995 by Jim Bumgardner, who at the time was a programmer for Time Warner Interactive. Since then other companies have owned the program, and the last company (Communities.com) stopped supporting the platform in January 2001. Nevertheless, Palace users continue to keep the servers running and The Palace scene keeps going.

The Palace is a two-dimensional multimedia sociability platform that provides an environment for synchronic interactions between users, represented as customizable images or 'avatars' (Figure 10.1).[3] The Palace servers are organized in rooms consisting of a double-layered two-dimensional image over which the avatars can move. Each server can have several rooms, which can be programmed to be accessed through the room list (shown in a specific window) or by clicking in predefined areas of the rooms. It is thus possible to build a Palace server resembling a house or any other physical place, where clicking on the doors gives access to rooms, corridors, and so on. The rooms can also be locked or made invisible on the room list. These configurations can be done 'on the fly' by Gods and Wizards, which allows a very dynamic use of the space, with rooms being created or disappearing according to the flow of the interaction.[4]

Avatars can be configured or 'dressed' in many ways, either by employing ready-made props or by making them from scratch (Figure 10.2). Interactions are performed through textual utterances shown over the avatars as text balloons following the iconography of comic books, through pre-programmed sounds, through pre-programmed facial expressions and through avatar movement (Figure 10.3). One notable feature of The Palace is the use of 'props', two-dimensional images that behave as objects. They can be worn, handed between the users or left in the rooms, acting as furniture or decoration. They can also be animated, as a bird flapping its wings or a person sensually moving her or his hips. There is an intense market created around the trading of props between users.

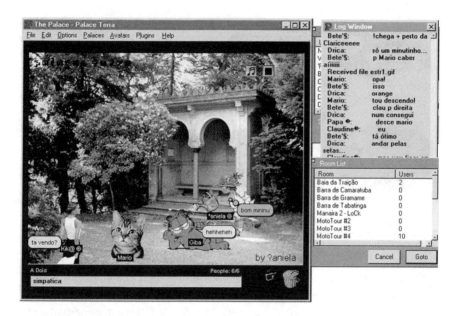

Figure 10.1 The Palace Platform.

Figure 10.2 Different avatars' clothing.

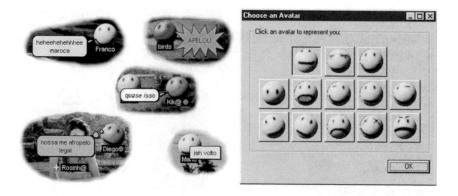

Figure 10.3 Different balloon types and the expressions of the default avatar.

The avatars' physical performance was one of the research targets, that is, how a bounded social group appropriates the platform resources and creates a set of social meanings through them. Effectively, it was found that body language was an important issue in the culture of the group. In a similar fashion to offline contexts, proxemics play a strong role in the interactions and are a way to recognize which group one is part of.[5]

Theoretical Framework

In order to apprehend the cultural meanings associated with the physical behaviour of avatars an anthropology of performance approach was employed. According to Bauman (1992b: 41) performance can be considered both as a mode of communicative behaviour and as a communication event. As a mode of communicative behaviour, performance allows understanding of the sociability practices of a culture through their manifestation in words, sounds, movements, dresses and so on, and in this way allows one to

> discover the patterns, functions, and meanings of those communicative resources in the conduct and interpretation of social life for the people among whom they are current, for whom they are available as equipment for living. (Bauman 1992a: xv)

The performance approach is related to a conception of culture as a process, a flux of facts embedded in a web of meanings that flow through time simultaneously supporting and creating social relations. Culture, therefore, is not homogeneous or fixed as the upshot of established traditions, but is continuously in motion and subject to change. This makes the study of the everyday performance of social practices an appropriate empirical element in the reading and interpretation of the local cultures established by the different groups that inhabit cyberspace.[6]

The term 'social groups' is intentionally used here instead of the more common expression 'communities', or in the case of cyberspace, 'virtual communities'. The everyday use (and to some extent *abuse*) of the word 'virtual' attributes a meaning to it that seems to refer to non-real entities, to experiences realized in a fantastic or imaginative sphere that lacks 'reality'. However, research has shown that in many cases users do not perceive their online experiences as 'not-real',[7] as Watson describes:

> My experience has been that people in the off-line world tend to see on-line commu-
> nities as virtual, but that participants in the on-line communities see them as quite real.
> (Watson 1997: 129)

The 'Living in the Palace' project came to similar conclusions. The informants demonstrated a range of perceptions about their online experience, from considering the Palace as a place to met new friends and develop acquaintances to seeing it as a pure fantasy world where they spent some of their spare time. Nevertheless, all of them were quite sure about the 'reality' of the feelings and personal relationships developed in cyberspace. Therefore, it is better to be cautious about using virtual-related concepts without taking into account the native perceptions of its meaning. The dichotomy online/offline instead of virtual/real seems more adequate to distinguish between these spheres of interaction.[8]

'Community' is also a concept which is widely used in different contexts and whose exact definition has become quite blurred. In social and cultural anthropology, for instance, every theoretical current employs the idea of community in a way that suits its own epistemological framework. Traditional anthropological approaches see community as an entity by itself, being determined by overall social structures. The community, therefore, is considered as self-contained, delimited by geographical limits, race, religion, language or any other identifiable issue. This approach helps to decide both the nature and the limits of the object of study, following the classical anthropological trend of studying small-scale groups.

Evolutionary flavours of thinking used to consider community as a primary stage of social gathering, ordered by traditional values. This stage would be fated to be overcome by society, a model of social grouping supposedly ordered by rational and contractual relationships. This way of thinking could be traced back to the origins of the nostalgic feelings regarding community. This nostalgia, that assumes many different ideological forms, associates with community the 'good' values of strong and close social bonds contrasting with the anonymity and loose-ness of social relationships in contemporary societies. It is not hard to foresee the multitude of different definitions of community that can arise from these two approaches. Hamman (1997), for instance, in the introduction to the *Cybersociology Magazine* thematic issue about virtual communities, quotes a paper that provides ninety-four different definitions for community.

Symbolic anthropologists, on the other hand, put themselves between those two extremes. For them community is not seen as a thing in itself, structuring social relationships. On the contrary, community is considered to be the outcome of social relationships that perform the idea and give a specific and contextualized meaning to it. This position is supported by Cohen (1985), stressing the relational nature of community. According to his position, a social group would call itself a community in order to assert its identity in relation to other social entities. This identity construction deals with the social construction of boundaries that characterise one's community. These processes occur on a symbolic level in the social life of communities, which are in this way continually performed and constructed. This approach shifts from a definition of community as a social-structural system to a conception of community as a set of shared meanings in the life of its participants that provides them with symbolic resources to build up their collective identity. The immediate outcome of the symbolic approach is that the quest for an exact definition of community loses its meaning. Every social and cultural context will be able to perform 'community' in its own and specific ways. The anthropological question hence switches from 'Are they a community?' to '*How* are they a community?' Naturally, there are some very basic and logically necessary conditions to the existence of any community, that is, which minimal conditions a group of people should fit in order to be able to perform a community. Hamman (1997) after being amazed by the amount of definitions for community compiled a set of these conditions:

> The sociological term community should be understood here as meaning (1) a group of people (2) who share social interaction (3) and some common ties between themselves and the other members of the group (4) and share an area for at least some of the time. (Hamman 1997)

Nevertheless, it seems that these conditions are enough only to determine a *group*. Whether a group performs a community or not is something to be investigated case by case, according to native impressions about being a community and regarding the nature of their boundaries. That is, 'community' is predominantly a matter of boundary construction through identity and shared systems of meaning. As Cohen points out: 'the reality of community lies in its members' perception of the vitality of its culture. People construct community symbolically, making it a resource and repository of meaning, and a referent of their identity' (Cohen 1985: 118).

Regarding virtual communities, the difficulties of a pinpointed definition are worsened by the questioning of the *possibility* of community in CMC environments.

In fact, there is a huge amount of writing dealing with the status of online communities. Much of this writing comprises a cultural critique of the possibility of community in cyberspace and another large proportion consists of responses to those criticisms.[9] The discussion is rather polarized between advocates of virtual communities (such as Rheingold 1993b) and their critics (such as Peck 1987). Discussion is usually framed in terms of whether the social gatherings mediated by CMC are 'real communities' or not, therefore employing as a premise the possibility of a consistent and universal definition of community. The immediate response to the critique of online communities would be to consider that there is not a static definition of 'community', but that the word is used as a *metaphor* whose meanings vary according to the context where it is applied and to the interests involved (Jones 1995; Watson 1997).

Jones (1995) reviews some of the key studies about communities and points out that many of them stressed geographical and spatial aspects in order to avoid the complexity of the overlapping groups in contemporary world. Jones also points to the ideological forces involved in the social construction of the 'community' category. The term is often employed rhetorically to refer to feelings of commonality and shared common interests. It is easy to perceive the pervasive and ideological use of 'communities' in many aspects of cyberculture. The idea of 'community' is quite often employed to refer to any group of users or potential customers. This will for 'community' can be tracked back to the origins of Internet. Many narratives about these 'good old times' are dominated by the image of an idyllic scenario of groups of people helping each other and therefore building the Net. E-business, nevertheless, is well aware of the profitable potential of user communities as can be seen in the many initiatives on the web using this concept.

To my surprise, after completing my fieldwork I realized that 'virtual communities' seems to be much more an emic than an etic concept for the group I investigated. Symptomatic evidence was that after searching the corpus of log files from the entire research, I found only ten occurrences of the word 'community'. From those ten, three were said by me and four by informants referring to my research. Despite this, the group where I did the ethnography was quite bounded and had a quite clear definition of its own identity and boundaries.

To avoid these problems associated with the notion of 'virtual community' I employed the expression 'online social groups'. This theoretical strategy allowed me to manoeuvre around the conceptual problems of 'virtual communities', and to keep the main feature of interest for an anthropologist: a group of people who share the same culture, belonging to the same 'web of meanings' (Geertz 1973). These online social groups are constituted by the social networks among members, which create a local culture. This culture provides a set of shared conceptions and representations about the social life developed by the group, as well as clues regarding the 'proper' behaviour that frames the way interactions develop. This cultural framework is accessible not only through the informant's discourse but also through many other everyday features such as physical behaviour, the form of interactions, how the acquaintances mature through time and many others. The group's identity is bounded by these cultural features, which at same time perform the boundaries of the social environments in cyberspace. These social environments can be either based on a single platform and server or spread through different servers and platforms.

Tracing the Fieldwork Boundaries

Tracing the boundaries of the chosen social groups remains a challenge for the ethnographer interested in the local cultures in cyberspace. Reviewing the literature, the amount of work which has studied online social relationships and which has employed the software platforms as the main – if not the only – criteria to determine the object is quite amazing (as in Reid 1991; Hamman 1996). This can be the natural approach if the question being researched relates to the specificity of the medium itself (as in McLaughlin, Osborne and Smith 1995). Nevertheless, when the focus is the culture developed inside bounded social groups, it is more appropriate to look at their actual behaviour and how they employ different resources in order to perform their social life.

The data gathered during the preliminary fieldwork revealed that it was possible to trace the group's boundaries through its network of social relationships and through the shared meanings that gave a sense of 'group' to its components. Nevertheless, it was very difficult to specify a single location in cyberspace where this group lived. The main platform employed was The Palace but the group used to travel around different Palace servers. Often instant messaging (specifically ICQ) was also used to counter temporary network 'lags' on the servers or to create another layer of interaction. Whenever Palace servers were down, web-based chat rooms or IRC were used. There was also an email list used to publicize events and web pages were maintained with news, pictures and links.

Social life in cyberspace has features similar to large urban centres, where the use of a particular urban space is not necessarily associated with being part of a specific social group.[10] In fact, the most popular Palace servers were frequented by very different groups, which managed to keep their specific boundaries despite sharing the same space. The eventual conflicts that arose from these contacts and consequent strategies employed to solve them provided valuable data about the group on which the ethnography was performed.

In order to conceptualize both the place of this group and its boundaries, I employed the idea of *social environment*, a symbolic space created in cyberspace through programs which allow communication between two or more users.[11] These environments are created and inhabited by social groups and can consist of different places (servers) and different software platforms. Environments keep their continuity due to the social and interpersonal networks that bind the members of the group. Online social environments are made up not only by 'places' (such as servers, rooms, URLs and so on) but also by time. The group that I followed used to meet in a specific time slot ranging from 7 p.m. till 2 a.m. The concept of social environment was indeed very helpful to trace the fieldwork borders and to understand the group's social identity.

Travelling to the Field

The immediate methodological outcome of this approach is the necessity to identify and gain access to the group's social networks. In the case of my research, since I chose The Palace as the multimedia platform to be studied, I spent some weeks hanging around at different times in Palace servers frequented by Brazilians. It was actually during this preliminary fieldwork, lasting about three months, that the idea of social environments came to my mind as I realized that sometimes in the same room there were very different activities going on, performed by different groups. During my long walks through the Brazilian Palace servers at this time I got the chance to know some people, was introduced to their acquaintances, collected contacts such as web pages, URLs, email lists and Palace servers addresses and was also able to master the technical features of the platform. All this material was very important to delineate the 'whole' of the Brazilian Palace scene, and to make the contacts that later would be my entry points to the chosen group.

Fortunately, in the first weeks of the fieldwork a big event in the Brazilian Palace scene happened. Some members of the group I researched organized the 'Palace Mototour', a motorbike ride through Brazilian Palace servers (Figure 10.4). An informant I contacted during the preliminary fieldwork was one of the coordinators of the event, and introduced me to other people as 'an anthropologist researching Palace', assuring them that I was 'a nice guy'. The event was a very important issue in the group's life for several weeks. While talking about the organization and the pleasures of motorbike riding and travelling (either online or offline), it was possible to introduce myself as an ethnographer and establish a rapport with some key members of the group as many of the organizers were Gods or Wizards.

This process of making myself visible, both as a member of the group and as a researcher, was very important in regards to one of the key ethical problems of online research: the possibility of hidden observation.[12] After the Mototour, practically all members of the group knew who I was, where I lived, and that I was there mainly to work as well as taking part in the group's activities. This 'work-related' aspect of my online identity was quite amusing to them. Many informants

Figure 10.4 Mototour, a motorbike tour across Palace servers.

were surprised to know that there was someone doing research in an environment they associated with their leisure time. This surprise was expressed in small jokes and gags about 'the hard life' of anthropologists and gave me the chance to make clear the purposes of my research.[13]

As the Mototour was a public event open to whoever owned a bike,[14] it was an excellent opportunity to meet people and to socialize within the group. Once I was accepted and made myself known within the group, it was possible to better figure out its boundaries regarding social networks, time and places. Thereby, it was possible to start making some sense of the group's culture, either through their behaviour, shared values or the overall interactions that took place during the Mototour. It was possible to figure out the important issues in the everyday life of the group, and how to develop rapport with the informants without making myself too intrusive.

Trying to write about how to develop rapport possibly plays against the ultimate meaning of the concept of 'rapport' as being something that lies in the subtleties and nuances of human contact. Nevertheless, on broad lines it could be said that the teachings of social anthropology and ethnography handbooks are valid for online contexts as well as offline ones. That is, the same skills of knowing how to listen to an informant, learning the proper way to behave and so on are as valuable online as offline. The main prerequisite for entrance to the group remained being attentive to the small details of everyday life and how they 'talk' about the broader culture of the environment. Reciprocity is also present in online social environments, and plays an important role. That is, the people gather there to *be* together, to share a common space where they can talk about their issues, and to listen to other members of the group. The symbolic exchange of attention and concern plays a very important role in the fabric of daily life, and must not be ignored. This kind of development is mainly detectable through an ethnographic approach where the researcher can afford to spend enough time to develop acquaintance and confidence with informants (although see also Kivits and Orgad, Chapters 3 and 4 in this volume, for discussion of the need for attention and concern in interview relationships).

Another form of reciprocity relates to objects and knowledge. One of the group's collective activities was building and decorating Palace servers or rooms. Despite the full resources to configure a room being available only to Gods and Wizards, the entire group participated in the creation of their space. There was trade in objects, pictures and sounds as well as the knowledge necessary to create and configure them. As it is relatively complex to build an avatar from scratch, there was an intense trade in 'tailored' avatars, as well as the knowledge of how to make them. The everyday small problems with computers and their solutions were also a topic of talk and mutual help among the members of the group.

Regarding fieldwork techniques, the way to apprehend the subtleties of bodily behaviour is by observing, learning through one's own experiences and sometimes making embarrassing mistakes. As this learning stage happens with every newcomer, experienced users already had some confidence in teaching the basics of everyday proxemics. There are many social resources available such as jokes and funny tales of past users that make the process easier. As a newcomer, I made many common mistakes, and my own process of learning was an excellent opportunity to grasp an insight into the role of the avatars and their physical performance.

During my first experiences in the field I found it hard to follow the many interactions going on in the environment and at same time keep the awareness of the 'whole' scene and make notes in the diary. This kind of experience is also common in offline ethnography, but the online contexts provide another level of difficulty: the possibility of simultaneously taking part in many conversations. These simultaneous interactions can take place: in public, addressing the different interlocutors by name or by the avatar's physical cues; in private, through utterances addressed for one specific person that can be 'heard' only by her or him; or even through the simultaneous use of different platforms such as ICQ or other chat applications such as IRC or web chat. This requires the researcher – as well as the users – to employ a peculiar range of cognitive skills to keep every interaction in its own track and give attention to all of them. Suler (1997) refers to the psychological mechanism of 'dissociation' as responsible for controlling attention to different things at the same time, which 'takes a great deal of online experience, mental concentration, and keyboarding skill (eye/hand co-ordination) to pull it off'. The learning of these skills was part of the socialization process to gain access to the group.[15]

Another peculiarity of online social life is the pace that seems to be rather 'speeded-up' if compared with the rhythm of offline life. Relationships that could take weeks or months to mature offline can reach great levels of intimacy in a few days online. This can bring some questions to the anthropological fieldwork myth of 'complete cycle of the informant's life'. It is usually assumed that one year of fieldwork is the minimum time span required to get a proper ethnographic grasp of the topic under research. As things do not necessarily happen in yearly cycles in cyberspace (in the same way as in many contemporary complex societies), it is up to the ethnographer's sensibility to perceive when to stop the fieldwork. A possible suggestion for an online group 'cycle' could be its demographic renewal. It seems that due to this 'speeding-up' of the social temporality in cyberspace some online groups have a very flexible dynamic of membership, with new people continuously arriving and old members ceasing to take part. This was the case with the group studied in the 'Living in the Palace' project, as well as some other online experiences I have came across, such as the fieldwork for my current project. This peculiar way of perceiving time still requires more detailed study, hopefully with the help of comparative approaches.

But Who *are* the Informants?

The pursuit of the 'online self' and its relationships with the multiple selves from which the individuals in contemporary complex societies are made has generated a considerable literature in the cyberculture field (the canonical example of which is Turkle 1996). Regarding research methodology, the outcome of this inquiry is the questioning of *who* the informants of an online ethnography are. Following my suggestion of pursuing the networks and experiences of users in their own context, the answer for this question is, again, related to each specific case. In cases like the project referred to in this chapter, which aimed to understand the local cultures that develop in cyberspace, the notion of social actor shifts from the user seated in front of a computer to the persona this individual incarnates within the environment.[16] According to Paccagnella (1997), 'In a perspective of ethnographic research on virtual communities the online world has its own dignity, as it is where the social groups gather and construct their local cultures.

The interactionist approach of Goffman (1959) is useful as an empirical tool to understand the performative aspect of the multiple belonging of individuals in contemporary societies. According to Goffman, in every context of social life actors play different roles consistent with the respective contexts that are dynamically negotiated with other actors. The social sciences are not necessarily concerned with persons as individuals, but as subjects of situated social relationships. Therefore, according to the topic under investigation and the empirical approach adopted, the informants of an online ethnography can be the personas that create the social environments in cyberspace. It is not always possible to equate one's online and offline personas in so far as the same individual can participate in many overlapping social groups playing different roles in each. The aim to find the 'truth' behind the social masks, therefore, must be abandoned because the intrinsic richness of the sociability created at the level of these masks could be lost in this quest. Either to create a character far away from one's own 'reality' or to be 'sincere' the individual must behave according to the environment's meaning framework, revealing in this way the culture of the group.[17]

In the Living in the Palace project, the informants were predominantly considered to be the online personas. Naturally, the individuals behind the keyboards were not ignored, but the empirical and analytical focus was the interactions and performances in cyberspace in so far as the informants themselves did not meet each other in contexts other than online.[18] The social life in cyberspace was considered by the members of the group as one aspect of their lives. In the same way as other domains of everyday sociability such as workplace, leisure activities or religion, cyberspace plays a role in their life which varies in intensity and importance according to the specificity of each individual case. Some informants consider the Palace as a leisure option and a place to meet interesting people. For Brazilians living abroad, life in the Palace is a chance to chat in Brazilian-Portuguese and to be in touch with the country. For some informants cyberspace can be their main place of social contact if access to other places is difficult for any reason. Some see cyberspace life as an interesting novelty that can lose appeal after some months while others frequent it daily, for long periods sometimes making it a workplace. Teenagers, elders, mothers, insomniacs, web-designers, cyber-anthropologists, children using the computer sneakily late at night, all of them met to create a culture through friendship, flirtation, information exchange, conflicts and all other features through which social life is created. Nevertheless, the informants of this research were not these persons, but the personas lived by them in the context of their online experiences. In other words, the research aimed to describe ethnographically the culture of a group constituted *in* cyberspace therefore taking account of the informant's online selves.

As a normal outcome of ethnographic work, even the researcher self was affected during the fieldwork. Despite the fact that I did not have to travel to an island far away in the Pacific Ocean to reach my 'tribe',[19] during the five months of the fieldwork I found myself quite distant from my own social networks. During this time, I lived in a time slot that isolated me from my acquaintances which, in addition to the everyday tasks of the research, contributed to increase the feeling of 'immersion' in the field.[20] Despite my efforts to develop an online persona as transparent as possible, there were some aspects of my offline self which were discordant with my online life. The most remarkable one was regarding my strong regional accent, which can be spotted even in text-talk. I came from Rio Grande do Sul, the southernmost state of Brazil, a region that has not only a very specific and strong accent but also some structural differences in the language that can be spotted in text-talk. As many of my informants were from other regions, I chose to talk in a way that did not make my regional identity very explicit or stereotypical in order to construct an identity as 'neutral' as possible in terms of regional origin. Another very important trace of my online identity was my personal web page at the time (http://www.cfh.ufsc.br/~guima). It was an essential element to legitimize my identity as a researcher and to create acquaintance with people who had similar interests. While developing the page, I tried to create both a 'serious' web page, putting academic material such as papers, the research proposal and my CV, as well as personal and relatively intimate stuff including a brief description of myself and my hobbies of photography and backpacking.

This persona, therefore, constructed himself through the interaction and the time spent with the group, sharing with them their local culture and social life. Despite being explicitly a researcher since my first contacts, during the fieldwork I found myself very involved in the daily life of the group in such a way that I was able to realize (and feel) that their life online, despite being developed in a 'virtual' environment, has many if not all the elements of human experience in society.

Conclusion

A qualitative, dense ethnographic approach can be made suitable for the enterprise of understanding social life in cyberspace in so far as the peculiarities of both social contexts and media are taken into account. This chapter aimed to suggest some possible approaches to this task through the solutions employed in a long-term ethnography of an online social group. I hope that these suggestions will be helpful to the development of other in depth qualitative studies of online social phenomena which will shed more light into how cyberspace is being inhabited and transformed by social life.

Notes

1. The research was conducted from 1998 to 2000 during my master's degree in Social Anthropology at PPGAS/UFSC, Florianópolis, Brazil. Its outcomes are in my MA dissertation 'Living at the Palace: The Ethnography of a Social Environment in Cyberspace' (Guimarães 2000a) as well as in some papers (Guimarães 1999, 2000b). The project was funded by CNPq.
2. 'Multimedia sociability platform' is used here to refer to software for communication in cyberspace that employs not only text-based resources but also audio, video, graphics and avatars. The distinction between environments and platforms is discussed later.
3. On the user side, The Palace requires the download of a client program that connects to the servers. At the time of the fieldwork a plug-in for web browsers was being developed, although this did not get much attention from the users and never achieved widespread use.
4. The software recognizes four categories of users: *Guests*, who can only chat but cannot change the appearance of their avatars or even choose their nicknames, *Members*, who can change their avatars, *Gods*, the server's managers, who can configure the rooms as well as moderate the interaction in the environment through disciplinary measures and *Wizards* whose role is to control the behaviour in the servers and have almost as many powers as the Gods.
5. It was found that users not only employ the resources provided by the platforms in order to collectively elaborate their culture but also transform and resignify those resources in ways often unforeseen by the applications' developers. These boundary negotiation processes between users and developers and the implications for online embodiment and personhood are the subject of the project 'Avatars: Technologies of Embodiment in Cyberspace' (Guimarães 2002, 2003).
6. The *Journal of Computer Mediated Communication* (http://www.ascusc.org/jcmc/index.html, accessed 16 February 2004), for instance, has a specific issue about online performance (vol. 2, issue 4 1997). See also Danet (2001) for a very comprehensive analysis of performative use of text in online communication.
7. Despite the fact that a philosophically informed discussion about the 'reality' of online experience is fascinating, it by far exceeds the limits of this chapter.
8. This move is also made by other scholars such as Jones (1995), Watson (1997), Wellman and Gulia (1999), among others.
9. In this chapter it is not possible to review this discussion in detail.
10. The theoretical development of this argument follows the references of Brazilian Urban Anthropology, which has a relatively long tradition of anthropological reflection in complex societies. Unfortunately, it is not possible to develop this discussion here.

11. The concept of social environment is further developed in Guimarães (1999).

12. Considering the characteristics of the group it would be very hard to perform any kind of hidden observation without deliberately masking my identity as a researcher, hence raising even more sensitive ethical issues.

13. This kind of empathy between subject and researchers in online contexts was also noted by other researchers such as Bernardo (1994) and Carneiro da Silva (2000). See also Rutter and Smith (Chapter 6 in this volume), for a different treatment of these issues.

14. The organizers spent many busy nights building motorbike-related avatars that were given for free to the participants. They also created a register system to avoid two persons getting the same bike.

15. On a very 'hands-on' note, I used to keep all the relevant applications running, switching back and forth between them using the Windows shortcut ALT+TAB. Both the database where I kept informants' details and the word processor with the diary had macros for the main tasks configured in short-cuts to minimize the time to access them. The screenshots taken and the log files were valuable as a way to recover the details eventually missed when the environment was too busy. For more details on these practical aspects of online ethnography check the document 'Doing Online Ethnography' at http://www.soc.surrey.ac.uk/virtualmethods/doingonlineethnography.pdf (accessed 4 November 2004).

16. MacKinnon (1995) uses the term 'persona' to refer to the identities built up inside cyberspace, that are negotiated and validated through the interaction processes.

17. Again, the discussion about reality here is taken for granted and roughly over-simplified. This discussion is developed further in Guimaraes (2000a, 2000b).

18. Adding to this theoretical perspective some logistical issues helped to support this approach. The members of the group were scattered through many different places in Brazil, and some were living abroad. The informant who lived closest to me was 705 km (438 miles) away.

19. In fact, I was already living on an island in the Atlantic Ocean: Florianópolis, Brazil.

20. The activity in the group was mainly in the evening and late at night. Usually the field sessions were done from 7 p.m. till 3 a.m.

–11–

Web Sphere Analysis: An Approach to Studying Online Action

Steven M. Schneider and Kirsten A. Foot

Online action – what people do (or do not do) – alone and together on the World Wide Web and via other Internet applications, is drawing the attention of a wide range of social researchers. The World Wide Web (hereafter referred to as 'the web') can be viewed as an evolving set of structures supporting online action, which manifests and enables the production, inscriptions and experience of cyber-culture – with a myriad of social, political and cultural dimensions. The hyper-linked, co-produced and evolving characteristics of the web necessitate reconsideration of traditional research methods, and the development of new ones. Each of these characteristics poses particular challenges for researchers. For instance, the hyperlinked and multilevel nature of the web makes the identification and demarcation of units of analysis a critical but difficult task. Seemingly straightforward questions, such as what constitutes a web site, and from what or whose perspective (that is, robot, browser or human) that question will be framed, require careful consideration. The co-produced nature of the web, evidenced in the joint production by multiple actors of many features and much content, makes problematic the attribution of authorship to producers of specific bits. The often rapid and unpredictable evolution of the web is one of the greatest challenges scholars face as they seek to develop methodological approaches permitting robust examination of web phenomena over time

Scholars from a variety of disciplines are interested in analyzing patterns within and across web materials – some in order to document and make sense of web-based phenomena, others to understand relationships between these patterns and factors exogenous to the web. We suggest online action can be explored, and at least partially explained, through an examination of web objects. These objects, including texts, features, links and sites, can be viewed both as inscriptions of web producers' practices and as potentiating structures for online action on the part of web users. In this approach, web objects and the technologies used to create them are considered as tools that are employed in and that mediate these practices as well as artefacts resulting from them.

In this chapter we describe an approach to research on online action that we call web sphere analysis. This approach centres on the concept of a web sphere as a unit of analysis, and provides an integrative framework for structural, rhetorical, and sociocultural methods of analysis. We propose three dimensions of web spheres -anticipatability, predictability and stability – and explain the implications of various web sphere characteristics for the study of online action within and across them. Finally, we assess the affordances and challenges of web archiving for the purpose of web sphere analysis. We highlight the interrelated set of choices facing researchers as they consider the dimensions of web spheres, select possible methods of analysis for analyzing online action within them, and evaluate techniques employed in identifying and archiving these web spheres.

Web Sphere Analysis

Web sphere analysis is a framework for web studies that enables analysis of communicative actions and relations between web producers and users developmentally over time (Foot and Schneider 2002; Foot et al. 2003b). We conceptualize a web sphere as not simply a collection of web sites, but as a set of dynamically defined digital resources spanning multiple web sites deemed relevant or related to a central event, concept or theme, and often connected by hyperlinks. The boundaries of a web sphere are delimited by a shared topical orientation and a temporal framework. A significant element in our conceptualization of web sphere is the dynamic nature of the sites to be included. This dynamism comes from two sources. First, the researchers involved in identifying the boundaries of the sphere are likely to continuously find new sites to be included within it. Second, the definition of a web sphere is recursive, in that pages that are referenced by other included sites, as well as pages that reference included sites, may be considered as part of the sphere under evaluation. Thus, as a web sphere is analysed over time its boundaries may be dynamically shaped by both researchers' identification strategies and changes in the sites themselves.

December's (1996) typology of units of analysis for Internet-related research is useful as a framework for understanding the nature of a web sphere as a unit of analysis. The five types of units of analysis December identifies are: (1) media space, consisting of the set of all servers of a particular type that may provide information in one or more protocols, the corresponding clients that are capable of accessing these servers, and the associated content available for access on these servers; (2) media class, a particular set of content, servers and clients; (3) media object, a specific unit in a media class with which the user can observe and interact; (4) media instance, a media object at a particular time; and (5) media experience, a particular user's perception of a set of media instances. In correspondence with December's definitions of each kind of unit of analysis, a web sphere could be considered a subset of an Internet media space, constituted by a single media class (web sites), which are comprised of elements or objects such as links, features and texts that are combined in larger media objects of web pages and web sites. What distinguishes our concept of a web sphere from December's definition of a web space is the addition of a shared thematic or event orientation and a temporal framework that is associated with 'the set of all Hypertext Transfer Protocol (HTTP) servers, web clients, and content on HTTP servers' that December (1996) identifies.

The web sphere can function as a macro, aggregate unit of analysis, by which historical and/or inter-sphere comparisons can be made. For example, the web sphere of the 2000 elections in the United States can be comparatively analysed with the electoral web sphere of 2002 and those that develop in later years. Similarly, this web sphere could be contrasted with electoral web spheres in other countries. Other, more micro and/or molar units such as a text, feature, link, site – or the multi-site web presence of an actor – can be employed in analyses simultaneously within a web sphere (for example, Schneider and Foot 2002, 2003). Defining any of these units operationally can be challenging, particularly when the temporal and malleable aspects of web objects are considered. For example, since any web text or feature can appear stable but actually be modified by its producer and/or rendered differently by technologies such as web browsers employed by users at particular moments, the point in time and the way in which a web object is observed must be part of the unit's definition for research purposes. Units such as an actor's web presence must also reflect the potential for change over time, by being situated in a particular temporal period. For instance, the web presence of a political party might be appropriately specified by the particular week or month of an election cycle.

Web sphere analysis provides a framework for investigating relations between producers and users of web materials as potentiated and mediated by the structural and feature elements of web sites, hypertexts and the links between them. In its fullest form, the multi-method approach of web sphere analysis consists of the following elements. Web materials related to the object or theme of the sphere are identified, captured in their hyperlinked context, and archived with some periodicity for contemporaneous and retrospective analyses. The identified constituent elements are annotated with human and/or computer-generated 'notes' and/or codes of various kinds, which creates a set of metadata. These metadata correspond to the unit(s) and level(s) of analysis anticipated by the researcher(s). Sorting and retrieval of the integrated metadata and URL files is accomplished through several computer-assisted techniques. Interviews, focus groups, experiments and/or surveys are conducted with producers and users of the web sites in the identified sphere, to be triangulated with web media data in the interpretation of the sphere.

Characterizing Web Spheres

Having defined the concept of a web sphere, and given a brief overview of web sphere analysis, we now turn to an explanation and illustration of web sphere dimensions, and an exploration of the challenges associated with discovering or establishing a web sphere and analyzing online action in the context of a web sphere. As Jones (1999) and Hine (2000) argue, Internet phenomena are in some ways extant for researchers to discover and in other ways constituted by the activity of any user, including a researcher. Thus, the first step in web sphere analysis – demarcating boundaries and identifying elements – is both a process of discovery and a process of creation. We identify three dimensions of web spheres that have bearing on how researchers demarcate a web sphere: thematic antici-patability, actor predictability and the stability of constituent web materials. The position of a web sphere of interest on these three dimensions, each of which we view as a continuum, may help researchers develop strategies for identification of elements to be included in the analysis. We should caution that these three dimen-sions are neither exhaustive nor mutually exclusive; they represent a starting point for the characterization of this new unit of analysis.

The first dimension measures the degree to which it is possible to *anticipate the emergence* of a web sphere. Part of the anticipatability of a web sphere is dependent on the extent to which it is defined by a specific event; some events, like elections and the Olympics, are highly anticipated, while others, such as accidents, tragedies and scientific discoveries, are less likely to be anticipated. Triggering events (Gamson and Modigliani 1989), which in general are unanticipated, may also provide the stimulus for a thematic web sphere. For example, a web sphere focused on cloning may have emerged in response to the announcement of Dolly, the first cloned mammal, suggesting that web spheres may emerge in response to specific events rather than be focused on specific events. In the absence of gener-alized and systematic web archiving (Kahle 1997; Schneider et al. 2003), antici-patability is often a crucial factor in whether a web sphere is researched. Web spheres emerging quickly after an unanticipated event may be more difficult to study, as a rapid investment of resources (for example, time, money, topical expertise) may be required. At the same time, a research design can be explicitly tailored to account for analysis of a web sphere 'in progress'.

A second dimension of web spheres is concerned with the ability of researchers to *predict the types of actors* who will produce materials encompassed within a web sphere in advance of its emergence. Some web spheres will be produced by a highly predictable set of actor types. Web spheres organized around electoral cam-paigns, for example, may (depending on the localized political context) include sites produced by parties, candidates, press organizations, advocacy groups, citi-zens and government agencies. Web spheres emerging around unanticipated natural disasters and accidents are likely to include sites produced by a predictable set of actors: government agencies, relief and charity organizations, press organizations, and citizens, for example. Other web spheres will be produced by a less predictable set of actor types. Following the terrorist attacks on New York and Washington of 11 September 2001, we observed significant and unpredicted activity on web sites produced by corporations and businesses, along with more predictable activity on sites produced by religious organizations, educational institutions and government agencies. Actor predictability can greatly affect the thoroughness with which relevant sites can be identified. A predictable set of actors enables researchers to identify a universe of sites to examine for evidence of web activity within a demarcated web sphere. A less predictable set of actors makes this task more difficult, and requires additional searching and identification activities.

Our third dimension is the *level of stability* in the development of sites, links and other objects within the web sphere. The level of stability has an impact on how frequently the boundaries of the web sphere need to be reconsidered, and how often the sites within the web sphere need to be examined. We have identified three determinants of the level of stability within a web sphere. First, consideration should be given to the frequency of entry and exit of new producers. The extent of new entrants into the web sphere (represented by specific producers, rather than types of producers) and the extent to which producers stop updating, maintaining or serving their sites, is a measure of the stability of the sphere; highly stable spheres have less entry and exit than unstable spheres. Second, stability is a measure of the degree to which sites being analysed change or add links to other web sites that ought to be considered within the sphere; frequent changes and substantial additions reduce stability. Third, the frequency and breadth of changes to content and features within the web sites under examination contribute to stability; highly stable web spheres include sites with infrequent and narrowly focused changes to content and features.

Of course, the object of some research projects may be to measure stability and/or to test assumptions about predictability, thus making it problematic to use the phenomenon under consideration as part of the selection process for objects to be studied. Nevertheless, prior research, preliminary examination and incremental evaluation can contribute both to estimates of these dimensions of the web sphere and to the research design itself.

The position of the web sphere on these dimensions may have bearing on whether the researcher 'fixes' the boundaries of the sphere at the beginning of a study, or engages in a dynamic bounding process. Bounding refers to the process of identifying constituent elements (sites or pages) within the web sphere and specifying a temporal frame for analysis. Identifying constituent elements of the web sphere to be examined may include both establishing the universe of sites or pages about which generalizations can be offered, and specifying a method of sampling sites or pages to be analysed. Constituent elements can be identified prior to analysis – following long-established practices in survey research (Hyman 1955) and content analysis (Berelson 1952). Alternatively, constituent elements can be identified as part of the analysis process, building on well-established techniques used in participant observation research (Whyte 1943), and more recently labelled as a snowball research strategy (Berg 1988; Atkinson and Flint 2001). Identifying constituent elements prior to analysis – in effect, fixing the boundaries of the web sphere under study – offers several advantages to the researcher. A clearly defined universe of sites within a web sphere makes representative sampling of sites possible for both archiving and structured observations. Fixed boundaries may also increase the possibility of replicating findings by subsequent analysts. Finally, fixing the boundaries of the web sphere may enhance options for collaboration in archiving or analyzing the web sphere, particularly with entities such as libraries (Schneider et al. 2003).

On the other hand, dynamic bounding allows the researcher to be responsive to unanticipated developments and emergent trends in the web sphere. Prior research in both the 11 September web sphere and electoral web spheres suggests that, even within anticipated, predictable and generally stable web spheres, unanticipated events precipitate the production or alteration of intertextual and interlinked web objects, sometimes in a matter of hours or over the course of a few days. We employ the concept of a web storm as a unit of analysis that reflects inter-actor and inter-site activity over a relatively brief period of time. For instance, a political scandal is likely to result in a web storm wherein actors such as news organizations, advocacy groups and individual citizens, (for example, producers of politically oriented weblogs), post texts, graphics and links regarding the scandal intensively for several days or weeks. Some web storms develop into web spheres that are durable on the web over a longer period, often through the migration of individual texts and pages pertaining to an event onto sites newly produced and dedicated to the event. For example, a web storm emerged quickly in the wake of the release of Kenneth Starr's report detailing US President Bill Clinton's affair with Monica Lewinsky and raising questions of perjury. The web storm of commentaries developed into a web sphere as sites were produced to advocate impeachment of the president (for example, http://impeach-clinton.org),[1] or oppose it (for example, http://moveon.org).[2]

Unless a researcher is engaged in dynamic bounding, he or she is likely to miss the opportunity to analyse these web storms, which may be significant bursts of online action. Dynamic bounding as a scholarly practice is also more consistent with how the web functions from a user perspective. It is critical, though, that dynamic bounding be implemented systematically to ensure representativeness and replicability.

Completely fixed and fully dynamic bounding represent two ends of a spectrum for identifying constituent elements within web spheres – most researchers will choose some blend of the two. Researchers need to decide, preferably before beginning a study, how frequently the web sphere boundaries will be redefined, and under what circumstances, and how often and according to what criteria and techniques the web will be searched for pages, sites or links comprising the web sphere. A further factor to consider is the correspondence between research goals and the bounding strategy. For instance, if the goal is to analyse the development of a web sphere, a fairly dynamic bounding strategy is needed. Finally, researchers should assume that increased dynamism in web sphere demarcation will increase resource needs – time, effort and storage – especially if systematic archiving is involved.

The process of discovering or establishing the web sphere under study also includes defining the steps or procedures to be taken to identify the specific elements to be examined. Depending on the characteristics of the web sphere, this process can involve a number of strategies. If the producer types are highly predictable, and the web sphere itself highly anticipated, existing and maintained directories of sites may be available. For example, if a researcher was interested in the web sphere related to a single season of a professional sports league, a preexisting directory of sites representing each of the participating teams could likely serve as a starting point for identification of relevant sites. Encompassing the preexisting directory in the research design (that is, by specifying sites to be examined as those identified by the directory on a specific date) both serves as a robust specification of identification strategy and provides a universe from which samples of sites to be examined can be reliably drawn.

On the other hand, some web spheres of interest, especially those that are not anticipated or predictable, may require a more search-oriented strategy to identify constituent elements. Using topical key words systematically in search engines may be fruitful in identifying constituent elements of a web sphere. However, this strategy, which relies on the presence of 'relevant' content within potential sites, may have significant drawbacks. The absence of relevant content on some web sites may reflect action on the part of a site producer that is just as strategic as the presence of relevant web content would be. Furthermore, if relevant material were to appear on a particular site at a later date, establishing its absence at the beginning of the study period would be critical for developmental analyses.

One alternative to content relevance as the primary criterion for inclusion in the web sphere is the identification of relevant actor types, and the inclusion of web sites produced by identified actors. Relevant actor types can be determined in several ways, beginning with whatever extant literature informs a particular study, as well as through methods of social network analysis. Once relevant actor types are established, the web sites of particular actors within each type can be selected through various indices and sampling techniques. Web sites produced by relevant actors may be significant in structuring online action – or the lack thereof – within the web sphere even if those actors have not (yet) produced web materials relevant to the theme of the sphere at the beginning of the study.

Another strategy for identifying constituent elements in a web sphere is to analyse patterns of inlinking to and outlinking from a core set of URLs. For instance, the web sphere of a sports team could be defined by tracing the inlinks to and outlinks from the URLs of the home pages of each player and the team itself. The origin pages of inlinks and the destination pages of outlinks can be analysed in the context of their base sites to identify their producers, then to specify the producer type. Further analysis of these producers' web presence may be helpful to ascertain their position or stance in the web sphere.

Approaches to Studying Online Action in a Web Sphere

The processes of demarcating/establishing web spheres, and of identifying constituent elements in a web sphere are foundational to tracking developmental trajectories of online action. In this section, we suggest a range of methods that can be adapted for studying online action within the integrative framework of web sphere analysis by identifying three sets of approaches that have been used in web-related research since the early 1990s (Schneider and Foot 2004). Although these approaches are not necessarily mutually exclusive, distinguishing between them enables examination of the affordances and challenges of each for studies of online action within a web sphere.

The first set of approaches employ *discursive or rhetorical* analyses of web pages or sites. Typically, this set of approaches is more concerned with the content of a web site than its structuring elements. Studies employing these approaches focus on the texts and images contained on web pages, and/or on web pages or web sites as texts in a Foucauldian sense (for example, Warnick 1998; Baym 2000; Benoit and Benoit 2000; Sillaman 2000). In an online action perspective, web texts are situated as inscriptions of communicative practices on the part of site sponsors and/or users, and methods of discursive or rhetorical analysis can help to illuminate social action. For example, discursive and rhetorical analyses were employed in the analysis of the post-11 September web sphere in studies of personal expression in general (Siegl and Foot 2004), and memorializing in particular (Foot, Warnick and Schneider, forthcoming) as forms of online action. As further illustration of the potential role of this set of approaches in web sphere analysis, rhetorical analysis was combined with quantitative content analysis of issue stance texts on campaign sites from 200 races to study campaign practices of position taking online (Xenos and Foot 2005). Discursive or rhetorical methods can also shed light on relations between web producers within a web sphere, particularly when hypertext intertextuality is included through analyses of cross-site linking (for example, Mitra 1999; Warnick 2001).

The second set of approaches are *structural/feature* analyses. Studies in this genre that use individual web sites as the unit of analysis focus on the structure of the site, such as the number of pages, hierarchical ordering of pages, or on the features found on the pages within the site, for instance, the presence of a search engine, privacy policy or multiple navigation options (D'Alessio 1997; McMillan 1999; Benoit and Benoit 2000; D'Alessio 2000; Hansen 2000). Other types of structural analysis employ computer-assisted macro level network analysis methods for mapping linking patterns (Jackson 1997; Rogers and Marres 2000; Thelwall 2001a; Rogers and Marres 2002; Park 2003; Park and Thelwall 2003; Park and Thelwall, Chapter 12 in this volume). Studies of this type enable understanding of network structures on the web, but the meaning or 'substance' of those network structures can be difficult to infer from large-scale mapping studies. We view features and other structural elements of sites as manifestations of (co)production activities that constitute 'online structure' (Schneider and Foot 2002). Online structure both inscribes particular forms of communicative, social and/or political action on the part of web producers, and enables or constrains particular forms of online and offline action on the part of web users. For example, a campaign's decision to create a database-driven web site feature for sending electronic letters to local newspaper editors enables online political mobilization. Methods for systematically analyzing features and other types of structure within a web sphere are being developed and employed in studies of online action both alone (for example, Foot et al. 2003b) and in combination with other methods that elicit user perspectives such as focus groups (for example, Stromer-Galley and Foot 2002) and surveys of web users (for example, Stromer-Galley et al. 2001; Schneider and Foot 2003).

A third set of approaches to web analysis has emerged for analyzing multi-actor, cross-site action on the web, based on adaptations of sociocultural methods of inquiry. Lindlof and Shatzer (1998) point in this direction in their article calling for new strategies of media ethnography in 'virtual space'. Hine (2000) presents a good example of sociocultural analysis of cross-site action on the web. Similarly, Howard's (2002) conceptualization of network ethnography reflects methodological sensitivity to processes of web production as a form of strategic online action. By appropriating the term 'sociocultural' to describe this set of approaches, we seek to highlight the attention paid in this genre of web studies to the hyperlinked context(s) and situatedness of web sites – and to the aims, strategies and identity-construction processes of web site producers (see several examples in Beaulieu and Park 2003; Beaulieu, Chapter 13 in this volume). Field research methods of participant observation and interviews, in combination with textual, structural and link analyses comprise this set of approaches. For studies of online action within a web sphere, sociocultural approaches are particularly helpful in analyzing complex, evolving processes such as collaborative mobilization and co-production

– of features, pages and whole sites, and across sites through links (Foot and Schneider 2002; Forte 2003; Forte, Chapter 7 in this volume).

In summary, the rubric for selecting and adapting social research methods for the study of online action is comprised of theoretical perspectives that situate web productions as socio-technical formations in combination with research design choices regarding levels and units of analysis. Within the framework of web sphere analysis, a wide range of methods can be adapted and used fruitfully in various combinations, in correspondence with particular kinds of research questions regarding online action. All of the methods described earlier will result in the generation of some kind of annotations or metadata about web materials, whether qualitative or quantitative. As we discuss in the next section, researchers may find it useful to create an archive or database of web materials in conjunction with their database of metadata.

Archiving Materials for Web Sphere Analyses

Methodological choices implicated in the identification of a web sphere and the selection of research methods for analyzing online action, have already been discussed. The third methodological issue entailed in analyzing online action within the framework of web sphere analysis concerns collecting or archiving 'born digital' web materials as data. Research design decisions about whether and how to archive for studies of online action may be influenced by the dimensions of the web sphere under consideration, and by the approach(es) selected for analyzing online action. For instance, in-depth rhetorical analysis of a relatively small number of web texts produced within a stable and predictable web sphere during a relatively brief period would not require the same level of archiving as a structural analysis of the development of a large number of web sites in an unstable and unpredictable web sphere over the course of several months. In this section, we focus on technical choices that may be involved in archiving for research projects within the framework of web sphere analysis in view of the nature of web materials, and on the specific challenges researchers face in collecting these materials as data.

Web materials are uniquely ephemeral and persistent. The ephemerality of web content comes from the way it is constructed and controlled. The availability of web content, once produced, is often solely under the control of the producer – a characteristic of born digital materials that holds significant implications for scholarly citation as well as data collection (Weiss 2003). From the perspective of web users, including social researchers, specialized tools and techniques are required to ensure that content can be viewed again at a later time. Additionally, web content, like theatre and other 'performance media' (Hecht, Corman and Miller-Rassulo 1993; Stowkowski 2002) is ephemeral in its construction: once presented, it needs to be reconstructed or re-presented in order for others to experience it. Although web pages are routinely reconstructed by computers without human intervention (that is, when a request is forwarded to a web server) it nevertheless requires some action by the producer, or the producer's server, in order for the content to be reproduced or reconstructed. Put another way, the experience of the web, as well as the bits used to produce the content, must be intentionally preserved in order for it to be reproduced (Arms et al. 2001). This is in contrast to older media – including printed materials, film and sound recordings, for example – that can be archived in the form in which they are presented without additional steps to re-create the experience of the original.

At the same time the web has a sense of persistence and even permanence that clearly distinguishes it from performance media. Unlike theatre, or live television or radio, web content must exist in a permanent form in order to be transmitted. Even dynamically generated web pages generally rely on data previously encoded in databases.[3] The web shares this characteristic with other forms of media such as film, print and sound recordings. The permanence of the web, however, is somewhat fleeting. Unlike any other permanent media, a web site may regularly and procedurally destroy its predecessor each time it is updated by its producer. That is, in the absence of specific arrangements to the contrary, each previous edition of a web site may be erased as a new version is produced. By analogy, it would be as if each day's newspaper was printed on the same piece of paper, obliterating yesterday's news to produce today's.

Researchers interested in studying online action may need to counter this ephemerality by taking proactive steps in order to facilitate a recreation of web experience (Arms et al. 2001) for future analyses. The permanence of the web makes this eminently possible. Although saving web sites is not as easy as, say, saving editions of a magazine, archiving techniques are evolving in such a way to facilitate scholarly research of web sites. In distinction to other ephemeral media, the web can be preserved in nearly the same form as it was originally 'performed' (Kahle 1997; Lyman and Kahle 1998; Lyman 2002) and analysed at a later time.

Decisions about archiving strategies should be made in view off research design, research operations and ethical considerations. The research design should include a specification of periodicity, breadth and depth. Periodicity refers to the frequency with which the researcher desires to capture or archive the web materials under examination. Depending on the stability of the materials, the researcher's objectives with respect to conducting developmental analyses measuring change over time, and the time frame anticipated for the research project, researchers may wish to capture materials daily, weekly, monthly, quarterly or even annually. Breadth in this context refers to the inclusion (or exclusion) of pages that are hyperlinked to the sites or pages under study. Pages with links to the sites under examination (inlinks), as well as pages that are linked by the sites under examination (outlinks), may provide critical context for understanding or evaluating the online action within the web sphere being analysed. One approach is to include pages one link away from those sites identified as being in the core of the web sphere. Inclusion of inlinked pages will, by definition, require additional searching for identification purposes. Inclusion of outlinked pages may present significant challenges for some archiving tools. Depth refers to the number of levels from a 'base' or starting web page, within the same domain or web site, that the researcher wishes to include within the web sphere. Many researchers may prefer to capture the whole web site without regard to depth. Periodicity may also interact with breadth and depth. For example, archiving strategies can be designed to capture 'deep' materials with a less frequent periodicity – perhaps capturing front pages of sites daily, and the second and subsequent levels of sites weekly or monthly.

Research operations concern the techniques that will be employed to conduct the analysis. First, the sheer quantity of materials to be archived will likely affect the techniques developed – capturing and maintaining an archive of several hundred gigabytes presents challenges substantially different than an effort involving several dozen gigabytes. Second, the number of individual researchers involved in the project may dictate specific choices. A collaborative project involving two or more researchers may require the use of a centralized server to host the archived materials, and the implementation of a system to allow web access to the archive. Alternatively, research projects may function quite well with single copies of archived materials stored on removable media like CDs or DVDs. Systems to track references to specific instances of archived objects (such as sites or pages) may also be dependent on the method developed to provide access to archived materials

Finally, archiving decisions should also be made with consideration of the intentions concerning the long-term use and availability of the captured materials. Scholars ought to consider the ethical issues associated with archiving (Schneider et al. 2003) such as current copyright laws, the phenomenon of artefacts being produced in the archiving process that were never actually available on the web, and the potential for digital repositories to be exploited in harmful ways by current and future users. Researchers may find it necessary to consult institutional policies concerning these issues, especially those involving copyright, fair use and consent. In addition, researchers may wish to consider the value of their archived materials to other scholars and to the wider community. Social science data archives and libraries represent two potential repositories for these materials. Choices made when capturing materials – for example, including HTTP header information – may increase the likelihood that archives match standards established by these types of institutions.

Conclusion

Web sphere analysis holds potential as an approach for studying online action. This approach is centred on the web sphere as a clearly specified, multidimensional unit of analysis. It provides an integrative framework encompassing multiple research methods. We have made explicit the set of challenges involved in identifying and collecting data responsive to the selected research method(s) and characteristics of the web sphere under examination. The framing of the web sphere, selection of research method and process of identifying and collecting data represent a set of interrelated choices to be made by researchers during the research design process.

Researchers interested in analyzing a web sphere should explicitly define its boundaries and the procedures to be employed in dynamically shaping those boundaries during the course of the study. Reflection on the three dimensions of a web sphere – the anticipatability of its emergence, the predictability of the types of actors producing materials and the level of stability – may contribute to decisions made as researchers approach a web sphere analysis. In particular, the dimensions of the web sphere under study may shape the data collection strategy.

Three approaches to studying online action illustrate the range of analysis methods that can be employed. Discursive or rhetorical analyses are more concerned with the content of web sites than its structuring elements. Structural/feature analyses focus on the structure of sites, and may employ macro level network analysis methods for mapping relations between sites. Sociocultural approaches focus on the hyperlinked context(s) and co-productive aspects of sites, features and texts, and of cross-site action through links. The type of web sphere that is under investigation has implications for the selection of one or more research methods, and may shape both the web sphere identification and data collection processes.

Data collection processes, which include both archiving web materials and the creation of metadata characterizing web materials, are highly dependent on a number of factors. The characteristics of the web sphere under examination and the research method selected will likely affect data collection. In addition, these processes will be affected by the availability of resources such as archiving expertise, computing facilities, time frame and research support. Web archiving is particularly useful for developmental analyses that are time sensitive (for example, Foot et al. 2003b) and in analyses of any kind in unstable and unpredictable web spheres. Regardless of the analytical methods employed, or the dimensions of the web sphere under investigation, web archiving enables more rigorous and verifiable research. Finally, consideration of ethical, policy and legal factors may affect archiving and data collection decisions.

The study of online action will continue to draw the attention of social researchers. Emerging practices of web production and use evoke questions about the traditional distinctions between producers and users. Casting this set of questions within the approach of web sphere analysis offers researchers a framework to productively and robustly conceptualize analyses of the hyperlinked, co-produced set of structures that manifest and enable the production, inscriptions and experience of cyberculture.

Notes

1. For an archival impression of this site captured shortly after the impeachment proceedings see http://web.archive.org/web/20000104071229/www.impeach-clinton.com/main/webmastersnote.htm (accessed 25 February 2004).
2. For an archival impression of this site captured during the impeachment proceedings, see http://web.archive.org/web/19981202172227/http://www.moveon.org/ (accessed 25 February 2004).
3. Application-based Web features, such as java applets, are not constrained in this way, and may include the presentation or generation of data not previously constructed by the producer.

–12–

The Network Approach to Web Hyperlink Research and its Utility for Science Communication

Han Woo Park and Mike Thelwall

Network approaches to research have rapidly developed since the late 1970s, principally in anthropology (Wolfe 1978), sociology (Galaskiewicz and Wasserman 1993), science studies (De Solla Price 1986) and communication science (Monge and Contractor 2000). In this chapter we focus on one set of network analysis techniques, those from social network analysis. In this field a set of social ties among entities of a social system is conceptualized as a network. Network techniques have been developed to examine concrete social relations among specific social actors as well as the effects of network structures on the way in which social systems operate. As a theoretical framework, the goal of one network approach is to identify patterns of relations that exist among social entities (Wellman and Berkowitz 1989; Richards and Barnett 1993; Wasserman and Faust 1994). Further, social network theory explains which factors influence the form and content of network structures. Also, the roles of different types of ties (that is strong and weak ties) and communication channels (ranging from traditional mass media to new interactive technologies) are valid research objects. In particular, the network approach uses a set of analytical techniques and tools (for example, density, centrality, cluster analysis, block modelling, and multidimensional scaling) derived from mathematical graph theory and, recently, statistical physics. These analysis methods provide a means to move beyond just thinking of ties, connections or networks as a metaphor (Rogers 1987). The network research approach has become not only a methodology but also a theoretical perspective. Network analysis is not a narrow set of tools but a broad intellectual approach (Wellman and Berkowitz 1989).

To illustrate the potential of network analysis, we describe its application to the study of science communication. More and more individual scientific researchers and research groups are seeking to communicate with each other via the web, making their research information such as specific results, research data, tools, pre-prints or academic interests available on their web sites. The web not only represents a technological development but also has become a new primary communication channel for some scientific research communities. However, there is a gap in the literature related to the role and use of the web in science communication. This is especially true when it comes to the quantitative examination of the science communication that takes place through new digital networks, in this case the web. The lack of understanding of the emerging form of scientific research communication on the web may adversely affect the establishment and promotion of an information society. Using hyperlink analysis, researchers can investigate an aspect of the structure of scientific and scholarly communication networks.

Social Network Analysis in CMC research

Electronic media are becoming an increasingly important channel for social interaction and information exchange. Several researchers have proposed a way in which the computer facilitates communication from the perspective of social networks (Garton et al. 1997; Wellman 2001; Park 2003). First of all, scholars have started to use the social network approach to examine the structural communication patterns among computer conference users (Danowski and Edison-Swift 1985). Following this approach, Marc Smith (2002) and others (Kang and Choi 1999; Paolillo 2001) analysed CMC networks among Usenetters and Internet Relay Chatters based on their text message exchanges and flows. Haythornthwaite (2000) investigated how distance learners in different physical locations use computer-supported educational applications such as electronic whiteboards to collaborate with one another. In contrast to these studies, some research (Hampton and Wellman 2000; Matei and Ball-Rokeach 2001) extended the study of CMC networks to offline life. They examined online social ties among people in relation to social interactions in their physical world.

The network approach has been employed to study the way in which an 'information society' operates on a national and global scale. Dodds, Muhamed and Watts (2003) conducted the first large-scale replication of Milgram's (1967) 'small world' experiment, which is also known as 'six degrees of separation'. Milgram discovered that people were able to deliver letters to unknown persons in a few steps by forwarding them to intermediate acquaintances. Following Milgram's approach, Dodds and his colleagues asked more than 60,000 email users to forward messages to acquaintances who seem to be closer to one of eighteen target persons in thirteen countries. Their study showed that a small world connected through the Internet may be found but the existence of global social networks with short chains are heavily dependent on individual incentives. Barnett et al. (2003) studied the relations between Internet network linkages and other social flows (such as migration, trade, air traffic and student exchanges) among the ten provinces in Canada. Gorman (2001) examined the fibre optic connection among cities in the United States, Europe and China. He claimed that the structures of fiber networks indicated some degree of freedom of Internet regulation policy in each country. The US fibre network has more scale-free characteristics than that of Europe and China. This was made possible by a minimum of regulation in the United States. Further, the scale-free network has lead to a high bandwidth capacity and more efficient allocation of data, thus reducing Internet traffic congestion. In the case of international relations, Hargittai (1999) investigated the global distribution patterns of Internet infrastructures such as the number of Internet hosts. She has shown that results from the Internet were consistent with other forms of international communication networks such as telephone calls: dominance of traditional core countries like the United States and the United Kingdom. These studies suggest that the network approach is helpful for analyzing the operating mechanisms of computer-mediated social systems.

Progress of the Network Approach for Hyperlink Analysis

The network approach has started to be employed to examine the structure of the World Wide Web through the analysis of configurations of hyperlink interconnections among web sites (Park 2003; Park and Thelwall 2003). Park and Thelwall (2003) provide an integrated review of hyperlink analyses of the web. This section extends the review to interesting and useful studies not covered in that article. First, there have been some attempts to explore whether a small world network exists in the online as well as the offline world (Albert, Jeong and Barabási 1999; Broder et al. 2000; Adamic and Adar 2003; Björneborn 2003). This type of research sought to measure distance between web sites to determine a small world phenomenon in the pattern of hyperlink connections (Scharnhorst 2003). Similar to Milgram's (1967) experiment, scholars measured how many steps you need to get from one web site to another site by clicking on hyperlinks, if you select two sites at random.

Second, the network methodology using hyperlink data was applied to e-commerce research. Krebs' (2000) study of Amazon.com indirectly revealed the role of hyperlinks in relation to mutual trust among online consumers. Palmer, Bailey and Faraj (2000) and Park, Barnett and Nam (2002) used the number of incoming hyperlinks to a web site as an indicator of the trust granted to an Internet dot com firm. Their research methods were similar to a traditional network analysis that measures an individual's prestige in terms of the number of the friends who choose the person as their representative. Adamic and Huberman (2000) examined the visiting patterns of AOL (America Online) users and found that the number of visitors per site had a power law distribution. That is a characteristic of a scale-free network, where a small number of sites receive the majority of visitors and most sites receive very few visits. The top 1 per cent of sites attracted more than half of the users. This is a signature of both winner-take-all markets and brand loyalty in cyberspace. But the extent to which web site popularity is highly concentrated among a few sites may vary across specific categories. Pennock et al. (2002) analysed the number of hyperlinks and visitors among eleven categories of sites and found that the winner-take-all phenomenon showed a significant difference between categories. The links to photography and wedding web sites are more evenly distributed than those to research and entertainment sites.

Third, the configuration of hyperlink networks themselves can be a source conveying useful overall information about the landscape of certain issues in a society. Adamic (1999) explored communication lines of an abortion issue in cyberspace. Rogers and Marres (2000) found that the private and public organizations involved with climate change produced a symbolic representation of their alliances through the selection of hyperlinks. Burris, Smith and Strahm (2000) showed that white supremacist organizations displayed a similar phenomenon in their web presence. The density of hyperlink connections is stronger among groups with similar ideological affinity or goals and weaker among organizations with different interests. From the perspective of network ethnography, Hine (2000) described the way hyperlink relations are formed and maintained between actors related to the case of the British au pair Louise Woodward. More recently, Garrido and Halavais (2003) described the hyperlink network structure of non-governmental organization (NGO) web sites related to the Zapatista movement and examined their role in the global NGO networks.

Fourth, some people see hyperlinks as potential new channels of political networking in achieving public recognition and serving as social symbols or signs of mutual cooperation. Foot et al. (2003b; see also Schneider and Foot, Chapter 11 in this volume) performed an exploratory analysis of outlinking practices exhibited on web sites produced by US Congressional candidates during the 2002 campaign season. They focused on the extent and development of outgoing links from the sites to other types of political web sites such as civic and advocacy groups, political parties, government agencies and press organizations. Further, they examined the effect of the characteristics of candidates – party type, incumbency status, level of competitiveness, and office sought – on the deployment of linking practices. On the other hand, Park, Barnett and Kim (2001) analysed the pattern of interlinking connectivity among political parties and National Assemblymen in South Korea. They found that the structure of their hyperlink network is significantly related to party membership. In other words, political actors form a community of 'birds of a feather'. More recently, Park, Kim and Barnett (2004) conducted a follow-up study and found that the hyperlink communication network rapidly evolved into a denser, more centralized and integrated network in one year. They suggested that the nation's move to informatization was a factor that, in part, determined the hyperlink structure among Korean political actors' web sites. In particular, this research is meaningful in that it attempted to explore the relationship between longitudinal hyperlink connectivity patterns among web sites and the social environment that surrounds their authors in a large context.

Some studies (Brunn and Dodge 2001; Thelwall 2001a, 2001b; Barnett and Park 2003; Thelwall, Tang and Price 2003) have examined hyperlink connectivity structures at the country level (see also Dodge, Chapter 8 in this volume). The studies of international hyperlink networks tend to focus on either the total volume of link connectivity from a country to other countries or a specific aspect of international hyperlinkage such as linguistic patterns. Additionally, the research conducted in computer and information science presents another good example of using a hyperlink analysis to find the most important pages on the web based on the distribution of hyperlinks among a group of personal or organizational sites devoted to a specific topic (Kleinberg 1999). In other words, their underlying assumption is that a network topology of hyperlinks conveys useful information about the quality and prestige of a web site.

Network Analysis and the Study of Science Communication

In the field of science communication, scientific structure generally refers to the communication and collaboration structure usually defined as the patterns or regularities of information exchange, co-authorship, citation of papers, authors or journals among members of scientific disciplines (Borgman and Furner 2002). The structure of a scientific system may be examined through the use of a social network framework that studies the relations that exist among social entities ranging over cultural symbols, people, groups and nation-states (Wellman and Berkowitz 1989; Richards and Barnett 1993; Wasserman and Faust 1994). Science communication network research (De Solla Price 1986; Perry and Rice 1998; Tomlinson 2002; Newman 2000) has examined the relationships among a scientific system's components (generally the individual documents, researchers or journals) based on the stable patterns of use of those system elements. Science communication is the process in which actors within scientific research communities exchange (in)tangible things such as information, knowledge, data, skill and social support. The process of exchange among actors can be represented as a network that is a set of ties describing the interconnections among those involved.

Interest in the field of science communication has been gradually focused on communication technologies used in scientific communities because the current growth in collaboration and communication in scientific research has been facilitated by the adoption and diffusion of new technologies among scientists (Gabbay 2000; McCain 2000). New technologies have a potential to play pivotal roles in promoting collaboration and communication by providing versatile functions for the exchange of scholarly information and informal messages among scientists. Past research indicates that a variety of novel forms of digital technologies may make possible more efficient and flexible modes of communication and collaboration in scientific research: online journals (Hawkins 2001); e-print servers (Kling, McKim and King 2001), groupware (Majchrzak et al. 2000), email (Cohen 1996), collaboratories (Finholt 2002), and instant messaging services (Nardi, Whittaker and Bradner 2000). Also, social network analysts (Koku, Nazer and Wellman 2000; Walsh et al. 2000; Matzat 2001; Walsh and Maloney 2002) have examined patterns of communication relations and new media use among scientific researchers, based upon their working and social relations such as scientific productivities, the frequency of collaborative communications, the information exchange relationships, and the types of communication technologies used. They found that those who had collaborative communication more frequently tended to be more productive (in terms of authored articles, see Walsh et al. 2000; Walsh and Maloney 2002) and were involved in more types of information exchange relationships and new communication media (see Wellman and his colleagues' works at http://www.chass.utoronto.ca/~wellman/publications/index.html, accessed 4 November 2004). The findings of network analyses also suggest that the closeness or strength of work ties (such as the frequency of co-authoring papers) is generally associated with the number of information exchanges, collaboration, and new technologies used among the researchers.

Hyperlinks and Science Communication

The development of network approaches for researching the web opens up possibilities and opportunities for analyzing the configuration of scientific and research communication networks on the web. Concepts and methods of network theory applied to various kinds of social relations on the web can also be used to study the role of web hyperlinks in the scientific and research communities. Individual researchers and academic organizations form and maintain communication relations, setting up hyperlinks to people, scholarly articles, journals, research tools, databases or institutions with shared interests and topics on their web pages or web-accessible documents. The advent of electronic journals transforms a traditional text into a hypertext that enables authors to hyperlink to cited literature (Zhang 1998; Kim 2000). Nowadays, many scientific and research conferences make their programs and abstracts available on the web and, occasionally, their participants' information such as email addresses or websites hyperlinked from conference sites. Audiences who want more detailed information are able to contact participants.

One use of hyperlinking is for collaborating researchers and institutes to connect to relevant materials, useful information, research tools and projects hosted on partners' locations without having to archive those resources in their own spaces. Of course, in the nature of the web, researchers can equally link to information and sites of people that they have never met. The convenience and usefulness of hyperlinking is a powerful draw to attract scientific community members. Logically, hyperlinks can *sometimes* reflect real world communication networks connecting individual researchers and research groups.

Communication relations in science can be divided into two types and four levels (Katz and Martin 1997; Genuth, Genuth, Chompalor and Shrum 2000). Types may be divided into information sharing (for example, email forwarding and bookmark sharing) and knowledge production (for example, collaborative writing). Levels can be classified as international, institutional, disciplinary and personal collaboration. From this perspective, some of the uses of hyperlinks discussed above can be classified as information sharing, although other uses fall outside the model, being social in nature. For example, scholars can link to the pages of collaborators not for the information that they contain but as a phatic communication device: a form of recognition (Thelwall 2003b). Hyperlinks clearly occur at all four levels of the model, however.

Scholarly Hyperlink Research

One of the key problems tackled by scholarly hyperlink research was to identify the particular type of communication represented by academic hyperlinks: links between two academic (for example, university) web pages. An early conjecture was that they would be analogous to citations, mainly representing cognitive connections between scholarly information. This would allow counts of links to a web page or site to be seen as a measure of its value or impact (Ingwersen 1998) in the same way that citation counts are used (Borgman and Furner 2002). A related early belief was that links could be seen as purveyors of trust (Davenport and Cronin 2000) with more highly targeted pages being more trustworthy information sources. This is also close to the rationale for Google's link based ranking mechanism (Brin and Page 1998), which assumes that better linked-to pages will be more useful. An opposite perspective has also been expressed: since anyone can create hyperlinks to anywhere, even at random, they are completely meaningless and not useful sources of information. For example, academics can and do link to cookery and restaurant pages in large numbers (A. G. Smith 1999; Thelwall 2001b). Moreover, there is no reason why collaboration should necessarily result in a hyperlink. A case in point is two academics, Ronald Rousseau and Leo Egghe, who frequently collaborate and both have published web research, yet there is no link on Rousseau's web site to any page authored by Egghe or containing information about him, nor any in the reverse direction (as of 6 October 2004).

Given the conflicting viewpoints above, how can we decide between them and find out the truth? A series of papers have attempted to do this and we report here the key outcomes of this line of research. First, why are links between academic

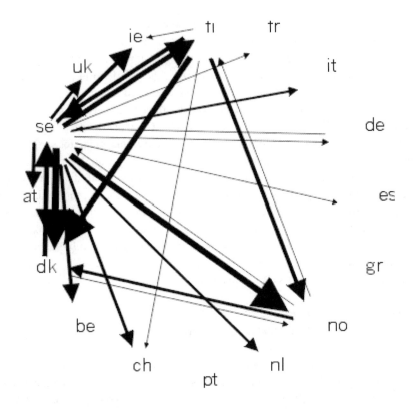

Figure 12.1 The strength of linking from Swedish language pages in European Union universities. Arrow widths are proportional to link counts. The letter pairs are international country codes (http://www.iso.org/iso/en/prods-services/iso3166ma/02iso-3166-code-lists/list-en1.html). Reproduced with permission from Thelwall, Tang and Price (2003).

web sites created? Since links within a web site are typically created for navigation purposes, it makes sense to ignore these and analyse only inter-university links. A random sample of these for UK universities was investigated, with the discovery that about 90 per cent were created for a wide range of reasons loosely related to research, with links to recreational pages (for example, food) being relatively insignificant, even though they do exist (Wilkinson et al. 2003). Nevertheless, less than 1 per cent of links were equivalent to citations, so the citation analogy thesis falls. Of particular importance, hyperlinks typically do not represent connections between people. Common targets of links include university home pages, unknown software publishers and information resources (Thelwall 2002b). As a result, hyperlinks cannot in general be conceived as reflecting interpersonal communication or as forming or representing social networks. Figure

12.1 gives an example of a network constructed from hyperlink data between European Union university web sites, one of a number of similar graphs available in Thelwall et al. (2003). It demonstrates interlinking, where the link pages are in Swedish. As would be expected, most Swedish links originate in Nordic countries (Sweden: se, Denmark: dk, Norway: no, Finland: fi) and Sweden in particular. A theory of linking is needed so that diagrams like this one can be interpreted with confidence.

Hyperlinks between academic web spaces are used for so many different purposes that it is difficult to describe what they represent in anything other than very general terms, such as a wide range of types of informal scholarly communication (Wilkinson et al. 2003), where communication does not necessarily mean interpersonal communication in this context. Despite this, however, strong patterns can be extracted from very large-scale analyses of collections of all university web sites within a country, if advanced data-mining techniques are used (Thelwall 2002a). At this large-scale level of analysis, hyperlinking is indirectly related to research productivity: more productive scholars publish more web pages, and attract more hyperlinks in total because they publish more (Thelwall and Harries 2004).

In summary, although patterns can be extracted from large-scale analyses of hyperlinks, on a small scale it is difficult to characterize hyperlinks in terms of meaning. It may seem clear that hyperlinks are at least always a communication device in the loosest possible sense, but even this statement is not true: sometimes they are created without any communicative intent, for example as part of an HTML creation practice exercise (Thelwall 2003b).

Prospects for Analyzing Web Science Communication with the Network Approach

Future research into hyperlinks in science communication should avoid jumping to conclusions about how hyperlinks should be interpreted, and be aware of the following two points in particular.

- The mere existence of a hyperlink does not necessarily imply any relationship between the documents interlinked or the document owners (Thelwall 2003b).
- A relationship between two individuals does not imply that their pages will be interlinked. Similarly, two related pages or sets of pages do not necessarily interlink (Menczer 2004; Thelwall and Wilkinson 2004).

A consequence of this is that future studies must be very carefully designed to ensure that interpretations placed upon links or link structures are genuinely evident from the data. This means that the links must be assessed individually to see why they were created or interpreted, in a research context where relationships are not assumed in advance (for example, Adamic, Buyukkokten and Adar 2003). Those with access to programming skills have the additional luxury of being able to automatically analyse other parts of the page in order to extract more information than from just the hyperlinks (Adamic and Adar 2003).

Researchers seeking to analyse hyperlink data should consider using small-scale preliminary pilot studies in order to assess whether hyperlink data is capable of yielding any information at all. For example, anyone studying the web interlinking patterns of historians is likely to be disappointed (Tang and Thelwall 2003) because real relationships translate into hyperlinks so rarely that there will be too little data to be useful.

Social network studies of hyperlink networks do have a promising future, however, if the topics are chosen carefully so that the scale and topic will yield enough data, or if the links are studied in the context of a larger problem scope, as is the case in web sphere analysis (see Schneider and Foot, Chapter 11 in this volume) or studies of particular kinds of rare links such as small world shortcuts (Björneborn 2003). There are interesting studies to be conducted, but not every topic and scale will yield interesting results and so great care must be taken with the initial stages. Additionally, since social network analysis statistics were designed for interpersonal communication networks, care must be taken when employing them to assess whether they are really meaningful in the new context.

There are two different approaches to hyperlink network analysis that future researchers may consider. The first is to assess how hyperlinks may be interpreted in a particular context. This would involve choosing a context, for example a set of web sites of a given type, and then using techniques to explore the way in which links are used in the chosen context. These techniques could include content analysis (Weare and Lin 2000) of the links, interviewing the authors of the pages containing the links (Kim 2000; Park 2002), or statistical techniques, particularly Spearman correlations with measures of known value (for example, Thelwall 2002a).

A second approach is to use links to infer structural properties of a set of web sites. In this case the interpretation of the meaning placed on links should be made explicit and steps taken to filter out the links that do not match the criteria. For example, many studies using personal web crawlers automatically eliminate duplicate pages and employ human intervention to identify and exclude mirror sites (collections of pages copied from another location). In small-scale studies it would be appropriate to form a set of rules for allowable links and then visit each link page to assess whether the rules are met, subsequently excluding unwanted links. Following a preliminary data-filtering step such as this, network analysis techniques could then be applied and interpreted with more confidence.

Conclusion

The marriage of arguably the most important communication network in the world, the web, with existing network analysis techniques is a natural and promising one. It has many pitfalls to catch the unwary researcher but, with care, the essential task of modeling and explaining web networks of various kinds can be a fruitful one.

Acknowledgements

The first author acknowledges that this work was partly supported by Korea Research Foundation Grant (KRF-2003–041–H00010). Further, he is grateful to Alexander Halavais, Mike Thelwall, George Barnett and his Royal Netherlands Academy ex-colleagues for helping him develop the concept of scientific communication through hyperlinking.

–13–

Sociable Hyperlinks: an Ethnographic Approach to Connectivity

Anne Beaulieu

The Internet can be conceptualized as communication medium, information infrastructure and 'space' of interaction. Thinking about which concept to use is especially central to ethnographic methods, since constituting 'the field' is determinant for the knowledge produced in this kind of research (Amit 2000).[1] The Internet is frequently seen as a mediated environment, constituted by a myriad of socio-technical interactions which often leave traces behind. Traces often seem ready-made (logs, files, archives of messages, hyperlinks), forming both a stimulus for renewed interest in ethnography on the Internet and a source of discomfort with the idea that the Internet might constitute a viable ethnographic site (Clifford 1997; Beaulieu 2004). These traces have also been perceived as potentially shared objects between quantitative and qualitative approaches. They are seductive for the researcher (Star 1999), but must be understood as representations constituted by the context, the users and last but not least, the researcher's own activities.

The term 'trace' is used in this chapter to evoke a sign left behind by an entity, the meaning of which must be understood and interpreted. The methods illustrated in this chapter address one particular kind of 'trace', the hyperlink, and its use as an ethnographic object to constitute a field of study. I suggest that an ethnographic treatment of hyperlinks can be a useful way to understand both social and technical dimensions of the Internet as a space for sharing and circulating data. Viewing hyperlinks as both functional and symbolic suggests ways in which traditional elements of ethnography might be adapted in order to constitute an online field site for the study of infrastructure. Specifically, this approach builds on the notion of connectivity as an important feature of networks on the Internet (Scharnhorst 2003) and suggests how connectivity can be further elaborated in an ethnographic approach. While the issues explored in this chapter arose from work in science and technology studies, the discussion may well be of interest to other streams of research in which ethnography plays an important role.

Ethnography of Knowledge Production

The methods discussed here were elaborated in the course of two projects using virtual ethnography (Hine 2000). Both focused on new infrastructures for knowledge production which had web interfaces, the first on a single large database, the functional Magnetic Resonance Imaging Data Center (fMRIDC) and the second on four public databases.[2] Common to both projects was the notion that these knowledge infrastructures might be involved in shifts in the locus of knowledge production. Studies of scientific fields like genetics and biodiversity have noted an increasing reliance on databases and information technologies (Fujimura and Fortun 1996; Lenoir 1999) and such databases tend to be especially large-scale and interdisciplinary (Bowker 2000). These trends complicate the issue of how to think about the location of scientific work.

'Public databases' were interesting to study because of their claimed potential to be more open to lay experts than other kinds of databases of scientific information. This could partly be witnessed in aspects of their design, for example, their non-password-protected interface on the web. In the case of fMRIDC, the role of the database was also to make data available in new ways to a wider audience, by enabling data-sharing practices among scientists. In these cases, new actors, new locations and new types of objects were meant to circulate, and to create new meaningful practices.

In what follows, I refer mainly to the work on the fMRIDC, and draw complementary examples from the other databases. The goals of the Center are to provide 'a publicly accessible repository of peer-reviewed fMRI studies and their underlying data', although its launch as a centralized database did raise a heated controversy. Currently, authors of articles published in the *Journal of Cognitive Neuroscience* are required to submit their data to the fMRIDC as a condition of publication. The database has both online and offline elements, and its various contents circulate in different ways (telephone, web interface, CD-Rom, email), with the ideal of having all aspects networked, possibly on a 'grid' type of infrastructure. This initiative was therefore a good case in which to study practices of data-sharing, in a network setting highly modulated by information and communication technologies.

The usual field site for ethnographies of knowledge production is the space of the laboratory. This had to be rethought to enable the study of data-sharing infrastructures in relation to our research questions about the 'novelty' and 'uptake' of these practices. The questions differed slightly in the two projects, but were deeply rooted in the notion from the sociology of science that knowledge requires sociality, via a community of 'knowers', in order to be validated, transmitted, applied and understood (Barnes 1985; Shapin 1995; Barnes, Bloor and Henry 1996). That this sociality might be mediated, rather than face-to-face, was one of the hypotheses guiding this work, with implications for defining the field – 'where' was this sociality to be explored? Potentially, the development of the infrastructure could have been studied from the location where the databases were being developed, defined as the 'host' institution (Newman 1998; Bowker and Star 1999). Another possible field site might have been one of the laboratories or places of work of potential contributors. Yet, the sharing of data, as the main theme, seemed to call for a multi-sited approach that might enable us to understand how connections were being made, how data circulated, and how social interactions embedded data into meaningful exchanges (and vice versa: compare Slater 2002b). The fieldwork thus took the shape of a combination of visits (of both sites of production and of users' local settings) and attendance at events where the initiatives would be discussed (see also Ratto 2004). We did a number of interviews (by telephone, email, face-to-face) and shared drafts of texts with informants. Another potential field site, which we have not yet been able to 'visit', could be constituted by pedagogical events to teach the use of these tools.

Connectivity and Hyperlinks

Throughout the early phase of the research, the web was used as place to gather information about the fMRIDC and the various persons involved with it, and to retrieve documents (journal and newspaper articles) in which it was discussed. The web site of the database was also explored thoroughly, and links on the site were followed. This enabled us to see how the site positioned itself in relation to others, and also what the site developers provided to the users (Hine 2001). Yet, something seemed to be missing from the information we were able to find about potential users. The fMRIDC claimed to have a few hundred registered 'users', and it further displayed prominently its numbers of visitors in sophisticated diagrams and tables from the log files, but this did not say very much about who these users were, nor about their use of the database and data. Furthermore, the only 'official' trace of use of the database was to be expected in eventual publications: the fMRIDC intended that users include in the acknowledgements sections of publications the reference number of the data sets.[3] The time cycle of publication is at the very least one calendar year, and waiting was not an attractive option. Since access to the database was embedded in a web interface, it seemed to make sense to assume that interactions with this interface, as traced via hyperlinks, could also be constitutive of the practices around the infrastructure.[4] I therefore started exploring how hyperlinks might be retrieved and analysed. Hyperlinks subsequently became a jumping-off point, which suggested different aspects of the fMRIDC and its various roles – among researchers, among other databases, in policy settings, and so on.

   In this sense, the significance of hyperlinks to the project was similar to their meaning for web designers. They also focus on links to their site as indicative of visibility, which in turn is taken to be the measure of success or failure (Hine 2000: 149). The importance of being hyperlinked is also built into the way search engines order their results.[5] Hyperlinks to and from the database therefore seemed one possible way to understand how data flow might be affected by the database, and how it might become embedded in the data-sharing practices of researchers. At this point, I was also aware of the body of work that operationalizes trust as the presence of hyperlinks (Davenport and Cronin 2000), but was critical of the assumption in this line of work that a hyperlink means an endorsement. It quickly became clear that a hyperlink to a site may be a positive endorsement, a negative one and may also be neutral. The hyperlink may be neutral in the case where it is included to make the linking site as thorough as possible (that is, cases where the primary criterion for including a hyperlink is inclusion of all sites, rather than the endorsement of a specific web site). The presence of a hyperlink can also be indicative of the automated construction of the linking web sites. For example, we found one site on rambling (in the sense of walking or hiking, as a leisure activity) in which the Walking with Woodlice web site was included. The word 'walking' in the title is used as a pun on a well-known BBC television show, but the Walking with Woodlice link had been included on the rambling site, putatively because it was retrieved from a search on the word 'walking'. Furthermore, the context of the link on the linking page can give indications of the way the linked site is perceived (what it is 'good for'). The specifics of linking also provide insight into the kind of information that is considered necessary to convey the identity or function of the web site. Finally, a hyperlink can be considered a special kind of expression, both functional and symbolic.[6] I therefore treated a hyperlink as a trace that can be used in terms of analytic categories as a text, and as a technology, as Hine (2000) suggests for the web. Metaphors of presence, connection and visibility were dominant by this point in the ethnography.

Looking for Users via Hyperlinks

The first attempt to use hyperlinks as a trace was the creation of what I later learned goes under the name of an 'ego network' in social network analysis, aiming to retrieve all hyperlinks to the site of interest (also called 'inlinks'). This was done using a number of search engines, because of their known instability and partiality of coverage (Lawrence and Giles 1998; Bar-Ilan 1999; Hellsten 2003; Wouters and Gerbec 2003). Searches for the fMRIDC case were done in the space of a few weeks, using six different engines, until no new hyperlinks could be found in the returned results. All hyperlinks were gathered into a table, the linking sites were subsequently visited and analysed, and notes taken about the presence of hyperlinks.

The mechanical aspect of this approach to creating the field was a double-edged sword which played on the anxiety, common to ethnographers, that something interesting is bound to happen if one leaves the field. On the one hand, using this kind of approach, (based on a specific trace, which would be either present or not) seemed to offer the promise of totally apprehending the field. On the other hand, the tools that were meant to perform this mechanical retrieval were known to be notoriously unstable and were a constant reminder that this approach is no less a filter than the embodied and co-present ethnographer.

In the second project, pursued with Elena Simakova, we still had lingering suspicions that there might be more out there, and that the field was being constituted through assumptions built into the search engines that might be discovered through the use of contrasting approaches. Specifically, we were concerned about the partiality of search coverage, and about the limitations of using the inlink search tools available on search engines. While we did not aim to retrieve data in a quantitative and exhaustive manner, we wanted to explore the potential diversity of users of databases and thus were interested in retrieving the greatest range possible. For this reason we chose to use two complementary strategies, via two search engines. First, we used the inlink function on Google advanced search, and retrieved web pages that contained a link to the web sites of interest. Second, we use the 'exact word combination' search function on AltaVista. We used word combinations that were highly specific to the web sites of interest. The first strategy generally provided fewer hits, while the second allowed us to retrieve sites that discussed the web site, without necessarily providing a hyperlink to it. The word combination search also provided more irrelevant links. For each set of results, we considered at least 100 hits, until the hits became repetitive.

For each linking site, we examined the context of the hyperlink (or textual reference), for the nature of the web site, the intended audience and the specific textual (or visual) context of the hyperlink. We see this approach as a way of operationalizing the notion that audiences are also active shapers of 'texts'. By indicating the qualities of the linked site (that is, a great site, an example not to be followed), links may also shape the perception of it (Beaulieu and Simakova, forthcoming). Partly because two researchers were pursuing the analysis from different locations, we set up a list of categories for labelling the features of linking sites. Figuring out which label to apply, however, still involved quite a bit of interpretive work, navigation and exploration of the linking sites and hyperlinks they contained. It is notoriously difficult to pinpoint the 'nature' of a web site. One common solution is to use indications contained in URLs, but this approach has serious shortcomings and can be very misleading. For example, in the Human Memory case, the site developers ensured that the 'popular' site contained the acronym uva (Universiteit van Amsterdam) in its URL as a trust-building mechanism, while the 'scientific' companion site did not. We chose to examine linking sites for the identity presented in terms of the content, rather than their URL addresses.

Hyperlinks helped us to elaborate the connectivity of the databases in terms of its embedding in particular contexts, and led to a number of potentially interesting actors and sites, including similar databasing projects in other countries, funding bodies interested in such initiatives, and other fields warning of possible controversies like that around the fMRIDC. Furthermore, we found certain information about the databases that was kept out of their official web sites. In this sense, the retrieval of hyperlinks to the databases pointed us to a kind of 'backstage' or to hidden agendas (Beaulieu and Simakova, forthcoming). Without stressing the value of an exposé of web site developers, we did find that other web sites pointed to less apparent aspects of the databases and highlighted 'silent partners' in the endeavours. As such, hyperlinks were telling of the alliances scientists are willing to make, in line with one of the original motivations of laboratory studies (Latour 1987). This may be one of the small ways in which the Internet provides more visibility to science, though it remains that presence on the web does not necessarily equate with accessibility of materials for all (Hine 2002).

Textured Connectivity

Our analysis of hyperlinks showed highly textured landscapes of hyperlinking contexts and roles of hyperlinks.

Context

We found pages on which the full URL of the site of interest was written out, but where the hyperlinking function was not implemented. We found this not only on parallel kinds of documents (PDF, PowerPoint files) but also on web pages, written in HTML. The reverse also holds: hyperlinks were found not only on HTML pages of individual or institutional web sites, but also in settings like discussion lists, where the URL of the database was part of a signature. These findings highlighted our assumptions about the way HTML might be used (or not, in this case). The way hyperlinks were also returned from places other than web pages further highlighted the difficulty in drawing boundaries of field sites using hyperlinks.

Specificity and Generality

Hyperlinks can vary enormously as to the way they are made specific or general. This is sometimes visible in the way the link is technologically implemented (to a specific photo), but we found many instances where the reference was very specific, although the URL given was to the general welcome page. For example, Walking with Woodlice was referred to as an example of a specific kind of web site and database design, for computer science students. This suggests that it might be useful to consider both specificity of presentation of a hyperlink, and of the way a hyperlink is constructed to lead to a more or less specific location in a site.

Timescapes of Hyperlinks

The creation of hyperlinks could frequently be situated in relation to a specific text and identifiable event (see also Schneider and Foot, Chapter 11 in this volume, for the concept of a 'storm' to describe a particular time dynamic of the creation of pages and hyperlinks). By looking at hyperlinks and their context closely, an 'origin' story could be reconstructed. Many hyperlinks were found in dated documents such as 'newsletters', and specifically embedded in sections of text that had been taken over from the press release announcing the databases. Typically, these hyperlinks had become 'buried' in their local settings. They were clearly visibly to search engines since we retrieved them, but they would be visible to a user of the site only with some effort, since the user would have to dig into the archives to see the hyperlink. This signals the need to distinguish a timescape or time value to hyperlinks. Some hyperlinks have a more 'temporary' prominence than others.

Embedded Hyperlinks

A further set of hyperlinks in the fMRIDC ethnography revealed an interesting aspect of connectivity of the database. These hyperlinks to the fMRIDC seemed to

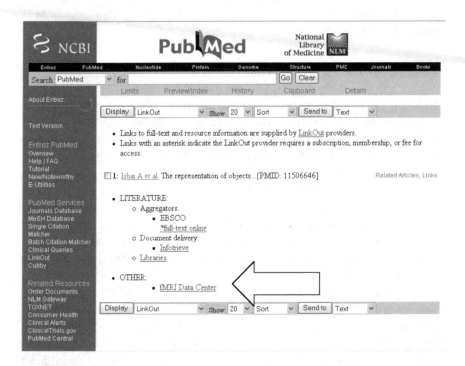

Figure 13.1 Linkout interface of PubMed, with hyperlink to the fMRIDC.

be located on PubMed web pages, but when we sought them out, an error message generated by the content management database indicated that the requested page could not be found. Only after exploring the PubMed web site and searching for articles contained in the fMRIDC did the source of these hyperlinks become clear. In other words, I had to find a way to elicit these traces, which the search engine had somehow picked up, by asking different questions via the site's search engine and examining the results very closely in a kind of ethnographic conversation with a database. It finally became clear that the hyperlinks were being automatically generated as part of a special function that served to connect to the fMRIDC with PubMed. In the PubMed database, abstracts of scientific articles are presented with a 'link out' function, which offers the reader a number of links to sources outside PubMed, to retrieve the full text of the article, information on the topic written for a general audience, or in this case, a link to the fMRIDC where the data associated with that particular scientific article can be found (Figure 13.1).

The way in which the fMRIDC piggybacks on the infrastructure of PubMed is potentially very significant, given the dominant role of PubMed for formal scientific communication in the biomedical field. The search for hyperlinks led to this discovery, though its significance became clear only through ethnographic exploration. An automated or formalized approach to hyperlink analysis would have treated these hyperlinks as noise.

Looking for the users' hyperlinks

Having retrieved and partly analysed these hyperlinks, I still wondered about the absence of 'users' in the set of hyperlinks retrieved. Few web sites of researchers or labs had been found, although I had expected they would exist since I knew these kinds of web pages often contained hyperlinks to community resources, such as software. I also wondered if the lack of hits leading to researchers' pages might not be simply due to the fact that their sites were not being crawled by search engines. The main change in emphasis that resulted, in terms of constituting the ethnographic field site, was that we shifted focus to 'potential linkers' rather than 'actual' linking sites. This was a way of changing the role of search engines in the creation of the site, so as to retrieve potentially contrasting patterns that might not be otherwise visible.

In order to check this, potential users, as articulated by the fMRIDC creators, were therefore sought.[7] At this point, the possibility of using social network analysis was considered. This move also seemed attractive as a way of 'scaling up' ethnographic methods.[8] Because social network analysis as a methodological tool tends to imply a flat, or undifferentiated, field of relations, however, it was difficult to incorporate into the ethnographic interpretative framework of this project. Where hyperlinks themselves are crucial and distinctions between patterns of linking are sought (Scharnhorst 2003), this combination of methods may be promising.

In this part of the project researchers who had submitted data to the database were identified. The first authors of the papers were especially targeted, since they are usually the ones who go through the process of inputting data into the database, and therefore have even greater contact with, and investment in it ('interested parties'). Personal web pages for a number of individuals were found in a first round, and this set was supplemented by the 'lab' web pages of these individuals (cognitive neuroscience is usually organized in labs of between four and ten researchers, working under the leadership of a senior researcher). All relevant pages were selected by human inspection, and hyperlinks were categorized.[9]

In the course of this process it became obvious that web sites and web pages themselves played a role in data-sharing activities that the fMRIDC itself was meant to support. While the sites were not cutting-edge instances of implementation of web technology, by exploring these web sites and being surprised by what they contained, I realized I had been treating these web sites as mainly 'text pages'. In this second phase of data collection, I came instead to consider web sites as little infrastructures for communicating and sharing data.

For example, researchers used web sites to provide images of their findings. Hyperlinks were also found which pointed to 'downloads' of computer programs for analysis, for building experiments or for calibrating instruments. Perhaps most striking in these results was that while researchers frequently listed their publications, with hyperlinks leading to abstracts and full texts, researchers (with a single exception) neither indicated that the data relating to an article were to be found in the fMRIDC, nor provided hyperlinks to it. There were also very few hyperlinks to the fMRIDC, thereby confirming to some extent the findings of inlink analysis.

The hyperlinks to other databases were especially closely examined, to try to understand why and how these were used. Of particular interest was the way hyperlinks to PubMed were implemented. In some cases, a hyperlink to PubMed was provided as part of a list of 'resources'. More often, however, the hyperlinks embedded a somewhat more complex function, and led to searches in the PubMed database. Researchers could embed into their personal page a link not only to PubMed, but also to the results of a search that yielded all their publications. Presumably this has a number of advantages for researchers, who do not need to update the page to have their publications up to date. It also indicates how a particular database comes to be aligned with the production of researchers (that is, the link implies that researchers believe their output will be found in PubMed). This also reinforces the point made above about the need to consider the specificity/generality of the implementation of a hyperlink.

Because of the relative prominence of PubMed as the main hyperlinked database in researchers' web sites, the results of the inlink analysis related to PubMed took on an increased importance. The embedding of the fMRIDC into the 'linkout' function of PubMed means that when researchers embed a search of PubMed into their hyperlinks, this move is also productive of connectivity to the fMRIDC. The alignment of PubMed and the fMRIDC had been raised explicitly in an early interview with the fMRIDC coordinator, but had not been considered to be particularly significant. The focus on hyperlinks, however, revealed that the embedding of the fMRIDC into the PubMed infrastructure may actually be one of the ways in which it has most visibility and integration into the ways of working of scientists. At this point in the research, web sites which had originally been conceived of as a place where hyperlinks were created, functioning as nodes to 'extend' the connectivity of the infrastructure of the database, were explicitly reconceptualized as 'little infrastructures' in their own right, working spaces as well as representational spaces.[10]

An Ethnographic View of Connectivity

It can be awkward to write a chapter on ethnographic methods, because so much of ethnography is about learning, and thus hard to convey without reproducing the entire ethnographic account. In this chapter, the shift from seeing hyperlinks as constitutive of a relevant field, to investigating how hyperlinks themselves are constituted, is presented in a somewhat more linear manner than occurred over a period of eighteen months. In constituting a field site through using hyperlinks as a trace, a number of dimensions of hyperlinks were highlighted which had not been considered at the outset of the project. It is a common trope in ethnographies that their main results show the complexity of phenomena and the difficulty in defining them. This is also the case here, although given the early stages of the exploration of knowledge production on the Internet this should not be an unforgivable result. In what follows I have tried to use instances where the results of the ethnography pointed to 'more complex' definitions to relate them to other frameworks for defining connectivity.

Defining Hyperlinks

In the work presented here, the unit of analysis was not strictly the hyperlink, but rather the use of a hyperlink as a trace that can contribute to constructing a field site. In order to understand the practices and meanings occurring in the context elaborated on the basis of hyperlinks, hyperlinks themselves had to be theorized. It became evident that different dimensions of hyperlinks exist, some more symbolic and others more technological. The symbolic value of hyperlinks has been noted by Slater and Miller, who drew an analogy between webrings and the anthropologically famous Kula ring where symbolic goods were exchanged (Miller and Slater 2000). The exact fit of this analogy is contested (Helmreich 2003), but a symbolic dimension is clearly present in hyperlinking practices and should not be ignored in favour of purely rational accounts of motivations for linking.

The complex nature of hyperlinks as illustrated here is useful in thinking about the possible transposition of practices like citation analysis to the context of the web. The way we examined hyperlinks resembles 'citation context analysis: the close examination of the text surrounding footnote numbers in scientific writing' (Cozzens 1985: 133), in order to discover social and cognitive relations in communities. But while the analogy with citations is powerful, the functional aspect of hyperlinks must not be neglected. As such, hyperlinks are themselves technologies which tell a story, and have value beyond their equivalence to citations (Rousseau 1997).

It was especially fruitful to see hyperlinks as a valuable trace that might enable the conjoined study of the meaning and context of connectivity of databases. In this research, considering what was being said about the databases, and by whom, provided insight into the meanings attributed to the database. But just as certain standard components of Internet practices can provide subtle contextualizing clues (Baym 1995b), hyperlinks are traces of both action and representation. The specificity of a hyperlink, in terms of the way in which it is discussed on the linking site, or the specificity of the functionality of the hyperlink (linking to a specific image on a site) is a good illustration of this point. Furthermore, hyperlinks not only are embedded in web sites which give them meaning, but also can trigger events (Wouters 2001) such as searches into another databased web site. Connectivity, as elaborated here, is a move away from studies that posit that behaviours are equivalent to text on the Internet. A focus on seeing the positive or negative 'endorsement' function of hyperlinks does not take into account the infrastructural aspects of hyperlinks, as structuring not only cognitive elements but also a space of action – in our case, the flow of data. Vann makes a similar point about the significance of representational infrastructures that enable institutional accounts of 'situated' work (Vann 2003).Without wanting to reify the distinction between action and language, there does seem to be a contrast here that is worth noting. A hyperlink is a trace of many things, and its functions can be more diverse than the usual 'linking one web page with another'.

Hyperlinks in Time

Hyperlinks can also be traces that have a punctual or structural character. The persistence of web pages has received attention (Koehler 2002), but as far as I know, the persistence or time-related prominence of hyperlinks has not been problematized. In the inlink studies of the various databases we repeatedly found subgroups of hyperlinks that could be traced to a specific event and text. This subgroup of hyperlinks hints at the use of the Internet as news medium, in which the function of the hyperlink is to provide further information or to illustrate a news story.

Other hyperlinks (found in frames, for example) seemed to indicate a more persistent interest in the databases. If hyperlinks are to be considered as indicators of social relations, these might usefully be differentiated on the basis of hyperlinks with a punctual versus structural character. Connectivity would then gain a time valence.

Connectivity and Infrastructure

Other approaches to studying the Internet have also taken connectivity as a key feature in creating their object. The creation of a web sphere, for example, also draws upon hyperlinks as meaningful indicators of relevance to a specific subject (Foot et al. 2003b; Schneider and Foot, Chapter 11 in this volume). Web sphere work to date has often used specific criteria to determine which hyperlinks are considered for further analysis (that is, official web sites produced by individual candidates), so that possible sources of hyperlinks are therefore determined a priori. As a consequence, the field is constituted in terms of standardized 'nodes'. This move enables statistical analyses about frequency of hyperlinking which remain beyond the reach of our approach. In being more open to the kinds of linkers we might find (things, infrastructures, as well as persons or institutions), we were able to give an account of the infrastructural layers that shape the relations with and visibility of the fMRIDC. As constructed in our approach, the field shows that linked sites are therefore not simply 'contiguous' or 'connected', but can rather display a range of connections that can vary greatly. Rather than a sphere around a single reference point, a field that takes infrastructure into account is closer to a complex origami figure in which multiple planes enfold each other.

Our examples show that infrastructural routines can constrain the way links are made and whether they come to exist at all. Social and institutional forces, personal preferences and infrastructural elements may have different weights in shaping how hyperlinks are created. To give one specific example of how these assumptions might be reviewed, the presence of hyperlinks in 'sidebars' (frames) is usually considered as an anomaly in webometric analyses. These 'violate . . . the implicit assumption of hyperlink analysis; that each hyperlink should be of approximately the same importance as the others. As an example, clearly a thousand automatically created hyperlinks should carry less weight than a hundred created by the decisions of different academics' (Park and Thelwall 2003). Arguably, the decision to incorporate a hyperlink into a sidebar can indicate structural involvement, which might be more meaningful than punctual inclusion of a hyperlink.[11] Whatever the case may be, this relative weighing might best be explored rather than assumed to be anomalous.

Conclusion

If connectivity is to be taken as a feature of a network structure, it is therefore best understood as a complex phenomenon. An ethnographic approach to investigate the components of connectivity has been presented here, and it is hoped will contribute to tracing the values and aspirations embedded in network structures (Scharnhorst 2003). If part of the original motivation for ethnography in the laboratory was to visit the place where knowledge was said to originate, the same holds for taking online settings seriously as a site where knowledge is also arising. Networked knowledge production, however, challenges the traditional approaches to constructing the field. The traces chosen as constitutive of the field in our research led to a complex, multilayered understanding of networks around the various databases investigated. They also enabled us to see the field as populated by various kinds of socio-technical actors. Paying attention to aspects of connectivity discussed here, including the specificity, origin, timescape, and symbolic and infrastructural dimensions of hyperlinks, may help to build a richer notion of various instantiations of the Internet. This approach also speaks to recent debates about over-investment of researchers in the textual view of the Internet. Given that we were looking for representations of infrastructure, and ended up finding more infrastructure in these representations, this approach may also do a better job of accounting for the material aspects of networks and activities on the web.

Notes

1. The association of a particular geographical area with a particular set of concerns in anthropology has been noted (Gupta and Ferguson 1997), and the same dynamic seems to be present in the study of the Internet, which has been constituted as the location for studies of community and identity.
2. The databases studied were:
   - Functional Magnetic Resonance Imaging Data Center (http://lx50. fmridc.org/f/fmridc) (accessed 4 November 2004).
   Four databases in the public databases project:
   - North American Reporting Center for Amphibian Malformations, NARCAM (http://www.npwrc.usgs.gov/narcam/narcam.htm, now incorporated into http://frogweb.nbii.gov/, both accessed 4 November 2004).
   - Walking with Woodlice, WWW (http://www.nhm.ac.uk/interactive/ woodlice/) (accessed 4 November 2004).
   - Brits in South America, BiSA (http://www.bisa.btinternet.co.uk/) (accessed 4 November 2004).
   - Human Memory (http://memory.uva.nl/) (accessed 4 November 2004).

The latter four databases were studied in a project on trust and databases open to the public, pursued with Elena Simakova, at the Science Culture and Communication Programme, University of Bath, UK and the Saïd Business School, Oxford. For further details on the project, see Simakova (2002).

3. Tracing such an accession number cannot be done using traditional biblio-metric techniques (that is, these are not included in references) and would require full text analysis techniques. The same problem is encountered if one wishes to analyse hyperlinks in scientific articles or references (see Wouters and De Vries 2004). This challenges database developers and funding agen-cies to look beyond traditional bibliometric tools for evaluations of databases and data-sharing.

4. The study of bookmarks on browsers is another approach to the study of users' practices, and requires close contact with individual users (Henwood et al. 2002).

5. Hyperlinks are relevant to search engines in two ways. First, a number of search engines use the number of inlinks to determine the relevance of certain web pages (including Google, which uses the PageRank algorithm). Second, all search engines use crawlers to collect links for their databases, and these crawl results are shaped by the hyperlink structures on the Web (Lynch 2001; Thelwall 2003a).

6. Rogers and Marres (2000) have developed a two-pronged approach to appre-hend these two aspects, though hyperlinks and content words are separated in the automated data retrieval and analysis process.

7. Han Park participated in some of the data collection and suggested possible processing of the data, using aspects of social network analysis.

8. The general need for this prompted by the study of infrastructures has been noted by Star (1999), while Newman (1998) has pointed to the need to develop ways of navigating shifting network topographies when doing multi-sited ethnography.

9. This is a community I have been studying since 1994.

10. The web pages have functions that fall quite squarely into the common defi-nitions of data-sharing. This was one indication of the ways researchers shared data, 'closer to home', in their own personal or lab spaces. Earlier fieldwork also showed that researchers have 'backstage' areas of their web sites, which are either accessible internally, to other insiders (of the lab, the university) or are simply not visible under most circumstances. These are spaces on web sites that are not hyperlinked, and are therefore 'protected' or made private by virtue of their being unlinked. Researchers may then invite collaborators to these spaces by providing them with a hyperlink.

11. Research on the use of hyperlinks in published texts has demonstrated that

structural embedding (rather than individual decision or disciplinary conventions) is the main determinant for the presence of hyperlinks (see Wouters and De Vries 2004).

–14–

Epilogue: Methodological Concerns and Innovations in Internet Research

Nicholas W. Jankowski and Martine van Selm

This book represents a valuable addition to the growing literature on Internet research methods. The authors address important and sometimes problematic features of empirically investigating Internet-based phenomena. At the same time, the collection – like previous forays into this methodological niche area – attends to only a portion of the entire array of issues and concerns. And, the chapters as a whole leave one wondering: what next, what still needs to be undertaken?

In this short epilogue we cannot cover the entire gamut of issues and concerns related to Internet research. We do, however, wish to indicate where methodological clarity is increasing and where more work is needed. In this regard, we wish to contribute to establishment of an agenda for methodological refinement of Internet studies.

As a first task related to that objective, we briefly review the history of new media and new methods. We consider the contributions of this present collection according to a typology of methodological innovations devised for a previous collection in this genre. This exercise produces insight into the kind of methodological innovations currently being developed.

The second task related to our overall objective in this epilogue is to share some of the tensions and problems one of us is encountering in co-launching an international cross-country comparative research project about the use of the Internet in political campaigns. These experiences may broaden our collective awareness of the complexities of doing certain kinds of Internet research not represented by the chapters in this book.

Third, we pose suggestions as to where energy should be spent in the search for solutions to some of the methodological issues and problems plaguing Internet research. In a sense, many of these suggestions are generic and applicable to other arenas of inquiry; still, we feel much is to be gained through attention to them in relation to the empirical study of the Internet.

On Methodological Innovations

A frequent swan song is that Internet research is, in some way, 'different' from other forms of social science investigation and, therefore, requires unique, yet-to-be-refined methods of study. Christine Hine examines this sentiment in the introduction to this volume; it has been voiced frequently elsewhere and constitutes the implicit message of the seminar series on which this book is based and other conferences about new media and new methods.[1] Our position is that this statement is suspect and that much more is to be gained through application of conventional research methodologies and practices than those who are on the vanguard of Internet research innovation seem willing to acknowledge.

That position having been stated, it is important to realize that innovation at a range of levels has been going on in the social sciences for a very long time. On taking an historical view of methodological development in the social sciences, it appears that innovation has been on the agenda for decades; it could be argued that innovation has been the order of the day since the inception of empirical social science itself. For example, both Robert Merton and Paul Lazarsfeld made contributions in this area, particularly with regard to the integration of social survey studies with in-depth interviews (for example, Merton, Fiske and Kendall 1956). Eugene Webb and his colleagues essentially invented unobtrusive observations, of which present-day examinations of log data are an extrapolation (Webb et al. 1966).

And, when we look at the historical development of a single method, content analysis, we see that the twentieth century has been characterized by methodological innovations induced by both developments in society and the social sciences. Examples of societal developments that had an influence on the method include increases in the popularity of and concern about newspaper content (for example, Speed 1893), narrative film (Payn Fund studies: Dale 1935) and television (Gerbner's Cultural Indicators studies, for example, Gerbner and Gross 1976). Other examples stem from developments around the Second World War and, later, the increased importance of election campaigns in the United States, resulting in publications such as *Propaganda Analysis* (George 1959) and *Language of Politics* (Lasswell and Leites 1965).

Somewhat later a qualitative turn took place in the social sciences, contributed to, among others, by Derek Phillips (1971, 1973) and by many of the authors in the Jensen and Jankowski (1991) volume on qualitative research methods. Extending the scope of interest to include the sciences as a whole, a large number of scholars have argued for acknowledgement of the human element and of power bases in the scientific enterprise (for example, Kuhn 1970 [1962]; Woolgar 1988).

Turning to new media, one of the classic volumes on research methods as applied to this area of study was prepared by Williams, Rice and Rogers (1988) in the late 1980s. As with present-day Internet researchers, they were concerned with how best to study the – then – *new* media. They proposed essentially four things. First, they suggested building on already existing research methods; second, they recommended looking, at the same time, for alternative methods and designs; third, they advocated consideration of triangulating the methods selected; and fourth, they urged attention to the three main paradigms prominent in social science research – the positivist, interpretative and critical approaches to empirical investigations.

Not long after the Williams, Rice and Rogers book, the Internet made its public entrance, and just a little more than a decade later the first volume appeared that examined Internet research methods (Jones 1999). The editor of that book, *Doing Internet Research*, brought together a group of scholars who were at the forefront of investigating this new mode of communication and information exchange. Chapters were included on network analysis, online surveys, unobtrusive measures, textual and literary analysis, participant observation and a form of action research.

Other books have since contributed to refinement of the research methods for studying the Internet. Mann and Stewart (2000), for example, produced a textbook-style volume devoted to online research. Batinic, Reips and Bosnjak (2002) compiled a reader reflecting a wide range of social science methods applied to online environments. Markham (1998) published a monograph with a detailed section on her ethnographic study of online discourse. And – obvious to the contributors of this book as well as to many of its readers – Hine (2000) laid the groundwork for understanding how ethnography can be performed in virtual environments.

Much of this work is generally considered pioneering and perhaps even 'innovative'. A basic definition of methodological innovation might serve as a good starting point for understanding what is meant by the term: 'Methodological innovation refers to the use of original or modification of conventional research approaches, designs and methods in the study of new media' (Jankowski 1999: 368). In the publication where that definition appeared, it was argued that innovations can take place at different levels of the research enterprise; three were suggested:

- The *macro* level, which deals mainly with epistemological issues and which often finds grounding in one of the three main approaches to social science research: positivism, interpretative investigation, and critical analytical studies.
- The *mezzo* level, which is mainly concerned with issues regarding research design and strategy, such as employment of multiple methods, development of longitudinal studies and consideration of different theoretical and disciplinary approaches.

- The *micro* level, which is concerned with specific methods and techniques and includes such topics as gathering log data and conducting web surveys.

This typology of levels of methodological innovation was applied to the chapters in *Doing Internet Research*. In a similar fashion, we have applied it to the chapters in this volume. Without delving into the categorization procedures, the exercise results in the overview presented in Figure 14.1.

The results are strikingly similar to those found when contributions to the Jones book were examined: most innovations presented reflect the micro level of methodological innovation. In this book, it is only the introductory chapter by Hine that can lay claim to substantial concern for innovations at the macro level. Two of the chapters emphasize issues related to research design (the mezzo level) and the remaining ten chapters address one or more forms of innovation at the micro level of research, although sometimes with more general, mezzo concerns. Some eight of the chapters treat one or more facets of ethnography or interpretive research; only four chapters deal with research methods generally considered distinct from the interpretatative approach. The book is, then, very much an exploration of innovations in interpretative research methods, which is perhaps its overriding strength. Still, other forms of research – the experimental method, survey research, systematic observation, unobtrusive research procedures – are either under-represented or just plain missing.

Chapter	Author	Topic	Methods, Issues	Main Level of Innovations
1	Hine	general overview	online ethnography, ethics	macro
2	Joinson	designing virtual methods	online surveys	micro
3	Kivits	online interviewing	email interviews	micro
4	Orgad	online and offline study	online ethnography	micro
5	Sanders	online sex work	online ethnography, ethics	micro
6	Rutter and Smith	presence and absence of researcher in online setting	online ethnography, ethics	micro
7	Forte	sites for ethnography	constructing sites	micro
8	Dodge	mapping in virtual research	visual displays	mezzo
9	Mackay	online and offline study	online ethnography	micro
10	Guimarães	anthropology in cyberspace	online ethnography	micro
11	Schneider and Foot	web sphere analysis	analysis of web content	mezzo
12	Park and Thelwall	network analysis and hyperlink study	network analysis	mezzo and micro
13	Beaulieu	linking and ethnography	link analysis	micro

Figure 14.1 Overview of chapter topics and levels of methodological innovations.

In a sense, these observations are not particularly surprising. Beginning with the emphasis on ethnography, it is entirely understandable that delegates at the seminars from which these chapters emerged felt affinity with the work in the area performed by Hine (2000), the organizer of the seminars. Regarding the attention given to micro level forms of innovation, it is generally the case that researchers tend to 'stick close to their data' and to their own research designs rather than philosophize about or reflect on broader issues like those represented at the mezzo and macro levels. Still, there is a consequence to such emphasis: the degree and kind of reflection so often advocated – including that by Hine in her introduction to the volume – is difficult to achieve.

Internet and Elections Project: Concerns and Tensions

It may be valuable to share information on a current research project to illustrate the tensions at play between traditional social science research methods and Internet studies attempting to be innovative. One of us is involved in coordinating, together with colleagues in Asia and North America, an international project on how the Internet is employed during election campaigns.[2] The project builds on previous Web sphere studies by Foot and Schneider (2002; Schneider and Foot 2002), who describe this research method in Chapter 11 in this book. The central research question of the Internet and Elections Project is: *In what ways and to what extent are online structures for political action produced within different political systems during electoral campaigns?* The project involves collaboration in data collection, methodological focus and analysis techniques among nationally based research teams distributed across Asia, Europe and North America.

Two dozen researchers from Asian and European countries met in Singapore in March 2004 for an intensive training workshop in the research methods being employed in the project. In the training, emphasis was placed on identification of political sites for selection in the study, quantitative coding of the presence of a range of site features, and provisions for open-ended note-taking on the sites examined.

Three fundamental issues arose during this training workshop relevant to the concerns of this epilogue:

- difficulties in creating a cross-national investigation
- differences in academic cultures regarding quality of data
- integration of interpretative and quantitative data.

The first point concerns one of the central features of the Internet – its global reach. Surprisingly and in contrast to this feature, most research on the Internet is centred in Anglo-American cultural contexts.[3] This project attempts to overcome this limitation by comparatively investigating the role of the Internet as played out in a nationally based political activity, elections. We have intentionally included a large number of countries outside the Anglo-American sphere with the intention of gaining insights from these other regions into how the Internet is being integrated into the political process.

This objective, however, is more easily stated than enacted. One of the things that became obvious during the training workshop was how difficult it is to construct an instrument for coding web sites across cultures. Both the suitability and interpretation of coding items by researchers from different cultures and countries was problematic. This is, of course, a classic problem in international comparative research for which there is not an entirely satisfactory solution. In the Internet and Elections Project we decided to employ a relatively basic quantitative instrument for identification of site features and are hoping that the open-ended note-taking about the observed features will provide substance and interpretation to the quantitative feature analysis.

The second issue, academic cultures and quality of data, refers to the strong desire among some members of the project to be able to generate data with sufficient 'respectability' and 'robustness' to be suitable for publication in major communication journals. During the training we placed considerable emphasis on the need for measuring intercoder reliability and noted that should some of the data for particular country elections not satisfy the established level of reliability, then that data would not be used for the comparative analyses in certain journal submissions. Intercoder reliability scores are considered an essential requirement in traditional content analysis. For some academic journals it is mandatory that these scores be reported in order for submissions to be considered and reviewed.

An alternative position, considered by the project coordinators, would have been to essentially disregard such journal requirements, which are maintained mainly by American academic institutions.[4] These two positions – adherence to certain standards for data versus a more open, explorative approach in which the focus is on developing meaningful measures that do not necessarily guarantee high intercoder reliabilities – date back to the classical division between qualitative and quantitative modes of research. For many decades, the dominant paradigm has been – and in some academic quarters, still is – the quantitative paradigm, from which concern for intercoder reliability stems.

The tension is in part culturally based: requirements are imposed by a variety of institutions (journal editors, university tenure committees, and other 'watchdogs' of research standards) to perform empirical study in a manner such that it is acceptable for publication in particular kinds of academic journals. These requirements, it should be clear, are not universal in nature, but are imposed by members of a segment of the scholarly community, often to the detriment of less established and less powerful sectors of the same community.

The third issue, integration of qualitative and quantitative findings, relates to the previous issue. During our training workshop we placed primary emphasis on instructing researchers in site identification and in handling the feature coding instrument and, because of time constraints and in the interest of achieving comparability of data, little attention was given to procedures for qualitative note-taking. We did, however, encourage participating researchers to develop more detailed guidelines in accordance with the political and cultural contexts in which they were working.

Towards an Agenda for Methodological Innovation

The third topic we wish to address in this epilogue is issues and concerns that merit placement on a methodological agenda for Internet research. We have organized our suggestions along two of the three levels of innovation introduced earlier: the macro and mezzo levels; suggestions at the micro level are more than adequately covered in the preceding chapters in this volume.

Macro Level

At the macro level, we have one overriding recommendation: acknowledgement of the mutual value and integration of the three approaches to social science research, the positivist, the critical analytical and the interpretative. All too often, researchers representing these traditions place themselves in opposing camps and engage in self-defensive tactics with regard to the 'others'. We regard such an oppositional stance as unproductive. There is, from our perspective, no single, authoritative way of knowing in the scientific enterprise. At the same time, we personally are reluctant to embrace Feyeraband's (1975) dictum of 'anything goes'. Rather, we advocate openness for the methodological stances and approaches of the various 'schools' and streams prominent in Internet research.

Mezzo Level

At the mezzo level we recommend four areas for further work. First, it is imperative that research designs be developed incorporating the three paradigms that Williams et al. (1988) identified. Concretely, this involves constructing research designs that include, for example, (quasi) experiments along with ethnographic studies. We are not, to be clear, advocating the conventional arrangement where a qualitative exploratory component precedes what the design is 'really' about: the quantitative measure of identified variables. This often reflects a biased and inappropriate combination of the qualitative and quantitative components in a research design.

A word of caution is important with regard to such integrative efforts. The term triangulation often is used to reflect this intent. Denzin (1970) introduced this term decades ago and then suggested a wide variety of forms of triangulation, involving data collection, data analysis, researchers, disciplines and theories. The metaphor triangulation implies that a closer approximation to 'truth' is possible through the intersection of different sources for data, or through employment of different researchers, sometimes coming from different disciplines and subscribing to different theoretical perspectives. In our view, the implication of the metaphor is misleading.

Taking the use of different datasets as an example, it does not follow that one of these datasets (say, open-ended interviews) necessarily provides more truth-value than another dataset (say, survey research findings). The easy case is when findings from the two datasets converge: more often than not, however, the findings from one dataset do not complement those from the other. In such a case the researcher is left with different, sometimes diametrically opposed, results from the two datasets. In such situations, the triangulation procedures followed do not contribute to greater truth-value; all we can really conclude is that differences result from different modes of measurement (see further Schrøder et al. 2003: 356–360).

Second, we recommend continued work on the ethical issues embedded in Internet research.[5] In the introduction to this volume, Hine elaborates on many of these issues and makes reference to the Association of Internet Researchers (AoIR) ethics committee work. As important as the contributions of this committee are, the relativistic stance taken by that committee is disturbing, when reduced to a position where all actions become ethically equal. Hine notes in the introductory chapter to this book that there is no universal set of ethical principles for Internet research; this observation, however, cannot be taken as an 'excuse' for researchers doing whatever they want.

Third, we have already noted the importance of developing cross-national studies, preferably longitudinal in nature. We believe it is time to go beyond the individual, often isolated case studies, and strive towards projects encompassing multiple methods, across time, intended to elaborate on central theoretical perspectives. At the same time, and this is our fourth area of recommendation, we are cognizant of the importance of what we like to call 'designs of engagement', whereby researchers take an active role in the formulation of policy and action within concrete settings. Typical designs of engagement are action research and participatory research forms of inquiry.

By way of general conclusion to this epilogue, we urge continued effort to develop innovative solutions to problems encountered in doing empirical research related to the Internet. Such innovations will increase in value when developed from a basis in traditional social science methodology, be that interpretative, positivistic or critical in nature. An ongoing structure would facilitate this endeavour and complement the usual opportunities for conference presentations, journal publications and contributions to edited volumes such as this. Hine refers in her introduction to the research group in Ljubljana that has concentrated on web-based and other online forms of survey research. We suggest that a similar initiative should be undertaken with a somewhat broader mandate, concerned with research methodology and the Internet, in which scholars from different disciplines and perspectives can exchange experiences and initiatives. This book and the seminar series on which it is based is, in fact, illustrative of such an initiative, as is the annual conference on new media and new research mentioned earlier. We would hope these important but dispersed initiatives could be brought together in such a manner as to improve deliberation and dissemination of methodological innovations for Internet research.

Acknowledgements

We wish to thank Kirsten Foot, Randy Kluver and Steve Schneider for their comments on an earlier draft of this epilogue, particularly as related to the second section.

Notes

1. Information on the 2003 and 2004 New Research for New Media conferences, held respectively in Minneapolis and Barcelona, may be found at: http://www.inms.umn.edu/convenings/newresearch/index.htm (accessed 4 November 2004).
2. For information on this project, see: http://oase.uci.kun.nl/~jankow/elections/ and http://www.ntu.edu.sg/home/trkluver/asefhome.html (accessed 4 November 2004). For a general overview of the project see document by Foot, Jankowski et al. (2003a) available on the first URL.
3. There are exceptions, such as the World Internet Project; see http://www.worldinternetproject.net (accessed 4 November 2004).
4. Some American communication departments are known to 'dictate' in which journals non-tenured staff members are expected to publish. The emphasis on certain journals, notably those that are included in the ISI database, is not only an American practice; institutions in the UK and in some countries on the Continent employ much the same criterion for acceptable publishing venues.
5. A theme issue of the journal *Ethics and Information Technology*, published in 2002, is illustrative of advances that can and are being made. See especially the contribution by Walther (2002).

References

Adamic, L. A. (1999), 'The Small World Web', *Proceedings of Third European Conference of Research and Advanced Technology for Digital Libraries*, ECDL, http://www.hpl.hp.com/shl/papers/smallworld/smallworldpaper.html (accessed 17 March 2004).

—— and Adar, E. (2003), 'Friends and Neighbors on the Web', *Social Networks*, 25(3): 211–30.

—— and Huberman, B. A. (2000), 'The Nature of Markets in the World Wide Web', *Quarterly Journal of Electronic Commerce* 1(1): 5–12.

—— Buyukkokten, O. and Adar, E. (2003), 'A Social Network Caught in the Web', *First Monday*, 8(6), http://www.firstmonday.dk/issues/issue8_6/adamic/ (accessed 27 January 2004).

Agre, P. (1994), 'Net Presence', *Computer-Mediated Communication Magazine*, 1(4), http://www.december.com/cmc/mag/1994/aug/presence.html (accessed 8 January 2004).

Akrich, M. and Méadel, C. (2002), 'Prendre ses médicaments / prendre la parole: les usages des médicaments par les patients dans les listes de discussion electroniques', *Sciences Sociales et Santé*, 20(1): 89–114.

Albert, R., Jeong, H. and Barabási, A.-L. (1999), 'Diameter of the World Wide Web', *Nature*, 401(9): 130–1.

Amit, V. (2000), 'Introduction: Constructing the Field', in V. Amit (ed.), *Constructing the Field: Ethnographic Fieldwork in the Contemporary World*, London and New York: Routledge, pp. 1–18.

Antoun, R. T. (1989), *Muslim Preacher in the Modern World*, Princeton, NJ: Princeton University Press.

Archer, J. L. (1980), 'Self-Disclosure', in D. Wegner & R. Vallacher (eds), *The Self in Social Psychology*, London: Oxford University Press, pp. 183–204.

Arms, W., Adkins, R., Ammen, C. and Hayes, A. (2001), 'Collecting and Preserving the Web: The MINERVA Prototype', *RLG DigiNews*, 5(2), http://www.rlg.org/preserv/diginews/diginews5-2.html (accessed 25 February 2004).

Atkinson, R. and Flint, J. (2001), 'Accessing Hidden and Hard-to-Reach Populations: Snowball Research Strategies', *Social Research Update*, summer 2001(33). http://www.soc.surrey.ac.uk/sru/SRU33.html (accessed 25 February 2004).

Bakardjieva, M. and Smith, R. (2001), 'The Internet in Everyday Life: Computer Networking from the Standpoint of the Domestic User', *New Media and Society*, 3(1): 67–83.

Bampton, R. and Cowton, C. J. (2002), 'The E-Interview', *Forum Qualitative Sozialforschung / Forum: Qualitative Social Research*, 3(2), http://www.quali-tative-research.net/fqs/fqs-eng.htm (accessed 23 January 2004).

Bargh, J. A. and McKenna, K. Y. A. (2004), 'The Internet and Social Life', *Annual Review of Psychology*, 55: 573–90.

Bargh, J. A., McKenna, K. Y. A. and Fitzsimons, G. M. (2002), 'Can You See the Real Me? Activation and Expression of the True Self on the Internet', *Journal of Social Issues*, 58(1): 33–48.

Bar-Ilan, J. (1999), 'Search Engine Results over Time – A Case Study on Search Engine Stability', *Cybermetrics* 2–3(1), http://www.cindoc.csic.es/cybermet-rics/articles/v2i1p1.html (accessed 17 March 2004).

Barnes, B. (1985), *About Science*, Oxford: Blackwell.

—— Bloor, D. and Henry, J. (1996), *Scientific Knowledge: A Sociological Analysis*, London: Athlone.

Barnett, G. A. and Park, H. W. (2003), 'The Structure of International Internet Flows', paper presented to the Fourth International Conference of the Association of Internet Researchers, Toronto, Canada, October.

Barnett, G. A., Sung, E. J., Lin, J., Hung, H. Y. and Park, H. W. (2003), 'An Examination of Canada's Interprovincial Networks', paper presented to the International Sunbelt Social Network Conference XXIII, Cancun, Quintana Roo, Mexico, February.

Barron, G. and Yechiam, E. (2002), 'Private E-mail Requests and the Diffusion of Responsibility', *Computers in Human Behaviour*, 18(5): 507–20.

Barthes, R. (1977) *Image, Music, Text*, London: Fontana.

Batinic, B., Reips, U.-D. and Bosnjak, M. (eds) (2002), *Online Social Sciences*, Göttingen: Hogrefe and Huber.

Bauman, R. (1992a), 'Introduction', in R. Bauman (ed.), *Folklore, Cultural Performances and Popular Entertainment*, Oxford: Oxford University Press, pp. xiii–xxi.

—— (1992b), 'Performance', in R. Bauman (ed.), *Folklore, Cultural Perform-ances and Popular Entertainment*, Oxford: Oxford University Press, pp. 41–49.

Baym, N. K. (1995a), 'The Emergence of Community in Computer-Mediated Communication', in S. Jones (ed.), *CyberSociety*, Newbury Park, CA: Sage, pp. 138–163.

—— (1995b), 'From Practice to Culture on Usenet', in S. L. Star (ed.), *Cultures of Computing*, Cambridge, MA; Blackwell, pp. 29–52.

—— (2000), *Tune In, Log On: Soaps, Fandom, and Online Community*, Thousand Oaks, CA: Sage.

Beaulieu, A. (2004), 'Mediating Ethnography: Objectivity and the Making of Ethnographies of the Internet', *Social Epistemology*, 18(2–3): 139–164.

—— and Park, H. W. (eds) (2003), *The Form and the Feel: Combining Approaches for the Study of Networks on the Internet*, special issue of *Journal of Computer Mediated Communication*, 8(4), http://www.ascusc.org/jcmc/vol8/issue4/ (accessed 25 February 2004).

—— and Simakova, E. (forthcoming), 'Databases on the World Wide Web: Exploring Trust and Data Gathering in Knowledge Production on the Internet'.

Bennett, T. and Woollacott, J. (1987), *Bond and Beyond: The Political Career of a Popular Hero*, London: Macmillan.

Benoit, W. J. and Benoit: J. (2000), 'The Virtual Campaign: Presidential Primary Websites in Campaign 2000', *American Communication Journal*, 3(3), http://acjournal.org/holdings/vol3/Iss3/rogue4/benoit.html (accessed 25 February 2004).

Ben-Ze'ev, A. (2003), 'Privacy, Emotional Closeness, and Openness in Cyberspace', *Computers in Human Behaviour*, 19(4): 451–67.

Berelson, B. (1952), *Content Analysis in Communication Research*, Glencoe, IL: Free Press.

Berg, S. (1988), 'Snowball Sampling', in S. Kotz and N. L. Johnson (eds), *Encyclopaedia of Statistical Sciences*, vol. 8, New York: John Wiley, pp. 528–532.

Bernardo, A. (1994), 'Um Novo Tipo de 'Impulso' na Cidade: Um Estudo do Serviço Telefônico Disque Amizade de Florianópolis', Social Anthropology master's dissertation, Federal University of Santa Catarina (UFSC), Florianópolis, Brazil.

Bijker, W. E. (1995), *Of Bicycles, Bakelite and Bulbs: Towards a Theory of Sociotechnical Change*, Cambridge, MA: MIT Press.

Birnbaum, M. H. (2004), 'Human Research and Data Collection via the Internet', *Annual Review of Psychology*, 55: 803–32.

Björneborn, L. (2003), 'Small-World Link Structures in an Academic Web Space – A Library and Information Science Approach', PhD thesis, Royal School of Library and Information Science, Copenhagen, Denmark.

Blaut, J. M., Stea, D., Spencer, C. and Blades, M. (2003), 'Mapping as a Cultural and Cognitive Universal', *Annals of the Association of American Geographer*, 93(1): 165–85.

Bodum, L. and Kjems, E. (2002), 'Mapping Virtual Worlds', in L. Qvortrup (ed.), *Virtual Space: Spatiality in Virtual Inhabited 3D Worlds*, London: Springer, pp. 75–92.

Booth-Kewley, S., Edwards, J. E. & Rosenfeld: (1992), 'Impression Management, Social Desirability, and Computer Administration of Attitude Questionnaires: Does the Computer Make a Difference?', *Journal of Applied Psychology*, 77(4): 562–6.

Borgman, C. and Furner, J. (2002), 'Scholarly Communication and Bibliometrics', in B. Cronin (ed.), *Annual Review of Information Science and Technology*, 36, Medford, NJ: Information Today.

Börner, K. and Penumarthy, S. (2003), 'Social Diffusion Patterns in Three-Dimensional Virtual Worlds', *Information Visualization*, 2(3): 182–98.

Bourdieu: (1984), *Distinction: a Social Critique of the Judgement of Taste*, London: Routledge and Kegan Paul.

Bowker, G. C. (2000), 'Biodiversity Datadiversity', *Social Studies of Science*, 30(5): 643–84.

—— and Star, S. L. (1999), *Sorting Things Out: Classification and its Consequences*, Cambridge, MA: MIT Press.

Brin, S. and Page, L. (1998), 'The Anatomy of a Large Scale Hypertextual Web Search Engine', *Computer Networks and ISDN Systems*, 30(1–7): 107–17.

Broder, A., Kumar, R., Maghoul, F., Raghavan:, Rajagopalan, S., Stata, R., Tomkins, A. and Wiener, J. (2000), 'Graph Structure in the Web', paper presented to the Ninth International World Wide Web Conference, Amsterdam, May, http://www9.org/w9cdrom/160/160.html (accessed 16 March 2004).

Brody, H., Rip, M. R., Vinten-Johansen:, Paneth, N. and Rachman, S. (2000), 'Map-Making and Myth-Making in Broad Street: The London Cholera Epidemic 1854', *Lancet*, 356(2000): 64–8.

Bruckman, A. (1992), 'Identity Workshop: Emergent Social and Psychological Phenomena in Text-Based Virtual Reality', ftp://ftp.cc.gatech.edu/pub/people/asb/papers/identity-workshop.ps (accessed 23 January 2004).

—— (2002), 'Ethical Guidelines for Research Online', http://www.cc.gatech.edu/~asb/ethics/ (accessed 17 March 2004).

Brunn, S. D. and Dodge, M. (2001), 'Mapping the "Worlds" of the World Wide Web: (Re)Structuring Global Commerce through Hyperlinks', *American Behavioural Scientist*, 44(10): 1717–39.

Brunsdon, C. and Morley, D. (1978), *Everyday Television 'Nationwide'*, London: British Film Institute.

Buchanan, T. and Joinson, A. N. (2004), 'Are Online–Offline Differences in Personality Test Scores due to Increased Self-Disclosure?', paper presented at German Online Research 2004 (Deutschen Gesellschaft für Online Forschung), University of Duisburg-Essen, Germany, March.

Buchanan, T., Joinson, A. N. and Ali, T. (2002), 'Development of a Behavioural Measure of Self-Disclosure for use in Online Research', paper presented at German Online Research 2002, Hohenheim, Germany, October, http://users.wmin.ac.uk/~buchant/downloads/Buchanan_Joinson_Ali_.pdf. (accessed 4 November 2004)

Bulmer, M. (ed.) (1982), *Social Research Ethics: An Examination of the Merits of Covert Participant Observation*, London: Macmillan.

Burris, V., Smith, E. and Strahm, A. (2000), 'White Supremacist Networks on the Internet', *Sociological Focus*, 33(2): 215–35.

Burrows, R., Nettleton, S., Pleace, N., Loader, B. and Muncer, C. (2000), 'Virtual Community Care? Social Policy and the Emergence of Computer Mediated Social Support', *Information, Communication and Society*, 3(1): 95–121.

Callon, M., Law, J. and Rip, A. (eds) (1986) *Mapping the Dynamics of Science and Technology*, London: Macmillan.

Card, S. K., Mackinlay, J. D. and Shneiderman, B. (1999), *Readings in Information Visualization: Using Vision to Think*, San Francisco, CA: Morgan Kaufmann.

Carneiro da Silva, A. M. A. (2000), 'Reconectando a Sociabilidade Online e Offline: Trajetórias, Poder e Formação de Grupos em Canais Geográficos no Internet Relay Chat', Sociology master's dissertation, State University of Campinas (Unicamp), Campinas, Brazil.

Chen: and Hinton, S. M. (1999) 'Realtime Interviewing Using the World Wide Web, *Sociological Research Online*, 4(3), http://www.socresonline. org.uk/socresonline/4/3/chen.html (accessed 23 January 2004).

Cisler, S. (1998), 'The Internet and Indigenous Groups', *Cultural Survival Quarterly* 21(4), http://www.culturalsurvival.org/publications/csq/csq_article. cfm?id=656A2AAD-FC3F-493B-8A83-29D3B4029AA2& region_id=10&subregion_id=32&issue_id=19 (accessed 19 March 2004).

Clifford, J. (1997), 'Spatial Practices: Fieldwork, Travel, and the Disciplining of Anthropology', in J. Ferguson (ed.) *Anthropological Locations*, Berkeley, CA: University of California Press, pp. 185–222.

Cohen, A. P. (1985), *The Symbolic Construction of Community*, London: Tavistock.

Cohen, J. (1996), 'Computer Mediated Communication and Publication Productivity among Faculty', *Internet Research*, 6(2/3): 41–63.

Collins, H. M. (1975), 'The Seven Sexes: A Study in the Sociology of a Phenomenon, or the Replication of Experiments in Physics', *Sociology*, 9(2): 205–24.

Coomber, R. (1997), 'Using the Internet for Survey Research', *Sociological Research Online*, 2(2), http://www.socresonline.org.uk/socresonline/2/2/2.html (accessed 17 September 2003).

Cooper, G. & Woolgar, S. (1996), 'The Research Process: Context, Autonomy and Audience', in E. S. Lyon and J. Busfield (eds), *Methodological Imaginations*, London: Macmillan, pp. 147–163.

Correll, S. (1995), 'The Ethnography of an Electronic Bar: The Lesbian Café', *Journal of Contemporary Ethnography*, 24(3): 270–98.

Couclelis, H. (1998), 'Worlds of Information: The Geographic Metaphor in the Visualization of Complex Information', *Cartography and Geographic Information Systems* 25(4): 209–20.

Cozzens, S. E. (1985), 'Comparing the Sciences: Citation Context Analysis of Papers from Neuropharmacology and the Sociology of Science', *Social Studies of Science*, 15(1): 127–53.

Crystal, D. (2001), *Language and the Internet*, Cambridge: Cambridge University Press.

Curtis: (1992), 'Mudding: Social Phenomena in Text-Based Virtual Realities', from the Proceedings of the 1992 Conference on Directions and Implications of Advanced Computing, Berkeley, CA, ftp://ftp.game.org/pub/mud/text/research/DIAC92.txt (accessed 23 January 2004).

Daft, R.L and Lengel, R. H. (1984), 'Information Richness: A New Approach to Managerial Behaviour and Organization Design', in L. L. Cummings and B. M. Staw (eds), *Research in Organizational Behaviour 6*, Homewood, IL: JAI Press, pp. 191–233.

Dale, E. (1935), *The Content of Motion Pictures*, New York: Macmillan.

D'Alessio, D. (1997), 'Use of the World Wide Web in the 1996 U.S. Election', *Electoral Studies*, 16(4): 489–500.

—— (2000), 'Adoption of the World Wide Web by American Political Candidates 1996–1998', *Journal of Broadcasting and Electronic Media*, 44(4): 556–68.

Damer, B. (1998), *Avatars! Exploring and Building Virtual Worlds on the Internet*, Berkeley, CA: Peachpit Press.

Danet, B. (2001), *Cyberpl@y: Communicating Online*, Oxford: Berg.

Danowski, J. and Edison-Swift: (1985), 'Crisis Effects on Intraorganizational Computer-Based Communication', *Communication Research*, 12(2): 251–70.

Dasgupta: (1988), 'Trust as a Commodity', in D. Gambetta (ed.), *Trust: Making and Breaking Cooperative Relations*, Oxford: Basil Blackwell, pp. 49–72.

Davenport, E. & Cronin, B. (2000), 'The Citation Network as a Prototype for Representing Trust in Virtual Environments', in B. Cronin and H. B. Atkins (eds), *The Web of Knowledge: A Festschrift in Honor of Eugene Garfield*, ASIS Monograph Series, Medford, NJ: Information Today, pp. 517–534.

De Angeli, A., Johnson, G. I., and Coventry, L. (n.d.), 'The Unfriendly User: Exploring Social Reactions to Chatterbots', http://www.alicebot.org/articles/guest/The per cent20Unfriendly per cent20User.html. (accessed 12 November 2002).

December, J. (1996), 'Units of Analysis for Internet Communication', *Journal of Computer Mediated Communication*, 1(4), http://www.ascusc.org/jcmc/vol1/issue4/december.html (accessed 25 February 2004).

DeCew, J. (1997), *In Pursuit of Privacy: Law, Ethics, and the Rise of Technology*, Ithaca, NY: Cornell University Press.

Denzin, N. K. (ed.) (1970), *Sociological Methods: A Sourcebook*, Chicago: Aldine.

—— (1999), 'Cybertalk and the Method of Instances" in S. Jones (ed.) *Doing Internet Research: Critical Issues and Methods for Examining the Net*, Thousand Oaks, CA: Sage, pp. 107–125.

Des Jarlais, D. C., Paone, D., Milliken, J., Turner, C. F., Miller, H., Gribble, J., Shi, Q., Hagan, H. and Friedman, S. (1999), 'Audio-Computer Interviewing to Measure Risk Behaviour for HIV among Injecting Drug Users: A Quasi-Randomised Trial', *Lancet*, 353(9,163): 1,657–61.

De Solla Price, D. J. (1986), *Little Science, Big Science . . . and Beyond*, New York: Columbia University Press.

Dillman, D. A. (2000), *Mail and Internet Surveys: The Tailored Design Method*, New York: Wiley.

Dodds: S., Muhamad, R. and Watts, D. J. (2003), 'An Experimental Study of Social Search in Global Social Networks', *Science*, 301: 827–9.

Dodge, M. (1999), 'Mapping How the Data Flows, *Mappa Mundi Magazine*, September, http://mappa.mundi.net/maps/maps_004/ (accessed 17 March 2004).

—— and Kitchin, R. (2000), 'Exposing the "Second Text" of Maps of the Net', *Journal of Computer-Mediated Communication*, 5(4), http://www.ascusc.org/jcmc/vol5/issue4/dodge_kitchin.htm (accessed 17 March 2004).

—— and Kitchin, R. (2001a), *Mapping Cyberspace*, London: Routledge.

—— and Kitchin, R. (2001b), *Atlas of Cyberspace*, London: Addison-Wesley.

—— and Kitchin, R. (2004), 'Mapping Internet Infrastructures', in R. Hanley (ed.), *Moving People, Goods and Information: The Cutting-Edge Infrastructure of Networked Cities*, New York: Routledge, pp. 146–167.

Doheny-Farina, S. (1996), *The Wired Neighbourhood*, New Haven, CT: Yale University Press.

Donath, J. S., Karahalios, K. and Viegas, F. (1999), 'Visualizing Conversation', *Journal of Computer-Mediated Communication*, 4(4), http://www.ascucs.org/jcmc/vol4/issue4/donath.html (accessed 17 March 2004).

Dorling, D. and Fairbairn, D. (1997), *Mapping: Ways of Representing the World*, London: Longman.

Durkin, K. and Bryant, C. (1995), '"Log on to Sex": Some Notes on the Carnal Computer and Erotic Cyberspace as an Emerging Research Frontier', *Deviant Behaviour*,16(3): 179–200.

Eaton, L. (2002) 'A Third of Europeans and Almost Half of Americans Use Internet for Health Information', *British Medical Journal*, 325(7,371): 989.

Emerson, R. M. (1981), 'Observational Field Work', *Annual Review of Sociology*, 7: 351–78.

Epstein, J. F., Barker, P. R. and Kroutil, L. A. (2001), 'Mode Effects in Self-Reported Mental Health Data', *Public Opinion Quarterly*, 65(4): 529–49.

Ess, C. and the Association of Internet Researchers Ethics Committee (2002), *Ethical Decision Making and Internet Research: Recommendations from the AoIR Ethics Working Committee*, approved by AoIR 27 November 2002, http://www.aoir.org/reports/ethics.pdf (accessed 23 January 2004).

Faugier, J. and Sargeant, M. (1997), 'Sampling Hard to Reach Populations', *Journal of Advanced Nursing*, 26(4): 790–7.

Ferguson, T. (2002), 'From Patients to End Users: Quality of Online Patient Networks Needs More Attention than Quality of Online Health Information', *British Medical Journal*, 324(7,337): 555–6.

Fernback, J. (1999), 'There Is a There There: Notes Towards a Definition of Cybercommunity', in S. Jones (ed.), *Doing Internet Research: Critical Issues and Methods for Examining the Net*, Thousand Oaks, CA: Sage, pp. 203–220.

Ferriter, M. (1993), 'Computer Aided Interviewing and the Psychiatric Social History', *Social Work and Social Sciences Review*, 4(3): 255–63.

Feyeraband: (1975), *Against Method*, London: Verso.

Finch, J. (1984), '"It's Great to Have Someone to Talk to": The Ethics and Politics of Interviewing Women', in C. Bell and H. Roberts (eds), *Social Researching: Politics, Problems and Practice*, London: Routledge, pp. 70–87.

Fine, G. A. and Smith, G. W. H. (eds) (2000), *Erving Goffman*, four volumes, London: Sage.

Finholt, T. A. (2002), 'Collaboratories', in B. Cronin (ed.), *Annual Review of Information Science and Technology*, 36, Medford, NJ: Information Today, pp. 74–107.

Fischer, C. S. (1992), *America Calling: A Social History of the Telephone to 1940*, Berkeley, CA: University of California Press.

Fisher, D. and Lueg, C. (2003), *From Usenet to CoWebs: Interacting with Social Information Spaces*, London: Springer.

Fiske, J. (1989), 'Moments of Television', in E. Seiter, H. Borchers, G. Kreutzner and E-M. Warth (eds), *Remote Control: Television, Audiences and Cultural Power*, London: Routledge, pp. 56–78.

Foot, K. A. and Schneider, S. M. (2002), 'Online Action in Campaign 2000: An Exploratory Analysis of the U.S. Political Web Sphere', *Journal of Broadcasting and Electronic Media*, 46(2): 222–44.

Foot, K. A., Jankowski, N. W., Kluver, R. and Schneider, S. (2003a), 'The Internet and Elections: An International Project for the Comparative Study of the Role of the Internet in the Electoral Process', available at http://oase.uci.kun.nl/~jankow/elections/ (accessed 4 November 2004)

Foot, K. A., Schneider, S. M., Dougherty, M., Xenos, M. and Larsen, E. (2003b), 'Analyzing Linking Practices: Candidate Sites in the 2002 US Electoral Web Sphere', *Journal of Computer Mediated Communication* (special issue: Internet

Networks: The Form and the Feel), 8(4), http:///www.ascusc.org/jcmc/vol8/issue4/foot.html (accessed 27 January 2004).

Foot, K. A., Warnick, B. and Schneider, S. M. (forthcoming), 'Web-Based Memorializing After September 11: Toward a Conceptual Framework'.

Forte, M. C. (2002), '"We are not Extinct": The Revival of Carib and Taino Identities, the Internet, and the Transformation of Offline Indigenes into Online "N-digenes"', *Sincronía: An Electronic Journal of Cultural Studies*, spring 2002, http://sincronia.cucsh.udg.mx/CyberIndigen.htm (accessed 6 June 2002).

—— (2003), 'Co-Construction and Field Creation: Website Development as both an Instrument and Relationship in Action Research', in E. Buchanan (ed.), *Virtual Research Ethics: Issues and Controversies*, Hershey, PA: Idea Publishing Group.

Fox, N. and Roberts, C. (1999), 'GPs in Cyberspace: The Sociology of a "Virtual Community"', *Sociological Review*, 47(4): 643–71.

Fox, S. and Fallows, D. (2003), *Internet Health Resources*, Washington, DC: Pew Internet and American Life Project, http://www.pewinternet.org/reports/pdfs/PIP_Health_Report_July_2003.pdf (accessed 17 September 2003).

Fox, S. and Rainie, L. (2002), *Vital Decisions: How Internet Users Decide what Information to Trust When They or their Loved Ones are Sick*, Washington, DC: Pew Internet and American Life Project, http://www.pewinternet.org/reports/pdfs/PIP_Vital_Decisions_May2002.pdf (accessed 17 September 2003).

Fox, S. and Schwartz, D. (2002), 'Social Desirability and Controllability in Computerized and Paper-and-Pencil Personality Questionnaires', *Computers in Human Behaviour*, 18(4): 389–410.

Frankel, M. S. and Siang, S. (1999), 'Ethical and Legal Aspects of Human Subjects Research in Cyberspace', report of a workshop held on 10–11 June 1999 in Washington DC. Washington DC: American Association for the Advancement of Science, http://www.aaas.org/spp/sfrl/projects/intres/report.pdf (accessed 23 January 2004).

Freedman, J. & Fraser, S. (1966), 'Compliance without Pressure: The Foot-in-the-Door Technique', *Journal of Personality and Social Psychology*, 4(2): 195–202.

Frick, A., Bächtiger, M. T. & Reips, U-D. (2001), 'Financial Incentives, Personal Information and Drop-Out in Online Studies', in U.-D. Reips & M. Bosnjak (eds), *Dimensions of Internet Science*, Lengerich: Pabst.

Fried, C. (1970), *An Anatomy of Values*, Cambridge, MA: Harvard University Press.

Friendly, M. and Denis, D. J. (2003), 'Milestones in the History of Thematic Cartography, Statistical Graphics, and Data Visualization', 25 July. http://www.math.yorku.ca/SCS/Gallery/milestone/ (accessed 17 March 2004).

Fujimura, J. and Fortun, M. (1996), 'Constructing Knowledge across Social Worlds: The Case of DNA Sequence Databases in Molecular Biology', in L.

Nader (ed.) *Naked Science: Anthropological Inquiry into Boundaries, Power and Knowledge*, New York: Routledge, pp. 160–173.

Gabbay, S. (2000), 'Connecting Minds: Computer-Mediated Communication in Scientific Work', *Journal of American Society for Information Science*, 51(14): 1,295–305.

Galaskiewicz, J. and Wasserman, S. (1993), 'Social Network Analysis: Concepts, Methodology, and Directions for the 1990s', *Sociological Methods & Research* 22(1): 3–22.

Gamson, W. A. and Modigliani, A. (1989), 'Media Discourse and Public Opinion on Nuclear Power: A Constructionist Approach', *American Journal of Sociology*, 95(1): 1–37.

Garland, K. (1994), *Mr Beck's Underground Map*, Harrow Weald, UK: Capital Transport Publishing.

Garrido, M. and Halavais, A. (2003), 'Mapping Networks of Support for the Zapatista Movement', in M. McCaughy and M. D. Ayers (eds), *Cyberactivism: Online Activism in Theory and Practice*, London: Routledge, pp. 165–184.

Garton, L., Haythornthwaite, C. and Wellman, B. (1997), 'Studying Online Social Networks', *Journal of Computer-Mediated Communication*, 3(1), http://www.ascusc.org/jcmc/vol3/issue1/garton.html (accessed 23 January 2004).

Geertz, C. (1973), *The Interpretation of Cultures*, New York: Basic Books.

—— (1988), *Works and Lives: The Anthropologist as Author*, Cambridge: Polity.

Genuth, J., Chompalov, I. and Shrum, W. (2000), 'How Experiments Begin: The Formation of Scientific Collaborations', *Minerva*, 38(3): 311–48.

George, A. L. (1959), *Propaganda Analysis: A Study of Inferences Made from Nazi Propaganda in World War II*, Evanston, IL: Row, Peterson.

Gerbner, G. and Gross, L. (1976), 'Living with Television: The Violence Profile', *Journal of Communication*, 26(2) 173–97.

Gluckman, M. (ed.) (1964), *Closed Systems and Open Minds: The Limits of Naivety in Anthropology*, London: Oliver & Boyd.

Goffman, E. (1959), *The Presentation of Self in Everyday Life*, New York: Doubleday.

—— (1989), 'On Fieldwork', *Journal of Contemporary Ethnography* 18: 123–32.

Gorman, S. P. (2001), 'The Network Advantage of Regions: The Case of the USA, Europe, and China', paper presented at the North American Regional Science Association Meeting, Charleston, SC, USA, http://www.networkgeography.org/network_advantage_prepub.pdf (accessed 14 August 2002).

Gray, C. H. (2001), *Cyborg Citizen: Politics in the Post-Human Age*, London: Routledge.

Greist, J. H., Klein, M. H. and VanCura, L. J. (1973), 'A Computer Interview by Psychiatric Patient Target Symptoms', *Archives of General Psychiatry*, 29: 247–53.

Grossberg, L. (1987), 'The In-Difference of Television', *Screen*, 28(2): 28–45.

Gueguen, N. (2002), 'Foot-in-the-Door Technique and Computer-Mediated Communication', *Computers in Human Behaviour*, 18(1): 11–15.

Guimarães, M. J.L., Jr (1999), 'Sociability at Cyberspace: Distinction between platforms and environments', paper presented at the Fifty-first Annual Meeting of Brazilian Society for the Progress of Science (SBPC), Porto Alegre, Brazil, July, http://www.cfh.ufsc.br/~guima/papers/plat_amb.html (accessed 24 December 2003).

—— (2000a), *Vivendo no Palace: Etnografia de um Ambiente de Sociabilidade no Ciberespaço*, Social Anthropology master's dissertation, Federal University of Santa Catarina (UFSC), Florianópolis, Brazil.

—— (2000b), 'O Ciberespaço como Cenário para as Ciências Sociais' (Cyberspace as a Scenario for the Social Sciences), *Ilha – Revista de Antropologia*, PPGAS/UFSC: Florianópolis, Brazil, 2(1): 139–53.

—— (2002), 'Avatars: the Social Dynamics of a Boundary-Crossing Artefact', paper presented at the workshop 'Engaging (Information) Technologies: Anthropological Objects and (con)texts' during the Seventh Bi-annual EASA Conference, Copenhagen, Denmark 14–17 August.

—— (2003), 'Technologies that are Bodies: Some Remarks about the Development and Use of Avatar-Related Technologies', paper presented at the panel 'Why are bodies machines' during the ASA Decennial Conference 'Anthropology and Science', Manchester.

Gupta, A. and Ferguson, J. (1997), 'Discipline and Practice: "The Field" as Site, Method, and Location in Anthropology', in A. Gupta and J. Ferguson (eds) *Anthropological Locations: Boundaries and Grounds of a Field Science*, Berkeley, CA: University of California Press, pp. 1–29.

Hadlaw, J. (2003), 'The London Underground Map: Imagining Modern Time and Space', *Design Issues*, 19(1): 25–35.

Halavais, A (2003), 'Networks and Flows of Content on the World Wide Web', International Communication Association conference, San Diego, CA, May, http://alex.halavais.net/research/halavais-ica03a.pdf (accessed 23 January 2003).

Hall, Stephen S. (1992), *Mapping the Next Millennium: How Computer-Driven Cartography is Revolutionizing the Face of Science*, New York: Vintage Books.

Hall, Stuart (1980), 'Encoding/Decoding', in S. Hall, D. Hobson, A. Lowe and P. Willis (eds), *Culture, Media, Language*, London: Hutchinson, pp. 128–138.

—— (1992), 'Cultural Studies and its Theoretical Trajectories', in L. Grossberg, C. Nelson and P. Treichler (eds), *Cultural Studies*, London: Routledge, pp. 277–294.

Hamman, R. (1996), 'Cyborgasms: Cybersex amongst Multiple-Selves and Cyborgs in the Narrow-Bandwidth Space of America Online Chat Rooms', http://www.socio.demon.co.uk/ (accessed 12 July 2003).

—— (1997), 'Introduction to Virtual Communities Research and Cybersociology Magazine Issue Two', *Cybersociology Magazine*, Issue Two: Virtual Communities, November, http://www.cybersociology.com/ (accessed on 16 February 2004).

Hammersley, M. and Atkinson: (1983), *Ethnography: Principles in Practice*, London: Tavistock.

Hampton, K. N. and Wellman, B. (2000), 'Examining Community in the Digital Neighborhood: Early Results from Canada's Wired Suburb', in T. Ishida and K. Isbister (eds), *Digital Cities: Technologies, Experiences, and Future Perspectives*, Heidelberg, Germany: Springer-Verlag, pp. 194–208.

Hansen, G. (2000), 'Internet Presidential Campaigning: The Influences of Candidate Internet Sites on the 2000 Elections', paper presented at National Communication Association, Seattle, WA, November 2000.

Hardey, M. (1999), 'Doctor in the House: The Internet as a Source of Lay Health Knowledge and the Challenge to Expertise', *Sociology of Health and Illness*, 21(6) : 1,545–53.

—— (2002), '"The Story of my Illness": Personal Accounts of Illness on the Internet', *Health: An Interdisciplinary Journal for the Social Study of Health, Illness and Medicine*, 6(1): 31–46.

Hargittai, E. (1999), 'Weaving the Western Web: Explaining Differences in Internet Connectivity among OECD Countries', *Telecommunications Policy*, 23(10/11): 701–18.

Harley, J. B. (1989), 'Deconstructing the Map', *Cartographica* 26(2): 1–20.

—— and Woodward, D. (1987), *The History of Cartography, Volume 1. Cartography in Prehistoric, Ancient and Medieval Europe and the Mediterranean*, Chicago: University of Chicago Press.

Harpold, T. (1999), 'Dark Continents: Critique of Internet Metageographies', *Postmodern Culture*, 9(2), http://muse.jhu.edu/journals/postmodern_culture/toc/pmc9.2.html (accessed 4 November 2004).

Harrington, C. L. and Bielby, D. D. (1995), 'Where Did You Hear That? Technology and the Social Organization of Gossip', *Sociological Quarterly*, 36(3): 607–28.

Harris Interactive (2003), 'No Significant Change in the Numbers of "Cyberchondriacs" – Those Who Go Online for Health Care Information', *Health Care News*, 3(4), http://www.harrisinteractive.com/news/newsletters/healthnews/HI_HealthCareNews2003Vol3_Iss04.pdf (accessed 17 September 2003).

Hawkins, D. T. (2001), 'Bibliometrics of Electronic Journals in Information Science', *Information Research*, 7 (1), http://informationr.net/ir/7–1/paper120.html (accessed 18 March 2004).

Haythornthwaite, C. (2000), 'Online Personal Networks: Size, Composition and

Media Use among Distance Learners', *New Media & Society*, 2(2): 195–226.

Hecht, M. L., Corman, S. R. and Miller-Rassulo, M. (1993), 'An Evaluation of the Drug Resistance Project: A Comparison of Film versus Live Performance Media', *Health Communication*, 5(2): 75–88.

Hellsten, I. (2003), 'Focus on Metaphors: The Case of "Frankenfood" on the Web', *Journal of Computer Mediated Communication*, 8(4), http://www.ascusc. org/jcmc/vol8/issue4/hellsten.html (accessed 4 November 2004).

Helmreich, S. (2003), 'Spatializing Technoscience', *Reviews in Anthropology*, 32(1): 13–36.

Hendricks, V. M., Blanken: and Adriaans, N. (1992), *Snowball Sampling: A Pilot Study on Cocaine Use*, Rotterdam: IVO.

Henwood, F., Wyatt, S., Hart, A. and Smith, J. (2002), 'Turned On or Turned Off? Accessing Health Information on the Internet', *Scandinavian Journal for Information Systems*, 14(2): 79–90.

Herring, S. C. (1997), 'Computer-Mediated Discourse Analysis: Introduction', *Electronic Journal of Communication*, 6(3), http://www.cios.org/www/ejc/v6n396.htm (accessed 23 January 2004).

—— (2003), 'Computer-Mediated Discourse Analysis: An Approach to Researching Online Behaviour', in S. A. Barab, R. Kling and J. H. Gray (eds), *Designing for Virtual Communities in the Service of Learning*, New York: Cambridge University Press, http://ella.slis.indiana.edu/~herring/cmda.html (accessed 23 January 2004).

Hiltz, S. R. and Turoff, M. (1978), *The Network Nation: Human Communication via Computer*, Reading, MA: Addison-Wesley.

Hine, C. (2000), *Virtual Ethnography*, London: Sage.

—— (2001), 'Web Pages, Authors and Audiences: the Meaning of a Mouse Click', *Information, Communication & Society*, 4(2): 182–98.

—— (2002), 'Cyberscience and Social Boundaries: The Implications of Laboratory Talk on the Internet', *Sociological Research Online*, 7(2), http://www.socresonline.org.uk/7/2/hine.html (accessed 4 November 2004).

—— and Eve, J. (1998), 'Privacy in the Marketplace', *Information Society*, 14(4): 253–62.

Howard: (2002), 'Network Ethnography and Hypermedia Organization: New Organizations, New Media, New Myths', *New Media & Society*, 4(4): 550–74.

Hubbard: (1999), 'Researching Female Sex Work: Reflections on Geographical Exclusion, Critical Methodologies and "Useful" Knowledge', *Area*, 31(3): 229–37.

Hyman, H. H. (1955), *Survey Design and Analysis: Principles, Cases, and Procedures*, Glencoe, IL: Free Press.

Illingworth, N. (2001), 'The Internet Matters: Exploring the Use of the Internet as a Research Tool', *Sociological Research Online*, 6(2), http://www.socreson-line.org.uk/6/2/illingworth.html (accessed 23 January 2004).

Ingwersen: (1998), 'The Calculation of Web Impact Factors', *Journal of Documentation*, 54(2): 236–43.

Jackson, M. (1997), 'Assessing the Structure of the Communication on the World Wide Web', *Journal of Computer-Mediated Communication*, 3(1), http://www.ascusc.org/jcmc/vol3/issue1/jackson.html (accessed 25 February 2004).

Jankowski, N. W. (1999), 'In Search of Methodological Innovation in New Media Research', *Communications: The European Journal of Communication Research*, 24(3): 367–74.

Jensen, K. B. and Jankowski, N. W. (eds) (1991), *A Handbook for Qualitative Methods for Mass Communication Research*, London: Routledge.

Joinson, A. N. (1999), 'Anonymity, Disinhibition and Social Desirability on the Internet', *Behaviour Research Methods, Instruments and Computers*, 31(3): 433–8.

—— (2001a), 'Knowing Me, Knowing You: Reciprocal Self-disclosure on the Internet', *CyberPsychology and Behaviour*, 4(5), 587–91.

—— (2001b), 'Self-Disclosure in Computer-Mediated Communication: The Role of Self-Awareness and Visual Anonymity', *European Journal of Social Psychology*, 31(2): 177–92.

—— (2003), *Understanding the Psychology of Internet Behaviour*, Basingstoke & New York: Palgrave.

—— (2004), 'Self-Esteem, Interpersonal Risk and Preference for E-Mail over Face-to-Face Communication', *Cyberpsychology and Behaviour*, 7(4): 472–8.

—— and Reips, U-D. (2004a), 'Salutation, Power and Behaviour in On-line Panels', paper presented at German Online Research 2004 (Deutschen Gesell-schaft für Online Forschung), University of Duisburg-Essen, Germany, March.

—— and Reips, U-D. (2004b), 'Self-Disclosure and the Use of "I Don't Want to Say" Options', unpublished manuscript.

Jones, S. G. (1995), 'Understanding Community in the Information Age', in S. G. Jones (ed.), *CyberSociety: Computer-Mediated Communication and Community*, London: Sage, pp. 10–35.

—— (ed.) (1999), *Doing Internet Research: Critical Issues and Methods for Examining the Net*, Thousand Oaks, CA: Sage.

Kahle, B. (1997), 'Preserving the Internet', *Scientific American*, 276(3): 82–3.

Kanayama, T. (2003), 'Ethnographic Research on the Experience of Japanese Elderly People Online', *New Media & Society*, 5(3): 267–88.

Kang, N. and Choi, J. H. (1999), 'Structural Implications of the Crossposting Network of International News in Cyberspace', *Communication Research*, 26(4): 454–81.

Kaplan, C., Korf, D. and Sterk, C. (1987), 'Temporal and Social Context of Heroin Using Populations: An Illustration of the Snowball Sampling Technique', *Journal of Nervous Mental Disorders*, 175(9): 566–74.

Katz, J. S. and Martin, B. R. (1997), 'What is Research Collaboration?', *Research Policy*, 26(1): 1–18.

Kendall, L. (2002), *Hanging Out in the Virtual Pub: Masculinities and Relationships Online*, Berkeley, CA: The University of California Press.

Kiesler, S. and Sproull, L. S. (1986), 'Response Effects in the Electronic Survey', *Public Opinion Quarterly*, 50(3): 402–13.

Kiesler, S., Siegel, J. and Mcguire, T. W. (1984), 'Social Psychological Aspects of Computer-Mediated Communication', *American Psychologist*, 39(10): 1123–34.

Kim, H. J. (2000), 'Motivations for Hyperlinking in Scholarly Electronic Articles: A Qualitative Study', *Journal of the American Society for Information Science*, 51(10): 887–99.

King, E. (1996), 'The Use of the Self in Qualitative Research', in J. Richardson (ed.), *Handbook of Qualitative Research Methods for Psychology and the Social Sciences*, Leicester: BPS Books, pp. 396–408.

King, S. (1996), 'Researching Internet Communities: Proposed Ethical Guidelines for the Reporting of Results', *Information Society*, 12(2): 119–27.

Kleinberg, J. M. (1999), 'Authoritative Sources in a Hyperlinked Environment', *Journal of the ACM*, 46(5): 604–32.

Kling, R., McKim, G. and King, A. (2001), 'A Bit More to IT: Scholarly Communication Forums as Socio-Technical Interaction Networks', http://www.slis.indiana.edu/csi/Wp/wp01–02B.html (accessed 14 August 2002).

Koehler, W. (2002), 'Web Page Change and Persistence – A Four-Year Longitudinal Study', *Journal of the American Society for Information Science and Technology*, 53(2): 162–71.

Koku, E., Nazer, N. and Wellman, B. (2000), 'Netting Scholars: Online and Offline', *American Behavioural Scientist*, 44(10):1750–72.

Krebs, V. (2000), 'Working in the Connected World Book Network', *IHRIM (International Association for Human Resource Information Management) Journal*, 4(1): 87–90.

Kuhn, T. S., (1970[1962]), *The Structure of Scientific Revolutions*, Chicago: University of Chicago Press.

Kvale, S. (1996), *Interviews: An Introduction to Qualitative Research Interviewing*, Thousand Oaks, CA: Sage Publications.

Lasswell, H. D. and Leites, N. (1965), *The Language of Politics: Studies in Quantitative Semantics*, Cambridge, MA: MIT Press.

Latane, B. & Darley, J. M. (1970), *The Unresponsive Bystander: Why Doesn't He Help?*, Englewood Cliffs, NJ: Prentice Hall.

Latour, B. (1987), *Science in Action: How to Follow Scientists and Engineers through Society*, Milton Keynes: Open University Press.

—— and Woolgar, S. (1986), *Laboratory Life: The Construction of Scientific Facts* 2nd edn, Princeton, NJ: Princeton University Press.

Lau, J. T. F., Tsui, H. Y., and Wang, Q. S. (2003), 'Effects of Two Telephone Survey Methods on the Level of Reported Risk Behaviours', *Sexually Transmitted Infections*, 79(4): 325–31.

Lawrence, S. and Giles, C. L. (1998), 'Searching the World Wide Web', *Science*, 280(5360): 98–100.

Lea, M. & Spears, R. (1991), 'Computer Mediated Communication, De-individuation, and Group Decision-Making', *International Journal of Man-Machine Studies*, 34(2): 283–301.

LeBesco, K. (2004), 'Managing Visibility, Intimacy, and Focus in Online Critical Ethnography', in D. Johns, S. S. Chen & G. J. Hall (eds), *Online Social Research: Methods, Issues, & Ethics*, New York: Peter Lang, pp. 63–79.

Lenoir, T. (1999), 'Shaping Biomedicine as an Information Science', in M. E. Bowden, T. Bellardo Hahn and R. V. Williams (eds), *Proceedings of the 1998 Conference on the History and Heritage of Science Information Systems*, ASIS Monograph Series, Medford, NJ: Information Today, pp. 27–45.

Lessler, J. T., Caspar, R. A., Penne, M. A. and Barker, P. R. (2000), 'Developing Computer-Assisted Interviewing (CAI) for the National Household Survey on Drug Abuse', *Journal of Drug Issues*, 30(1): 19–34.

Lindlof, T. R. and Shatzer, M. J. (1998), 'Media Ethnography in Virtual Space: Strategies, Limits, and Possibilities', *Journal of Broadcasting and Electronic Media*, 42(2): 170–89.

Lull, J. (1990), *Inside Family Viewing: Ethnographic Research on Television Audiences*, London: Routledge.

Lyman, P. (2002), 'Archiving the World Wide Web', in *Building a National Strategy for Digital Preservation*, Council on Library and Information Resources report, http://www.clir.org/pubs/reports/pub106/web.html (accessed 25 February 2004).

—— and Kahle, B. (1998), 'Archiving Digital Cultural Artifacts: Organizing an Agenda for Action', *D-Lib Magazine*, July/August, http://www.dlib.org/dlib/july98/07lyman.html (accessed 25 February 2004).

Lynch, C. A. (2001), 'When Documents Deceive: Trust and Provenance as New Factors for Information Retrieval in a Tangled Web', *Journal of the American Society for Information Science and Technology*, 52(1): 12–17.

Lyon, D. (1994), *The Electronic Eye: The Rise of the Surveillance Society*, Cambridge: Polity.

McCain, K. W. (2000), 'Sharing Digitized Research-Related Information on the World Wide Web', *Journal of the American Society for Information Science*, 51(14): 1321–7.

McClintock, A. (1993), 'Sex Workers and Sex Work', *Social Text*, 37(winter): 1–10.

MacEachren, A. M. (1995), 'Visualization in Modern Cartography: Setting the Agenda', in A. M. MacEachren and D. R. F. Taylor (eds), *Visualization in Modern Cartography*, Oxford: Pergamon, pp. 1–12.

Mackay, H. and Ivey, D. (2004), *Modern Media in the Home: An Ethnographic Study*, Rome, Italy: John Libbey.

McKenna, K. Y. A. and Bargh, J. (1998), 'Coming Out in the Age of the Internet: Identity Demarginalization through Virtual Group Participation', *Journal of Personality and Social Psychology*, 75(3): 681–94.

McKenna, K. Y. A. Green, A. S. and Gleason, M. E. J. (2002), 'Relationship Formation on the Internet: What's the Big Attraction?', *Journal of Social Issues*, 58(1): 9–31.

MacKinnon, R. C. (1995), 'Searching for the Leviathan in Usenet', in S. G. Jones (ed.), *CyberSociety: Computer-Mediated Communication and Community*, London: Sage, pp. 112–137.

McLaughlin, M. L., Osborne, K. K. and Smith, C. B. (1995), 'Standards of Conduct on Usenet', in S. G. Jones (ed.), *CyberSociety: Computer-Mediated Communication and Community*, London, pp. 90–111.

McMillan, S. J. (1999), 'Health Communication and the Internet: Relationships between Interactive Characteristics of the Medium and Site Creators, Content, and Purpose', *Health Communication*, 11(4): 375–90.

Madge, C. and O'Connor, H. (2002), 'On-Line with E-Mums: Exploring the Internet as a Medium for Research', *Area*, 34(1): 92–102.

Majchrzak, A., Rice, R., King, N., Malhotra, A. and Ba, S. (2000), 'Computer-Mediated Inter-Organizational Knowledge-Sharing: Insights from a Virtual Team Innovating Using a Collaborative Tool', *Information Resources Management Journal*, 13(1): 44–53.

Malinowski, B. (1922), *Argonauts of the Western Pacific*, London: Routledge and Kegan Paul.

Mann, C. and Stewart, F. (2000), *Internet Communication and Qualitative Research: A Handbook for Researching Online*, London: Sage.

Mantovani, G. (1994), 'Is Computer-Mediated Communication Intrinsically Apt to Enhance Democracy in Organizations?', *Human Relations*, 47(1): 45–62.

Markham, A. M. (1998), *Life Online: Researching Real Experience in Virtual Space*, Walnut Creek, CA: AltaMira Press.

—— (2004), 'The Internet as Research Context', in C. Seale, G. Gobo, J. Gubrium and D. Silverman (eds), *Qualitative Research Practice*, London: Sage.

Marx, G. (1998), 'An Ethics for the New Surveillance', *Information Society*, 14(3): 171–85.

Mason, B. (1999), 'Issues in Virtual Ethnography', in K. Buckner (ed.) *Esprit i³*

Workshop on Ethnographic Studies in Real and Virtual Environments: Inhabited Information Spaces and Connected Communities, Edinburgh: Queen Margaret College.

Matei, S. and Ball-Rokeach, S. (2001), 'Real and Virtual Social Ties: Connections in the Everyday Lives of Seven Ethnic Neighborhoods', *American Behavioural Scientist*, 45(3): 550–63.

Matheson, K, and Zanna, M. P. (1988), 'The Impact of Computer-Mediated Communication on Self-Awareness', *Computers in Human Behaviour*, 4(3): 221–33.

Matzat, U. (2001), *Social Networks and Cooperation in Electronic Communities: A Theoretical-Empirical Study on Academic Communication and Internet Discussion Groups*, Amsterdam: Thela, http://www.ub.rug.nl/eldoc/dis/ppsw/u.matzat/ (accessed 4 November 2004).

Menczer, F. (2004), 'Lexical and Semantic Clustering by Web Links', *Journal of the American Society for Information Science and Technology*, 55(14).

Merton, R. K., Fiske, M. and Kendall: L. (1956), *The Focused Interview*, New York: Free Press.

Milgram, S. (1967), 'The Small World Problem', *Psychology Today*, 1(1): 60–7.

Miller, D. and Slater, D. (2000), *The Internet: An Ethnographic Approach*, Oxford: Berg.

Miller, J. (1995), 'Gender and Power on the Streets', *Journal of Contemporary Ethnography*, 24(2): 427–51.

Mitra, A. (1999), 'Characteristics of the WWW Text: Tracing Discursive Strategies', *Journal of Computer-Mediated Communication*, 5(1), http://www.ascusc.org/jcmc/vol5/issue1/mitra.html (accessed 4 November 2004).

Mnookin, J.L. (1996), 'Virtual(ly) Law: The Emergence of Law in LambdaMOO', *Journal of Computer-Mediated Communication*, 2(1), http://www.usc.edu/dept/annenberg/vol2/issue1/lambda.html (accessed 8 January 2004)

Molotch, H. (1994), 'Going Out', *Sociological Forum*, 9: 221–40.

Monge, P. and Contractor, N. S. (2000), 'Emergence of Communication Networks', in F. M. Jablin and L. L. Putnam (eds), *The New Handbook of Organizational Communication: Advances in Theory, Research, and Methods*, Thousand Oaks, CA: Sage, pp. 440–502.

Monmonier, M. (1993), *Mapping It Out: Expository Cartography for the Humanities and Social Sciences*, Chicago: University of Chicago Press.

Moon, Y. (1998), 'Impression Management in Computer-Based Interviews: The Effects of Input Modality, Output Modality, and Distance', *Public Opinion Quarterly*, 62(4): 610–22.

—— (2000), 'Intimate Exchanges: Using Computers to Elicit Self-Disclosure from Consumers', *Journal of Consumer Research*, 27(4): 323–39.

Moores, S. (1993), *Interpreting Audiences*, London: Sage.

Morley, D. (1980), *The 'Nationwide' Audience: Structure and Decoding*, London: British Film Institute.

—— (1986), *Family Television: Cultural Power and Domestic Leisure*, London: Comedia.

—— (1992), *Television, Audiences and Cultural Studies*, London: Routledge.

Mulkay, M., Gilbert, G. N. and Woolgar, S. (1975), 'Problem Areas and Research Networks in Science', *Sociology*, 9(2): 187–203.

Murdock, G. (1989), 'Critical Inquiry and Audience Activity', in B. Dervin, L. Grossberg, B. O'Keefe and E. Wartella (eds), *Rethinking Communication Volume 2*, London: Sage, pp. 226–249.

Nardi, B., Whittaker, S. and Bradner, E. (2000), 'Interaction and Outeraction: Instant Messaging in Action', *Proceedings of the ACM 2000 Conference on Computer Supported Cooperative Work*, http://www.shef.ac.uk/uni/academic/I-M/is/people/stafpage/whittake/outeraction_cscw2000.pdf (accessed 18 March 2004).

Nass, C. I., Fogg, B. J. and Moon, Y. (1996), 'Can Computers be Teammates? Affiliation and Social Identity Effects in Human–Computer Interaction', *International Journal of Human–Computer Studies*, 45(6): 669–78.

Neice, D. C. (2000), 'Shifting Research Relationships from On-line to Face to Face', paper presented at 'Virtual Methodology?' conference, Brunel University, February. http://www.brunel.ac.uk/depts/crict/neice.htm (accessed 16 March 2004).

Newman, M. E. J. (2000), 'The Structure of Scientific Collaboration Networks', *Proceedings of the National Academy of Sciences*, 98(2): 404–9, http://www.pnas.org/cgi/content/full/98/2/404 (accessed 8 February 2002).

Newman, S. (1998), 'Here, There and Nowhere at all: Distribution, Negotiation and Virtuality in Postmodern Ethnography and Engineering', *Knowledge and Society*, 11: 235–67.

Nicholas, D., Huntington:, Williams: and Blackburn: (2001), 'Digital Health Information Provision and Health Outcomes', *Journal of Information Science*, 27(4): 265–76.

Nicholas, D., Huntington, P., Williams, P. and Gunter, B. (2003), '"Search-Disclosure": A Concept to Aid the Understanding of Digital Information Platform Preference and Location in a Health Environment', *Journal of Documentation*, 59(5): 523–39.

Oakley, A. (1981), 'Interviewing Women: A Contradiction in Terms', in H. Roberts (ed.), *Doing Feminist Research*, London: Routledge, pp. 30–61.

—— (1999), *Experiments in Knowing: Gender and Method in the Social Sciences*, Cambridge: Polity.

O'Connor, H. and Madge, C. (2001), 'Cyber-Mothers: Online Synchronous Interviewing using Conferencing Software', *Sociological Research Online*,

5(4), http://www.socresonline.org.uk/5/4/o'connor.html (accessed 23 January 2004).

Orford, S., Dorling, D. and Harris, R. (1998), *Review of Visualization in the Social Sciences: A State of the Art Survey and Report*, report for the UK Advisory Group on Computer Graphics, no. 41, http://www.agocg.ac.uk/train /review/cover.htm (accessed 4 November 2004).

Orgad, S. (2004), 'Help Yourself: The World Wide Web as a Self-Help Agora', in D. Gauntlett and R. Horsley (eds), *Web Studies: Rewiring Media Studies for the Digital Age* 2nd edn, London: Arnold, pp. 146–157.

Paccagnella, L. (1997), 'Getting the Seats of your Pants Dirty: Strategies for Ethnographic Research on Virtual Communities', *Journal of Computer Mediated Communication*, 3(1), http://www.ascusc.org/jcmc/vol3/issue1/ paccagnella.html (accessed 16 February 2004).

Palmer, J. W., Bailey, J. P. and Faraj, S. (2000), 'The Role of Intermediaries in the Development of Trust on the WWW: The Use and Prominence of Trusted Third Parties and Privacy Statements', *Journal of Computer-Mediated Communication*, 5(3), http://www.ascusc.org/jcmc/vol5/issue3/palmer.html (accessed 22 June 2000).

Paolillo, J. C. (2001), 'Language Variation on Internet Relay Chat: A Social Network Approach', *Journal of Sociolinguistics*, 5(2): 180–213.

Park, H. W. (2002), 'Examining the Determinants of Who is Hyperlinked to Whom: A Survey of Webmasters in Korea', *First Monday*, 7(11), http://www.firstmonday.org (accessed 27 January 2004).

—— (2003), 'Hyperlink Network Analysis: A New Method for the Study of Social Structure on the Web', *Connections* 25(1): 49–61.

—— and Thelwall, M. (2003), 'Hyperlink Analyses of the World Wide Web: A Review', *Journal of Computer-Mediated Communication* (special issue: Internet Networks: The Form and the Feel), 8(4), http://www.ascusc. org/jcmc/vol8/issue4/park.html (accessed 27 January 2004).

—— Barnett, G. A. and Kim, C-S. (2001), 'Internet Communication Structure in Korean National Assembly: A Network Analysis', *Korean Journal of Journalism & Communication Studies*, special English edition: 185–203.

—— Barnett, G. A. and Nam, I. Y. (2002), 'Hyperlink-Affiliation Network Structure of Top Websites: Examining Affiliates with Hyperlink in Korea', *Journal of the American Society for Information Science and Technology*, 53(7): 592–601.

—— Kim, C-S. and Barnett, G. (2004), 'Socio-Communicational Structure among Political Actors on the Web in South Korea', *New Media & Society*, 6(3): 403–23.

Parks, M. R. and Floyd, K. (1996), 'Making Friends in Cyberspace', *Journal of Computer-Mediated Communication* 1(4), http://www.ascusc.org/jcmc/ vol1/issue4/parks.html (accessed 18 March 2004).

Paulhus, D. L. (1984), 'Two-Component Models of Socially Desirable Responding', *Journal of Personality and Social Psychology*, 46(3): 598–609.

Peace, A. (1998), 'Anthropology in the Postmodern Landscape: The Importance of Cultural Brokers and their Trade', *The Australian Journal of Anthropology*, 9(3): 274–84.

Peck, M.S. (1987), *The Different Drum: Community-Making and Peace*, New York: Simon & Schuster.

Pennock, D. M., Flake, G. W., Lawrence, S., Glover, E. J. and Giles, C. L. (2002), 'Winners Don't Take All: Characterizing the Competition for Links on the Web', *Proceedings of the National Academy of Sciences*, 99(8): 5207–11, http://modelingtheweb.com/ (accessed 27 January 2004).

Perkins, C. (2003), 'Cartography and Graphicacy', in N. J Clifford and G. Valentine (eds), *Key Methods in Geography*, London: Sage, pp. 343–368.

Perry, C. A. and Rice, R. E. (1998), 'Scholarly Communication in Developmental Dyslexia: Influence of Network Structure on Change in a Hybrid Problem Area', *Journal of American Society for Information Science*, 49(2): 151–68.

Peterson, M. P. (2001), 'The Development of Map Distribution through the Internet', *Proceedings of the Twenty-first International Cartographic Conference*, Beijing, China, 6–10 August.

Phillips, D. L. (1971), *Knowledge from What? Theories and Methods in Social Research*, Chicago: Rand McNally.

—— (1973), *Abandoning Method: Sociological Studies in Methodology*, San Francisco, CA: London: Jossey-Bass.

Ratto, M. (2004), 'From Beasts to Bits and Back Again: Biobanks and the New Informationalism', paper presented at EASST/4S Annual Meeting, August, Paris.

Reid, E. M. (1991), 'Electropolis: Communication and Community on Internet Relay Chat', http://eserver.org/cyber/reid.txt (accessed on 16 February 2004).

—— (1996), 'Informed Consent in the Study of On-line Communities: A Reflection on the Effects of Computer-Mediated Social Research', *Information Society*, 12(2): 169–74.

Reips, U-D. (2002), 'Standards for Internet Experimenting', *Experimental Psychology*, 49(4): 243–56.

Rheingold, H. (1993a), *The Virtual Community: Homesteading on the Electronic Frontier*, London: Secker and Warburg.

—— (1993b), 'A Slice of Life in my Virtual Community', in L. M. Harasim (ed.), *Global Networks*, Cambridge, MA: MIT Press, pp. 57–80.

Rice, R. E. & Love, G. (1987), 'Electronic Emotion: Socioemotional Content in a Computer-Mediated Network', *Communication Research*, 14(2): 85–108.

Richards, W. D., Jr and Barnett, G. A. (eds) (1993), *Progress in Communication Science* 12, Norwood, NJ: Ablex.

Robins, K. (1995), 'Cyberspace and the World We Live in', in M. Featherstone and R. Burrows (eds), *Cyberspace, Cyberbodies, Cyberpunk: Cultures of Technological Embodiment*, London: Sage, pp. 135–155.

Robinson, R. & West, R. (1992), 'A Comparison of Computer and Questionnaire Methods of History-Taking in a Genito-Urinary Clinic', *Psychology and Health*, 6(1): 77–84.

Rogers, E. M. (1987), 'Progress, Problems and Prospects for Network Research: Investigating Relationships in the Age of Electronic Communication Technologies', *Social Networks*, 9(4): 285–310.

Rogers, M. (1996), 'Beyond Authenticity: Conservation, Tourism, and the Politics of Representation in the Ecuadorian Amazon', *Identities*, 3(1–2): 73–125.

Rogers, R. and Marres, N. (2000), 'Landscaping Climate Change: A Mapping Technique for Understanding Science & Technology Debates on the World Wide Web', *Public Understanding of Science*, 9(2): 141–63.

Rogers, R. and Marres, N. (2002), 'French Scandals on the Web, and on the Streets: A Small Experiment in Stretching the Limits of Reported Reality', *Asian Journal of Social Science*, 30(2): 339–53.

Rousseau, R. (1997), 'Sitations: An Exploratory Study', *Cybermetrics*, 1(1), http://www.cindoc.csic.es/cybermetrics/vol1iss1.html (accessed 4 November 2004).

Rutter, J. (1997), 'Standup as Interaction: Performance and Audience in Comedy Venues', PhD thesis, University of Salford, http://les1.man.ac.uk/cric/Jason_Rutter/papers/rutter_phd.pdf (accessed 8 January 2004)

—— (2000), 'The Introductions of Stand-up Performers: Comparing Comedy Compères', *Journal of Pragmatics*, 32(4): 463–83.

—— and Smith, G. (1999), 'Ritual Aspects of CMC Sociability', in K. Buckner (ed.) *Esprit i³ Workshop on Ethnographic Studies in Real and Virtual Environments: Inhabited Information Spaces and Connected Communities*, Edinburgh: Queen Margaret College.

Sacks, H. (1992), *Lectures on Conversation*, 2 volumes, Oxford: Blackwell.

Sanders, T. (2004a), 'Controllable Laughter: Managing Sex Work through Humour', *Sociology*, 38(2): 273–92.

—— (2004b), *Sex Work: A Risky Business*, Cullompton, Devon: Willan.

Scambler, G. and Scambler, A. (1997), *Rethinking Prostitution*, London: Routledge.

Scharnhorst, A. (2003), 'Complex Networks and the Web: Insights from Nonlinear Physics', *Journal of Computer-Mediated Communication* (special issue: Internet Networks: The Form and the Feel), 8(4), http://www.ascusc.org/jcmc/vol8/issue4/scharnhorst.html (accessed 27 January 2004).

Schneider, S. M. and Foot, K. A. (2002), 'Online Structure for Political Action: Exploring Presidential Web Sites from the 2000 American Election', *Javnost (The Public)*, 9(2): 43–60.

Schneider, S. M. and Foot, K. A. (2003), 'Crisis Communication & New Media:

The Web after September 11', in P. N. Howard and S. Jones (eds), *Society Online: The Internet in Context*, London: Sage, pp. 137–154.

Schneider, S. M. and Foot, K. A. (2004), 'The Web as an Object of Study', *New Media & Society*, 6(1):114–22.

Schneider, S. M., Foot, K., Kimpton, M. and Jones, G. (2003), 'Building Thematic Web Collections: Challenges and Experiences from the September 11 Web Archive and the Election 2002 Web Archive', paper presented at the European Conference on Digital Libraries, Workshop on Web Archives, Trondheim, Norway, August. http://bibnum.bnf.fr/ecdl/2003/proceedings.php?f=schneider (accessed 25 February 2004).

Schrøder, K., Drotner, K., Kline, S. and Murray, C. (2003), *Researching Audiences*, London: Arnold.

Schroeder, R. (ed.) (2002), *The Social Life of Avatars: Presence and Interaction in Shared Virtual Environments*, London: Springer.

Selwyn, N. and Robson, K. (1998), 'Using Email as a Research Tool', *Social Research Update* issue 21, http://www.soc.surrey.ac.uk/sru/SRU21.html (accessed 23 January 2004).

Shapin, S. (1995), *A Social History of Truth: Civility and Science in Seventeenth-Century England*, Chicago: University of Chicago Press.

Sharp, K. and Earle, S. (2003), 'Cyberpunters and Cyberwhores: Prostitution on the Internet', in Y. Jewkes (ed.), *Dot Cons: Crime, Deviance and Identity on the Internet*, Cullompton, Devon: Willan, pp. 36–52.

Sharpe, K. (2000), 'Sad, Bad and (Sometimes) Dangerous to Know: Street Corner Research with Prostitutes, Punters and the Police', in R. King and E. Wincup (eds) *Doing Research on Crime and Justice*, Oxford: Oxford University Press, pp. 362–372.

Sharrock, W. W. (1974), 'On Owning Knowledge', in R. Turner (ed.) *Ethnomethodology*, Harmondsworth: Penguin, pp. 45–53.

Siegl, E. and Foot, K. A. (2004), 'Expression in the Post-September 11th Web Sphere', *Electronic Journal of Communication*, 14 (1–2), http://www.cios.org/www/ejc/v141toc.htm (accessed 3 November 2004).

Sillaman, L. (2000), 'The Digital Campaign Trail: Candidate Images on Campaign Websites', master's thesis, Annenberg School of Communication, University of Pennsylvania, Philadelphia, PA.

Silverstone, R. (1999), *Why Study the Media?*, London: Sage.

—— and Morley, D. (1990), 'Families and their Technologies: Two Ethnographic Portraits', in C. Newton and T. Putnam (eds), *Household Choices*, London: Futures, pp. 74–83.

Simakova, E. (2002), 'The Public Face of Databases: the Relationships of Trust within Epistemic Communities on the WWW', master's dissertation, University of Bath, UK.

Singh, S. (2001), 'Gender and the Use of the Internet at Home', *New Media and Society*, 3(4): 395–416.

Skupin, A. and Fabrikant, S. I. (2003), 'Spatialization Methods: A Cartographic Research Agenda for Non-Geographic Information Visualization', *Cartography and Geographic Information Science*, 30(2): 95–115.

Slater, D. (2002a), 'Social Relationships and Identity Online and Offline', in L. Lievrouw, & S. Livingstone (eds), *The Handbook of New Media*, London: Sage, pp. 533–546.

—— (2002b), 'Making Things Real: Ethics and Order on the Internet', *Theory, Culture & Society*, 19(5–6): 227–46.

Smith, A. G. (1999), 'A Tale of Two Web Spaces: Comparing Sites Using Web Impact Factors', *Journal of Documentation*, 55(5): 577–92.

Smith, G. W. H. (ed.) (1999), *Goffman and Social Organization*, London and New York: Routledge.

—— (2001), 'Techniques of Neutralization, Techniques of Body Management and the Public Harassment of Runners', in S. Cunningham-Burley and K. Backett (eds), *Exploring the Body*, Basingstoke: Palgrave, pp. 163–182.

Smith, M. (1998), 'Invisible Crowds in Cyberspace: Measuring and Mapping the Social Structure of Usenet', in M. Smith and P. Kollock (eds), *Communities in Cyberspace*, New York: Routledge, pp. 195–219.

—— (2002), 'Tools for Navigating Large Social Cyberspaces', *Communications of the ACM*, 45(4): 51–5.

Snowdon, D. N., Churchill, E. F. and, Frécon, E. (2003), *Inhabited Information Spaces: Living with your Data*, London: Springer.

Sparke, M. (1998), 'A Map that Roared and an Original Atlas: Canada, Cartography, and the Narration of Nation', *Annals of the Association of American Cartographers*, 88(3): 463–95.

Spears, R. and Lea, M. (1992), 'Social Influence and the Influence of the Social in Computer-Mediated Communication', in M. Lea (ed.), *Contexts in Computer-Mediated Communication*, London: Harvester Wheatsheaf, pp. 30–64.

Spears, R. Lea, M., & Lee, S. (1990), 'De-Individuation and Group Polarization in Computer-Mediated Communication', *British Journal of Social Psychology*. 29(2): 121–34.

Spears, R., Postmes, T., Lea, M. and Wolbert, A. (2002), 'When are Net Effects Gross Products? The Power of Influence and the Influence of Power in Computer-Mediated Communication', *Journal of Social Issues*, 58(1): 91–107.

Speed, G. J. (1893), 'Do Newspapers Now Give the News?', *Forum*, 15, 705–11.

Spender, D. (1995), *Nattering on the Net*, North Melbourne: Spinifex.

Sproull, L. & Kiesler, S. (1986), 'Reducing Social Context Cues: Electronic Mail in Organizational Communication', *Management Science*, 32(11): 1,492–512.

Sproull, L. and Kiesler, S. (1991), *Connections: New Ways of Working in the*

Networked Organization, Cambridge, MA: MIT Press.

Standage, T. (1998), *The Victorian Internet*, London: Phoenix.

Star, S. L. (1999), 'The Ethnography of Infrastructure', *American Behavioural Scientist*, 43(3): 377–91.

Stowkowski: A. (2002), 'Languages of Place and Discourses of Power: Constructing New Senses of Place', *Journal of Leisure Research*, 34(4): 368–82.

Stromer-Galley, J. and Foot, K. A. (2002), 'Citizen Perceptions of Online Interactivity and Implications for Political Campaign Communication', *Journal of Computer-Mediated Communication*, 8(1), http://www.ascusc.org/jcmc/vol8/issue1/stromerandfoot.html (accessed 25 February 2004).

Stromer-Galley, J., Foot, K. A., Schneider, S. M. and Larsen, E. (2001), 'How Citizens Used the Internet in Election 2000', in S. Coleman (ed.) *Elections in the Age of the Internet: Lessons from the United States*, London: Hansard Society, pp. 26–35.

Suler, J. (1997), 'TextTalk: Psychological Dynamics of Online Synchronous in Text-Driven Chat Environments', http://www.rider.edu/~suler/psycyber/texttalk.html (accessed 16 February 2004).

Swirsky, R. and Jenkins, C. (2000), 'Prostitution, Pornography and Telephone Boxes', in J. Radford, M. Friedberg and L. Harne (eds), *Women, Violence and Strategies for Action*, Buckingham: Open University Press, pp. 57–71.

Tang, N. (2002), 'Interviewer and Interviewee Relationship Between Women', *Sociology*, 36(3): 703–21.

Tang, R. and Thelwall, M. (2003), 'Disciplinary Differences in US Academic Departmental Web Site Interlinking', *Library & Information Science Research*, 25(4): 437–58.

Thelwall, M. (2001a), 'Extracting Macroscopic Information from Web Links', *Journal of the American Society for Information Science and Technology*, 52(13): 1,157–68.

—— (2001b), 'Results from a Web Impact Factor Crawler', *Journal of Documentation*, 57(2): 177–91.

—— (2002a), 'Conceptualizing Documentation on the Web: An Evaluation of Different Heuristic-Based Models for Counting Links Between University Web Sites', *Journal of the American Society for Information Science and Technology*, 53(12): 995–1005.

—— (2002b), 'The Top 100 Linked Pages on UK University Web Sites: High Inlink Counts are Not Usually Directly Associated with Quality Scholarly Content', *Journal of Information Science*, 28(6): 485–93.

—— (2003a), 'Can Google's PageRank be Used to Find the Most Important Academic Web Pages?', *Journal of Documentation*, 59(2): 205–17.

—— (2003b), 'What is this Link Doing Here? Beginning a Fine-Grained Process of Identifying Reasons for Academic Hyperlink Creation', *Information Research*, 8(3): 151, http://informationr.net/ir/8–3/paper151.html (accessed 27 January 2004).

—— and Harries, G. (2004), 'Do Better Scholars' Web Publications have Significantly Higher Online Impact?', *Journal of the American Society for Information Science and Technology*, 55(2): 149–59.

—— and Wilkinson, D. (2004), 'Finding Similar Academic Web Sites with Links, Bibliometric Couplings and Colinks', *Information Processing & Management*, 40(3): 515–26.

—— Tang, R. and Price, E. (2003), 'Linguistic Patterns of Academic Web Use in Western Europe', *Scientometrics*, 56(3): 417–32.

Thrower, N. (1996), *Maps and Civilization: Cartography in Culture and Society* 2nd edn, Chicago: University of Chicago Press.

Tidwell, L. C. & Walther, J. B. (2002), 'Computer-Mediated Communication Effects on Disclosure, Impressions, and Interpersonal Evaluations: Getting to Know One Another a Bit at a Time', *Human Communication Research*, 28(3): 317–48.

Tomlinson, M. (2002), 'The Academic Robotics Community in the UK: Web Based Data Construction and Analysis of a Distributed Community of Practice', DRUID Working Paper no. 02–07, http://www.druid.dk/wp/pdf_files/02–07.pdf (accessed18 March 2004).

Tourangeau, R. (2004), 'Survey Research and Societal Change', *Annual Review of Psychology*, 55: 775–801.

—— Smith, T. W. (1996), 'Asking Sensitive Questions: The Impact of Data Collection Mode, Question Format, and Question Context', *Public Opinion Quarterly*, 60(2): 275–304.

Tufte, E. R. (1983), *The Visual Display of Quantitative Information*, Cheshire, CT: Graphics Press.

Turkle, S. (1996), *Life on the Screen: Identity in the Age of the Internet*, London: Weidenfeld & Nicolson.

Vann, K. (2003), 'Practical Tautology: On Performativity and the Posited Actions of Labor', paper presented at the Nineteenth Colloquium of the European Group for Organization Studies, Stream on Materialities of Organizing, Copenhagen Business School, Denmark.

Wallace: (1999), *The Psychology of the Internet*, Cambridge: Cambridge University Press.

Wallace, R. (n.d.), 'The Anatomy of A.L.I.C.E.', A.L.I.C.E. Artificial Intelligence Foundation, http://www.alicebot.org/anatomy.html (accessed 11 November 2002).

Walsh, J. P. and Maloney, N. G. (2002), 'Computer Network Use, Collaboration Structures and Productivity', in P. Hinds and S. Kiesler (eds), *Distributed Work*,

Cambridge, MA: MIT Press, pp. 433–458, http://tigger.uic.edu/~jwalsh/ Collab.html (accessed 10 June 2002).

—— Kucker, S., Maloney, N. G. and Gabbay, S. (2000), 'Connecting Minds: Computer-Mediated Communication and Scientific Work', *Journal of the American Society for Information Science*, 51(14): 1,295–305.

Walther, J. B. (1996), 'Computer-Mediated Communication: Impersonal, Interpersonal, and Hyperpersonal Interaction', *Communication Research*, 23(1): 3–43.

—— (2002), 'Research Ethics in Internet-enabled Research: Human Subjects Issues and Methodological Myopia', *Ethics and Information Technology*, 4(3): 205–16.

Ward, K. J. (1999), 'The Cyber-Ethnographic (Re)Construction of Two Feminist Online Communities', *Sociological Research Online*, 4(1), http://www.socresonline.org.uk/socresonline/4/1/ward.html (accessed 8 January 2004).

Warnick, B. (1998), 'Appearance or Reality? Political Parody on the Web in Campaign '96', *Critical Studies on Mass Communication*, 15(3): 306–24.

—— (2001), *Critical Literacy in a Digital Era: Technology, Rhetoric, and the Public Sphere*, Mahwah, NJ: Lawrence Erlbaum.

Wasserman, S. & Faust, K. (1994), *Social Network Analysis: Methods and Applications*, Cambridge: Cambridge University Press.

Watson, N. (1997), 'Why We Argue about Virtual Community: A Case Study of the Phish.net Fan Community', in S. G. Jones (ed.), *Virtual Culture: Identity and Communication in Cybersociety*, London: Sage, pp. 102–132.

Weare, C. and Lin, W. Y. (2000), 'Content Analysis of the World Wide Web: Opportunities and Challenges', *Social Science Computer Review*, 18(3): 272–92.

Webb, E. J., Campbell, D. T., Schwartz, R. D. and Sechrest, L. (1966), *Unobtrusive Measures: Nonreactive Research in the Social Sciences*, Chicago: Rand McNally.

Weisband, S. and Kiesler, S. (1986), 'Self-Disclosure on Computer Forms: Meta-Analysis and Implications', Proceedings of CHI96, http://www.acm.org/ sigchi/chi96/proceedings/papers/Weisband/sw_txt.htm (accessed 11 March 2004).

Weiss, R. (2003), 'On the Web, Research Work Proves Ephemeral', *Washington Post* 24 November: A08.

Wellman, B. (2001), 'Computer Networks as Social Networks', *Science*, 293(14): 2,031–34.

—— and Berkowitz, S. D. (1989), *Social Structures: A Network Approach*, New York: Cambridge University Press.

—— and Gulia, M. (1999), 'Virtual Communities as Communities: Net Surfers Don't Ride Alone', in M. A. Smith and P. Kollock (eds), *Communities in Cyberspace*, London: Routledge, pp. 167–194.

—— Salaff, J., Dimitrova, D., Garton, L., Gulia, M. and Haythornthwaite, C. (1996), 'Computer Networks as Social Networks: Collaborative Work, Telework and Virtual Community', *Annual Review of Sociology*, 22: 213–38.

Whyte, W. F. (1943), *Street Corner Society: The Social Structure of an Italian Slum*, Chicago: University of Chicago Press.

Wilkinson, D., Harries, G., Thelwall, M. and Price, E. (2003), 'Motivations for Academic Web Site Interlinking: Evidence for the Web as a Novel Source of Information on Informal Scholarly Communication', *Journal of Information Science*, 29(1): 59–66.

Williams, F., Rice, R. and Rogers, E. (1988), *Research Methods and the New Media*, New York: Free Press.

Wilson, S. M. and Peterson, L. C. (2002), 'The Anthropology of Online Communities', *Annual Review of Anthropology*, 31: 449–67.

Wise, J.A. (1999), 'The Ecological Approach to Text Visualization', *Journal of the American Society for Information Science*, 50(13): 1224–33.

Wittel, A. (2000), 'Ethnography on the Move: From Field to Net to Internet', *Forum Qualitative Sozialforschung/Forum: Qualitative Social Research*, 1(1), http://www.qualitative-research.net/fqs-texte/1–00/1–00wittel-e.htm (accessed 8 January 2004).

Wolfe, A. W. (1978), 'The Rise of Network Thinking in Anthropology', *Social Networks* 1(1): 53–64.

Wood, D. (1992), *The Power of Maps*, New York: Guilford Press.

Woolgar, S. (1988), *Science, The Very Idea*, London: Routledge.

—— (2002), *Virtual Society? Technology, Cyberbole, Reality*, Oxford: Oxford University Press.

Wouters: (2001), 'The Semiotics of the Hyperlink', paper presented at the Society for the Social Study of Science (4S) Conference, Cambridge, MA, 1–4 November.

—— and De Vries, R. (2004), 'Formally Citing the Web', *Journal of the American Society for Information Science & Technology JASIST*, special issue on Webometrics.

—— and Gerbec, D. (2003), 'Interactive Internet? Studying Mediated Interaction with Publicly Available Search Engines', *Journal of Computer Mediated Communication*, 8(4), http://www.ascusc.org/jcmc/vol8/issue4/wouters.html (accessed 4 November 2004).

Xenos, M. and Foot, K. A. (2005), 'Politics as Usual or Politics Unusual? Position-taking and Dialogue on Campaign Web Sites in the 2002 US Elections', *Journal of Communication*, 55(2): 168–184.

Xiong, R. and Donath, J. (1999), 'PeopleGarden: Creating Data Portraits for Users', *Proceedings of the Twelfth Annual ACM Symposium on User Interface Software and Technology*, New York: ACM.

Yook, S-H., Jeong, H. and Barabási, A-L. (2002), 'Modeling the Internet's Large-Scale Topology', *Proceedings of the National Academy of Science*, 99(21): 13,382–86.

Zhang, Y. (1998), 'The Impact of Internet-Based Electronic Resources on Formal Scholarly Communication in the Area of Library and Information Science: A Citation Analysis', *Journal of Information Science*, 24(4): 241–54.

Index